Alice

Alice

MEMOIRS OF A BARBARY COAST PROSTITUTE

Edited by Ivy Anderson and Devon Angus
Foreword by Josh Sides

Heyday, Berkeley, California
California Historical Society, San Francisco, California

Library of Congress Cataloging-in-Publication Data
Names: Smith, Alice (Prostitute), author. | Anderson, Ivy, 1990- editor. | Angus, Devon, editor.
Title: Alice : memoirs of a Barbary Coast prostitute / edited by Ivy Anderson and Devon Angus.
Other titles: Bulletin (San Francisco, Calif. : 1895) | Voice from the underworld.
Description: Berkeley, California : Heyday ; San Francisco, California : California Historical Society, [2016] | Includes bibliographical references. | Originally published in 1913 in the San Francisco Bulletin as a serialized memoir entitled "A voice from the underworld".
Identifiers: LCCN 2016029378 (print) | LCCN 2016034563 (ebook) | ISBN 9781597143615 (pbk. : alk. paper) | ISBN 9781597143769 (e-pub) | ISBN 9781597143776 (amazon kindle)
Subjects: LCSH: Smith, Alice (Prostitute) | Prostitutes—California—San Francisco—Biography. | Prostitutes—California—San Francisco—Social conditions—20th century. | Prostitution—California—San Francisco—History—20th century.
Classification: LCC HQ146.S4 S65 2016 (print) | LCC HQ146.S4 (ebook) | DDC 306.74090794—dc23
LC record available at https://lccn.loc.gov/2016029378

Cover photo courtesy of the San Francisco History Center, San Francisco Public Library.

Book Design: Ashley Ingram
Printed in East Peoria, IL, by Versa Press, Inc.

Alice: Memoirs of a Barbary Coast Prostitute was published by Heyday and the California Historical Society. Orders, inquiries, and correspondence should be addressed to:

Heyday
P.O. Box 9145, Berkeley, CA 94709
(510) 549-3564, Fax (510) 549-1889
www.heydaybooks.com

10 9 8 7 6 5 4 3 2 1

MIX
Paper from responsible sources
FSC
www.fsc.org
FSC® C005010

We dedicate this work to all of the current and former sex workers we have spoken with who have supported and shaped this project, and to the sex worker rights organizations that continue to bring their struggle to the national and international stage.

Contents

Foreword

Historical scholarship takes many forms. From writing articles, monographs, and multivolume books to curating museum exhibitions and leading historical tours, the practice of revealing history is multifaceted, painstaking, and almost always illuminating. And for Ivy Anderson and Devon Angus, it is also exciting, for they found what so many historians seek in vain: a long-forgotten, almost indescribably rich primary document that has never been reprinted until now—in this case a serialized memoir of sorts titled "A Voice from the Underworld." In *Alice: Memoirs of a Barbary Coast Prostitute*, Anderson and Angus have not only resurrected "A Voice from the Underworld" but also provided, in the form of an expansive introduction, a broad context for the narrative. Students and scholars of California, the Progressive era, and sexuality are in their debt.

"A Voice from the Underworld"—originally published in Fremont Older's *San Francisco Bulletin* in 1913—is a first-person account by a prostitute named Alice Smith. That Smith was possibly not a real person but rather a composite of many working-class women and prostitutes in San Francisco at the time does nothing to diminish the power of the narrative (which was almost certainly ghostwritten by *Bulletin* staff). In fact, as Anderson and Angus suggest, it was the very amalgamated nature of the Alice Smith narrative—which touches on countless aspects of the working-class experience that probably wouldn't have arisen in an account by a single individual—that encouraged so many prostitutes to respond to the narrative by writing their own letters to the *Bulletin*, some of which were published alongside installments of "A Voice from the Underworld." According to Anderson and Angus, the *Bulletin* received more than four thousand letters in response to Alice's story, many of which came from women, and from working-class women in particular. Above all, "Alice" and these women wanted to be heard.

And what they said was worth hearing. Among the details most notable to a modern reader is that both Alice and her many respondents spoke eloquently about issues that would not become popular causes until the arrival of second-wave feminism in the 1960s and the sex workers' rights movement of the 1970s. Further, the interplay between the "Voice" narrative and the letters to the *Bulletin*—abundantly detailed in the following pages—reveals that prostitutes were generally not the social misfits Progressive-era reformers often portrayed them to be. True, they were considered by "decent" society to be of compromised morality, but in turn-of-the-century San Francisco they also fulfilled a role that was more or less accepted as a necessary evil. Even then, however, it was a hard life and not one many women would choose if they could afford to do otherwise. The plight of single, working-class women of that time was essentially this: they lived in a society that simultaneously denied them livable wages for "legitimate" work while also circumscribing, criminalizing, and moralizing against sex work. "When one goes to bed hungry many times," one prostitute wrote in to the *Bulletin*, "the demarcation between right and wrong becomes much less in evidence and it requires some rubbing of the eyes to distinguish it at all."

Once a woman's reputation was tarnished by sex work, it became nearly impossible to escape the stigma of the profession and the social alienation it engendered. Often, the only way out of this quagmire was through marriage, although more than one respondent shared the view that seeking remuneration through a loveless marriage was essentially legal prostitution. "Morality," wrote fabled anarchist Emma Goldman, "compels a woman to sell herself as a sex commodity for a dollar per, out of wedlock, or for fifteen dollars a week, in the sacred fold of matrimony." Alice and her respondents detailed the ways in which, for single, working-class women, prostitution was less a moral failing than it was a social inevitability.

But it was the official closure of San Francisco's vice district, the Barbary Coast, in 1917 that was the most detrimental to the well-being of the city's prostitutes. Evicting at least fourteen hundred sex workers, the closure marked the end of the sanctioned brothel (although some, like those of the legendary Sally Stanford, continued into the 1940s). A triumph for moral reformers, the end of the Barbary Coast was disastrous for sex workers because it directly endangered their safety, and sometimes their lives. Without romanticizing the brothel, Alice and her respondents generally agreed that the institution generated a sisterhood of women watching out for one another's safety, whereas streetwalking, by contrast, offered no such safety, and more than its share of danger.

Although Alice was not particularly political, she and many of her respondents gave voice to a viciously marginalized segment of American society. In doing so they participated in something truly groundbreaking, and the fact that they did it through the *Bulletin*, whose readership was already at 45,000 at the turn of the century, meant they reached a large number of people from a broad cross-section of the community. Most importantly, they called on society to recognize their common humanity. "Can't people understand," Alice asked, "that they are all responsible for each other in lots of ways?" It was the question of her time and may just be the question of ours.

JOSH SIDES, Whitsett Chair in California History
at California State University, Northridge,
and author of *Erotic City: Sexual Revolutions
and the Making of Modern San Francisco*

Preface

When we began researching the story behind "A Voice from the Underworld," we were startled and delighted to discover that there was hardly a trace of it on the Internet. Particularly here in the tech capital of the world, we are bombarded with the idea that everything worth knowing and doing is accessible through the colloquial "touch of a button"; from a cab ride to a new romance, we purportedly can find everything we want— and more—in the massive data network. Take that away, however, and you open yourself to a different kind of possibility: the possibility of discovering something new, something not already accessible to anyone on the planet with an Internet connection. Finding "A Voice from the Underworld," after hours holed up behind the screen of a microfilm reader, is confirmation of this belief. There are hundreds of books about the history of San Francisco, a handful about the history of sex work in America at the turn of the twentieth century, and even a few volumes on the history of the *San Francisco Bulletin* newspaper. But up until now, this unique document existed only on a few pieces of microfilm thankfully archived in a library. It is in this analog world of fragile reels and dusty old equipment that the act of pure discovery still awaits, despite the pervading belief that everything has already been catalogued on Wikipedia.

Our hunt for the narrator, "Alice Smith," began with a love of outlaw literature and a fascination with Fremont Older, the enigmatic editor of the *San Francisco Bulletin*, who gained fame as a vitriolic crusader during the graft trials of the first decade of the twentieth century but soon after suffered an existential turnabout, becoming a Dostoyevskian champion of the downtrodden. Our love of Jack Black's underworld autobiography *You Can't Win*, originally published by Older, led us to the many other memoirs of merit that were serialized in the *Bulletin*, and through them we began to see Older as an early link to a distinct form of California literature, which, like Steinbeck's *Cannery Row*, Bukowski's *Factotum*, or Didion's *White Album*, aims to dignify and scrutinize the full sociological diversity of human life. The candid tales of poverty and vice published in the *Bulletin* contain a kernel of the soul of San Francisco, and even as tech money sweeps away more of the SROs, free clinics, dive bars, diners, and taquerias that have made this city livable for many in the lower economic rungs of society, Fremont Older's appeals to the diverse classes of San Francisco are not only still relevant for a modern audience but absolutely necessary to revisit.

While *You Can't Win* has become a cult classic, "A Voice from the Underworld" curiously remained lost for more than a hundred years. We can't explain why or how that happened, but once we saw reference to it—in Older's own autobiography—we knew we wanted to know more. The mention of a prostitute's memoir in turn-of-the-century San Francisco sent us into a research frenzy. One early online reference we found placed the publication of the story in 1917, a date we knew must be wrong because by that time Older was wrapped up in the defense of radical labor activists Thomas Mooney and Warren K. Billings—California's own Sacco and Vanzetti—who were framed for the bombing of a prowar parade as the United States prepared to enter into the Great War. In search of the original document, we settled into the San Francisco Main Library's 5th Floor, split up the reels of microfilm, and began scanning forward from 1911 until, in June 1913, "A Voice from the Underworld" emerged on the screen. It was itself an eye-opening piece of journalism, but adding to its impact were the published letters from hundreds of women reacting to the serialized memoir—women writing candidly about being women, about sex, labor, crime, politics. More than 4,000 letters were received by the *Bulletin* on the subject, and nearly 300 were published in the paper. Of those, 114 were written by women who said they were or had been themselves sex workers, and 30 were by working-class women who had at one point in their lives considered turning to sex work. We knew we had stumbled upon something of critical importance.

The question of authenticity is a significant one for historians. We'd hoped to find the raw material of Alice's memoirs and the many letters written to the *Bulletin* in some magical archive tied up with a bow, but of course tracking down history rarely works that way. The *Bulletin*, following Fremont Older's firing in 1919, appears to have cleaned house before its eventual purchase by the Hearst-owned *San Francisco Call*. As far as we know, the original source material simply doesn't exist.

Because of the *Bulletin*'s history as a sensationalist publication, not to mention our own doubts as well as the doubts of academics we consulted, we wondered if we could find a definitive record of Alice Smith. There are a few brief descriptions of her by Fremont Older himself, a fuller description by newspaper editorialist John Barry published during the serial, and a later recollection by newspaperman R. L. Duffus written in 1960. Other than that, we had little to go on.

In the spring of 2015, we drove down from San Francisco into the Santa Cruz Mountains to visit Woodhills, Fremont Older's home, which also served as a bohemian salon and (failed) cooperative. Standing with the rest of the history buffs there to tour the property, we noticed an old guestbook in the living room. Ignoring the docent's talk, we consumed the pages, photographing and taking notes on this simple book that had somehow escaped the archives. There we found a remarkable list of visitors to Woodhills spanning decades, including Clarence Darrow, Lincoln Steffens, Carl Sandburg, Emma Goldman, Alexander Berkman, David Starr Jordan, James Rolph, Hiram Johnson, and many others from the world of letters and politics. Among the names of such luminaries, however, were a great deal of names unknown to us, a testament to Older's habit of mixing company of all types. He hosted regular dinners bringing together, as he put it, "world savers, economists, psychics, ex-prisoners, fortune tellers, insane people, underworld characters, and religious fanatics." If the "real" Alice Smith—or Alma Greene or Violet Brown or any of the other letter writers, who may or may not have used their actual names—was amongst those listed in the guestbook, we had no way of knowing.

Our failure to corroborate Alice's existence might very well suggest that her ghostwritten memoir is at best a composite portrait of multiple women, if not pure fiction. Certainly the context of the era suggests as much: salacious "exposés" and white slave narratives of dubious authenticity—most of them written by vice reformers and editors looking to capitalize on public hysteria over prostitution—flooded the nation's media. On the other hand, as you'll read in our introduction to this volume, Older's career in the years preceding "A Voice from the Underworld" might suggest a different conclusion, which we invite you to consider.

In any case, over the course of our research we have realized that the obsession with finding the "real" Alice Smith borders on delicate ethical territory. It is challenging as historians, as passionate as we are about evidence gathering, to work with documents from a community in which anonymity is the norm. Sex workers throughout history have donned pseudonyms not just as a performative choice but as a safety mechanism to protect themselves and their families from abuse and criminal charges. Even today, sex worker narratives are often cast off as unworthy of serious consideration because of the continued use of pen names. And yet many of these documents—whether essays, memoirs, letters, news articles, or interviews by, with, or about contemporary sex workers—deserve our attention, even as they allow their narrators to protect their identities. In readings of many of these works, we have uncovered a salient detail about the urge to find "Alice": perhaps society's readiness to cast off as invalid the stories from anonymous sex workers is but one more way in which the public refuses to relate to them as fellow humans, as if simple disconnection from their given names reinforces the tradition of diminishing their personhood. As much as we hoped to find evidence of the "real" Alice, we did not want to fall into invasive, voyeuristic territory by obsessing over her identity, nor could we with good conscience cast aside her story despite questions of her existence as a single, verifiable person. Whoever Alice Smith was or wasn't, we strive here to preserve the integrity of her voice.

This project has defined both of our lives for the last few years, and any editorial decisions were made with careful and pained consideration. The memoir, which ran six days a week between June 23 and August 12, 1913, has been edited from its original length of almost 91,000 words down to 71,000. Every excision was made with the intention of retaining the bulk of the original narrative while forming a more manageable book-sized whole. For the sake of creating a cohesive story, we have removed the original chapter breaks and the repetitious plot summations that occurred at the beginning of almost every new section. The section breaks that appear here are our own, although many do coincide with original breaks. Aside from these small changes, no creative measures were taken with editing.

We would have liked to include every one of the letters sent to the *Bulletin* in response to "A Voice from the Underworld," but it would have made this a book of impossible length and weight. Instead we have selected twelve of the letters written by women in response to Alice's story. While the *Bulletin* did publish a number of letters written by men—including local politicians, philosophers, and clergy—these letters are notably missing here, since it is relatively easy to find other documentation of powerful men discussing prostitution in the Progressive era. We also believe that this choice remains true to the original intent of the *Bulletin*, which aimed to elevate the voices of the "voiceless." We hope that by emphasizing the stories of the *Bulletin*'s most marginalized readers, we will also honor them, their courage, and the courage of contemporary sex workers who struggle to be taken seriously in a world that pushes them so shamefully into exile.

Introduction

On January 25, 1917, more than two hundred prostitutes gathered inside a San Francisco church and staged what might have been the first sex workers' rights protest in modern history. Since the gold rush of 1849, prostitutes in San Francisco had plied their trade openly, but by 1917, the wave of Progressive-era reforms that swept the nation had reached the shores of the Paris of the West, and San Francisco's red-light district came under the scrutiny of moral reformers. While these self-appointed guardians of decency saw the closure of the brothels as a means to not only purify society of sin but also protect the sex workers themselves, many of the prostitutes saw it as a mass eviction. With few options left to them, hundreds of the women stormed the church of one of the city's most virulent anti-vice reformers, the Reverend Paul Smith, and demanded that he answer their cry: "You want...the city cleaned up...but where do you want the women to go?"[1]

It would be generations before the concept of a sex workers' rights movement existed in any official form (COYOTE, which stands for Call Off Your Old Tired Ethics, was founded in California in 1973 and is considered the first sex workers' rights organization), but in 1917, two madams named Reggie Gamble and Maude Spencer organized a political demonstration and demanded their voices be heard. Spencer and Gamble enlisted the help of their friend Fremont Older, the editor of the *San Francisco Bulletin*, who in 1913 had earned their trust by publishing "A Voice from the Underworld," the serialized memoir of a prostitute going by the name "Alice Smith." The publication sparked public reaction, and the paper also published 291 letters sent to the *Bulletin* by sex workers and others. We must of course question the historical authenticity of the narrative and accompanying letters—the *Bulletin* was notoriously sensationalistic, and nationwide media was rife with dubious "true" accounts of prostitution and white slavery—and we must even go so far as to ask whether or not "Alice Smith" was a real person. And yet regardless, Alice Smith certainly existed for the women who followed "A Voice from the Underworld" in 1913 and marched with Gamble and Spencer four years later. The madams in fact approached Fremont Older to help them organize local prostitutes for their march because it was his publication of Alice Smith's narrative that provided a public platform from which echoed the stories of these women who had long been silenced.

The marginalization of sex workers' voices is a critical issue that still shapes debates about sex work today. On August 11, 2015, Amnesty International adopted a policy calling for the worldwide decriminalization of consensual sex work. "As a global human rights organization…it is right and fitting that we should look at one of the most disadvantaged groups of people in the world, often forced to live outside the law and denied their most basic human rights: sex workers," wrote the organization's policy advisor several days later.[2] Certain prominent anti-trafficking organizations argued against the policy, claiming that decriminalization would allow vicious pimps, johns, and brothel owners to exploit innocent victims of the sex trade without fear of legal recourse. The debate ran in international newspapers for weeks, and a letter—penned by the Coalition Against Trafficking Women—opposing AI's policy drew attention after it was signed by a number of Hollywood celebrities, including actors Kate Winslet, Meryl Streep, and Lena Dunham. Dozens of editorials filled the pages of the *New York Times*, the *Guardian*, and the *Washington Post*, highlighting the illustrious signatures backing the opposition. On the other side, journalist and sex worker Molly Smith (a pseudonym) openly criticized these news sources for failing to consult actual sex workers on the topic, in effect putting the opinions of multimillionaire actors at the center of the argument. "If this criminalization is so beneficial for us," wrote Smith, a sex worker in Europe, "it's hard to imagine why the organizations campaigning for it are unable to find and quote even one sex worker in the world in support of it....We are hopeful that the quieter voices of sex workers remain audible next to those of Hollywood stars."[3]

What Molly Smith and many other contemporary sex workers are demanding is the same request that Alice Smith and the letter writers to the *Bulletin* insisted upon in 1913: to be heard. As politicians, clergymen, and clubwomen across the state of California debated an anti-vice law that would finally close California's brothels, the prostitutes whose lives would inevitably be changed by this law went largely ignored. In publishing Alice Smith's memoir and the accompanying letters, *Bulletin* editor Fremont Older was undoubtedly capitalizing on the national obsession with prostitution in order to sell papers and increase circulation, but, taking into consideration Older's political and philosophical transformation during the years leading up to the publication of "A Voice from the Underworld," one can argue that he was also taking a stance: one that said everyone deserved a chance to be heard, no matter how "criminal" or how outside of proper society one was.

Nevertheless, we must always take the accuracy of "A Voice from the Underworld" with a grain of salt, as we must with all memoirs and all popular media. But whether it is read as a story of one woman's life or as a revealing portrait of the role and attitudes of the media in Progressive-era San Francisco, this narrative has great value as a direct link between the shantytown brothels of gold rush San Francisco and the potent sex workers' rights movement today.

SHANTYTOWN METROPOLIS

In 1848, the discovery of gold at Sutter's Mill caused an immediate influx of thousands of new settlers from all around the globe, each one seeking fast fortunes far from the rule of civilized society. The vast majority of these hopeful travelers were male, and by 1850 more than thirty-five thousand of them had made their way to San Francisco, which would quickly become the financial center of the gold rush. The culture that developed in the early years of this shantytown metropolis was a haven for licentious behavior; transient bachelors and married men, far from the watchful eyes of their families, spent their money freely on gambling, liquor, and sex. San Francisco's instantaneous wealth, geographic isolation, gender imbalance, and mixing of multiethnic cultures contributed to a laissez-faire attitude in contrast with the tightly buttoned morality of the East. Prostitution flourished, and professional sex workers traveled from around the world to capitalize upon the sudden blitz of wealth. Living conditions for these women varied widely based on such factors as race and age, although in general, life was notably worse for Chinese women, who were more likely to be kidnapped or tricked in China and then forced into sexual slavery in California. At least in the first few years of the city's development, many sex workers were able to amass individual wealth, social status, and political power. In fact, one illustrious hotel and brothel, the El Dorado, sat just adjacent to San Francisco's City Hall in Portsmouth Square, a fitting symbol of gold rush morality.

Ironically, those sex workers who were able to thrive in gold rush San Francisco were capitalizing upon the same gender roles that aimed to prevent women's engagement in the economic sphere. Although the patriarchal social structure had long been established in the United States, by the 1830s society had adopted new Jacksonian-era ideas surrounding gender to match changes in the geography of economics. The country was developing from a subsistence-based economy into a market economy, the result being a shift in the economic locus from the private sphere of the family farm to the public sphere of the marketplace. As market goods replaced those that were traditionally made by women in the home, women's role in the economy was considered less valuable, and they were left to care for domestic necessities while men alone engaged in the public market, effectively becoming the sole breadwinners.

Jacksonian gender roles dictated that men, who had long controlled the public sphere, continue to test their mettle in the arenas of economics and politics, and masculinity was considered both naturally authoritative and passionate to a fault. Where men were thought to be inherently violent and sexual, women were expected to balance them by being demure and virtuous. Without a clear economic role, the Jacksonian woman's primary social purpose was to mitigate male energy by dictating the moral foundation of the home and family. According to this structure, decent women were by nature asexual. It was believed that the two sexes could not exist without the other, and a man's success in the public sphere depended upon the counterbalance of the moral private sphere as embodied by the respectable woman.

In general, prostitutes were thought to exist outside that circle of society; they were "underground," seen as betrayers of the social contract by failing in their domestic role and by engaging in the male-controlled economic sphere. In the instant city of San Francisco, however, where, in 1849, men outnumbered women fifty to one, things were different, and a window opened through which sex workers might gain greater social mobility. Prevailing sexual codes that demanded a balance of men in the public sphere and women in the private were so strong that isolated men of status often used their relationships with prostitutes to substitute for the usual private sphere of wife, home, and family. Thus, for a time, a sex worker walking down the street would not be shunned or ignored but instead be greeted by doffed hats and gallant bows; she could go to the theater like any other citizen or even meet a client at a respectable restaurant.[4]

San Francisco's relationship with prostitution changed as it grew into a modern city, however. As California's surface-level gold stores began to dwindle, following a peak in 1852, the nature of labor shifted, and so did the work of its citizens. Large-scale hydraulic mining replaced the independent gold miner, and these itinerant entrepreneurs instead became wage laborers, merchants, and financiers. This transition encouraged the more permanent settlement of San Francisco, and the shanty-town quickly developed into a bona fide city, with buildings of brick and metal replacing the canvas tents and ersatz structures that had been built around the bones of grounded ships.

The ephemeral metropolis was developing a feeling of permanence, and as the newly established population put down roots, they sent for their families, initiating yet another new era in the social world of San Francisco. As wives, mothers, and other "decent" women settled in the city, outnumbering prostitutes two to one by 1852, the role of the prostitute as a tempering counterbalance to the harsh masculinity of the boomtown changed from something accepted to something illicit. Even as sex work moved underground, however, it was considered by many to be a "necessary evil," an industry that sacrificed some women in order to shield the majority from the uncontrollable lust of men. If it could not be eradicated, at least it could be contained.

Vice could be found across the city of San Francisco, but by the 1860s the Barbary Coast stood tall as the primary destination for "underground" activity. Named after a stretch of North African coastline infamous for piracy, "The Coast" had grown out of two neighborhoods with reputations for sex, gambling, and crime, Sydney Town and Little Chile. Intertwined with the development of the Barbary Coast was the surge of vigilantism that rose up against the perceived lawlessness of the city. As early as 1851 a Committee of Vigilance had formed to confront a spate of offenses with the efficient and ruthless method of public lynching. Although their influence was sporadic, their reputation survived and their cause was eventually taken up by a vigilante newspaperman who also sought to rid the city of vice, criminality, and political corruption.

James King of William, a failed banker turned newspaper editor following the bank collapse of 1855, turned his vitriol onto the ills of the city through the organ of his paper, the *San Francisco Evening Bulletin*. Chief amongst his targets was the Broderick political machine, a powerful engine of corruption under former lieutenant governor David C. Broderick, whose unethical maneuverings King believed kept the city in a state of lawlessness. The municipal government, in cahoots with a criminal class of thugs, ballot-stuffers, and confidence men, was seen as a roadblock on the path to legitimacy. How could a "wide-open" town that turned a blind eye to vice and corruption ever be the capital of the western United States? Painting with a sensationalist brush, King played fast and loose with facts, believing in his own sense of right over careful argument—a tradition that would weave throughout the *Bulletin*'s history. Said one historian of King, "He flayed the politicians, the prostitutes, the barbarous custom of dueling, the defaulting bankers, the gamblers, the toughs, the police, and just about everything else in sight while championing the home, the church, the school, and reform—and the city loved him for it."[5] The good people of San Francisco would clean the city with a broad broom, all to the music of his passionate and stirring editorials.

In 1856, James King of William was gunned down by James Casey, a political enforcer who worked for the Broderick faction and was himself a particular target of King's poison pen. The editor's assassination helped to usher in a second vigilance committee, in 1856, yet it too disbanded within a year, and by the 1860s San Francisco remained as "wide open" as ever. Another attempt at cleaning up the city would come in the 1870s, but, such efforts being tidal in nature, it also receded as usual. By the turn of the century, the *Bulletin* was ready to rise again as a vehicle of vigilantism, but this time under a different editor, and with very different results.

THE CRUSADING EDITOR

Fremont Older, a farm boy from Wisconsin with grand dreams of becoming a journalist, had long been enchanted with San Francisco's rough-and-tumble past. Arriving in 1873 with an empty belly and open eyes, he fell in love with his new home, seeking out the dark alleyways, gangplanks, and promenades of the wild, mythic city by the bay. There the seventeen-year-old sought out vestiges of the past, in search of his own future. He frequented the watering holes and haunts that had attracted the young Samuel Clemens before he became Mark Twain, and he found history walking the streets, lifting a glass with Samuel Brannan, the newspaperman who had announced the gold rush to the sleepy hamlet in 1848, and with the strange shuffling figure of Judge Ned McGowan, who had escaped the noose of the vigilantes in 1856 by wearing a disguise and being smuggled out of danger in a rolled-up carpet. Broke, Older was nevertheless charmed enough to buy a few drinks for a colorful madman named Emperor Norton, a favor paid back in kind with Norton's famous "million-dollar bond with his imperial signature affixed."[6] San Francisco breathed history for Older, a trait lost on his contemporaries, he feared. As he later wrote, "I could see that the city was rapidly losing the flavor of its romantic past. A new generation had grown up, and the young people were not especially interested in the '49 stories told by their fathers."[7] Deciding to follow the journalistic trail of his hero, Samuel Clemens, Older left the city to learn his trade in the boomtowns of Nevada and the eastern Sierra, always intending to return to the bustling vibrancy of the legendary bayside city to make his mark.

Although Fremont Older would in turn become a champion of the alienated and disenfranchised, it would take time. When he grabbed the reins of the *Bulletin* as managing editor in 1895, he was both a conservative and a reactionary. Early in his career he had been virulently anti-immigrant and especially anti-Chinese, a trait he sadly shared with many in the city. He patriotically supported the expansion of Manifest Destiny into the Pacific during the Spanish-American War, and he was pro–law and order, showing little patience for lawbreakers. He advocated for the return of whipping-post punishment for wife beaters, as well as the harsher treatment of prisoners, prescribing poor food, the ball and chain, and long terms of rock smashing. Punishment, to Older, was "the only means of teaching the rising generation that it is better to be good than bad."[8] He was skeptical of the ward politics of the city's past and was a firm believer in the efficacy of vigilante justice, both fitting platforms for the man taking over the editorship in the hallowed tradition of the *Bulletin*. All in all, he was following the path of his predecessor, James King of William, despite his obvious romance with the city's messy, protean gold rush beginnings. His first piece of reportage in the city took him to a gunfight on the infamous Barbary Coast, by then a vestige of San Francisco's shadowy past. The experience left him shaken: "It was a night of horrors to me. I had never realized that there was such a place on earth."[9] It was his destiny, he felt, to help clean the city of the corruption that had so long defined its civic life.

Older quickly returned the *Bulletin* to its vigilante glory days as a political force to be reckoned with. Following the lead of William Randolph Hearst's innovative paper the *San Francisco Examiner*, Older took advantage of cutting-edge techniques and technology to bring the *Bulletin* into the twentieth century. Employing attention-grabbing headlines splashed across the cover, an increased use of photography, sensationalist editorials, and a grab bag of stunts and theatricalities, Older increased readership from 9,000 in 1895 to more than 45,000 by the turn of the century.

Alongside his editorial success came considerable political clout. Fearing that the city would relapse into the corruption of the past decades following a short burst of reform in the 1890s, Older convinced one of the richest businessmen of San Francisco, James D. Phelan, to run for mayor in 1897. He believed that a man of independent wealth such as Phelan could withstand the corrosive graft elements of the dominant players in California politics, not least of which was the dreaded monopoly of the Southern Pacific Railroad, derided popularly as "the Octopus" for the way its tentacles stretched across the state both literally and figuratively.

Phelan was a popular, reform-minded mayor, yet his political antennae proved deficient in the face of labor unrest. In 1901, an association of business interests came together with the intent of destroying organized labor. The unions responded with a bitter, violent strike that proved Phelan's downfall once he allowed police protection of strikebreakers. Phelan, in the face of labor's ire, decided to not run for re-election, leaving a noticeable power gap. Taking advantage of voter mistrust of the two major parties, the pro-labor Union Labor Party (ULP) came to power, pushing through the mayoral election the charismatic and handsome Eugene Schmitz. And with Schmitz came the ULP's real source of power: lawyer and political boss Abe Ruef.

The publication of "A Voice from the Underworld" can be traced back to Older's complicated relationship with Ruef. The editor, from day one, nursed an aversion to the corrupt lawyer, and with good reason. For one, Older's handpicked candidate, Phelan, was no longer mayor, and with that came a diminishing of the *Bulletin*'s political sway. But more than that, Older hated political bosses, who, among other machinations, controlled party tickets, handpicked candidates, and manipulated the vote to stay in power. The memory of the corrupt "Blind Boss" Buckley, who had fled San Francisco just a handful of years before Older took over the *Bulletin*, was still fresh in the minds of city reformers, and the editor was part of a generation of reform-minded activists who saw in bossism a gross cancer attacking law and democracy.

For Older, Ruef represented a dark return of the legacy of lawless San Francisco. The editor, convinced of Ruef's corrupting influence, became obsessed with bringing the political boss down. He threw accusations against the wall like spaghetti, hoping something would stick, but he had little success. Believing that vice and civic corruption went hand in glove, reforming vice became one of his primary goals, and it took many forms. He examined graft in the selling of liquor to saloons in the Barbary Coast; he used an undercover operative to expose police corruption amidst underground gambling in Chinatown; he sought federal aid when he went after a "yellow slavery" trafficking ring, which dealt in Chinese women sold into Chinatown brothels; and he hired two prostitutes to infiltrate the so-called Municipal Brothel, which paid out a quarter of its profits directly to Ruef for his protection from police raids. Older and his paper railed against Ruef's many associations with the "kings of the tenderloin"*—pimps and saloon owners who had close ties with the boss and his political machine. As the *Bulletin* put it, "The saloon and the brothel can swing an election for a candidate by the certainty of the number of votes they control,"[10] and from Older's perspective, men like Ruef were the single greatest obstacle keeping San Francisco from becoming a great city. From the highest circles of industry to the lowly bunko artist, Older was convinced corruption began and ended with men like Ruef. He insisted that City Hall had to be cleaned up at any cost, but to his growing frustration, for many years nothing would stick to Ruef.

And then eventually the accusations started to take hold. For much of the decade, Older, along with fellow graft hunters James Phelan, Rudolph Spreckels, William Burns, and Francis J. Heney, doggedly pursued Ruef and Schmitz. After members of the Board of Supervisors were caught trading in bribes during a sting operation (after which they agreed to testify in exchange for immunity), Ruef and Schmitz, along with the president and attorney of the streetcar company United Railroads of San Francisco (who had given $200,000 in graft to Ruef) appeared ready for San Quentin. Older was ecstatic, yet cracks of doubt began to trouble him.

The problem for Older was the involvement of United Railroads. Under the influence of his friend and fellow muckraker Lincoln Steffens, Older had begun to question his approach to the graft hunt, and he now realized that with so much of his energy pointed toward the bribed, he had lost sight of the bribers. This changed in 1907, the year an explosive streetcar

---

* Not to be confused with today's Tenderloin neighborhood, the term "tenderloin" here is simply period slang referring to a vice district. At that time, the Barbary Coast was still the city's primary "tenderloin" district.

strike was violently put down by United Railroads amidst the chaos and fears of the post-earthquake city. Patrick Calhoun, the president of the streetcar company, was publicly lauded as a hero, but Older, who had come far from his reactionary roots, held great sympathy for the strikers and, in fact, had raised considerable funds to keep the strike alive. Once the $200,000 bribe was uncovered, Older began to steer his investigations toward Calhoun. This disturbed many of the business elite of the city, who, while they supported the graft hunt targeting the pro-labor party, thought it was a mistake to go after a city hero like Calhoun. Older found himself on the receiving end of cold shoulders and hard stares from the higher circles of society. The editor feared that Calhoun and the rest of the bribers would escape prosecution.

Older's worries proved to be true. When the dust and smoke cleared after several long years of concentrated assault on the forces that kept the city down, Ruef alone was sent to prison. The graft hunters were disappointed and angry, but it shook the editor to his core. Ruef was behind bars, yet Calhoun was free? Was this justice? Was Lincoln Steffens correct, that it was in fact business that corrupted politics, not the other way around? Something felt wrong about the entire affair. Older began to question the very nature of his crusade.

Historians have asked whether Abe Ruef can be truly considered a "political boss."[11] According to multiple sources, the Schmitz administration was not overly corrupt in the early years, and Ruef did not have a unified enough machine behind him to pull the necessary strings. In fact, according to Ruef, Older's insinuations contributed to the corruption; the constant accusations of graft began to take hold in the popular imagination, with the result that many interests in the city believed them to be true even when they weren't. Graft became expected of the administration because the newspapers said so. The editor's actions during his crusade began to weigh heavily upon his conscience. He decided to visit Abe Ruef in prison.

Fremont Older crossed the bay to San Quentin to visit the man he'd put away, and once inside the prison he was thoroughly shocked by the inhumane conditions within its walls. To the surprise of the city, and to the bitter anger of the graft hunters, Older ran an editorial the next day under the bold block-print headline MERCY FOR ABRAHAM RUEF! Many dismissed Older as an eccentric; President Theodore Roosevelt thought he'd gone "too far." Older pleaded his case with surprising candor:

> I have asked for mercy to Ruef because I felt that I, above all others, had done most to bring about his downfall. If you have followed the long fight the *Bulletin* has made during the past eight or nine years, you will recall that I was fighting Ruef long before the city woke up. You will also recall that I attacked him bitterly with all the invectives that I could personally command, and all that I could hire....At last, after eight years of a man-hunting and man-hating debauch, Ruef crossed over and became what I wanted him to be—...a convict, stripped of his citizenship, stripped of everything society values except the remnant of an ill-gotten fortune.
>
> It is then I said to myself, "I have got him. He is in stripes. He is in a cell. His head is shaved. He is in tears. He is helpless, beaten, chained—killed, so far as his old life is concerned. You have won. How do you like your victory?..."
>
> My soul revolted. I thought over my own life and the many unworthy things I had done to others, the injustice, the wrongs I had been guilty of, the human

hearts I had wantonly hurt, the sorrows I had caused, the half-truths I had told, and the mitigating truths I had withheld, the lies I had allowed to go undenied. And then I saw myself also stripped, that is, stripped of all pretense, shame, self-righteousness, holding the key to another man's cell. I dropped the key. I never want to hold it again. Let it be taken up and held by those who feel they are justified in holding it. I want no more jail keys. For the rest of my life I want to get a little nearer to the forgiving spirit that Christ expressed.

Isn't what I'm accusing myself of true of all of us?[12]

Older realized that the best way he could serve Ruef was to offer him the *Bulletin* as a platform to defend himself. Ruef was skeptical yet enthusiastic, and on May 21, 1912, the first installment of his serialized memoirs were published under the title "The Road I Traveled: An Autobiographic Account of My Career from University to Prison, with an Intimate Recital of the Corrupt Alliance between Big Business and Politics in San Francisco." Throughout its three-month publication, Older continued to seek a pardon for his now close friend. He appealed to Hiram Johnson, a lawyer who had joined Older's graft fight toward the end and had used the exposure to launch his political career to become the governor of California in 1911. Although Older had been a confidant and advisor to the progressive governor, Johnson refused to touch Ruef. Older continued to publish Ruef's serialized memoir for three months before it was discontinued for legal reasons. Although the results were mixed, Older was proud of what they'd done, and his effort on behalf of Ruef would begin a tradition at the *Bulletin* of using the memoir as a tool of social change.

During one of his many visits to San Quentin, the editor met a young convict who was writing his own memoirs.

Donald Lowrie, a "slender, wistful young fellow in prison stripes, with an anemic body and a look of tragedy,"[13] had little hope of getting his story out to the public (he'd planned on smuggling the work out of the prison through his lawyer), but Fremont Older, under the influence of his experiences with Abe Ruef, decided to help Lowrie himself. Using his political connections, the editor secured an early parole for the prisoner and promptly put him to work as a reporter at the *Bulletin*.

Older pitched an idea to Lowrie, hoping the ex-con would agree: What about publishing his memoirs as a serial in the *Bulletin*, like Abe Ruef's? Lowrie was eager to publicize abuses within the California prison system, yet he was nervous putting his own story out so publicly. "But I'm just out of prison.... I don't want to put myself in prison for life," he told Older. "I'll have to stand in front of the whole world as an ex-convict... and you know how ex-convicts are regarded."[14] The editor finally convinced him, arguing that his memoir could enact change by its very candor. "The old spirit of life-long condemnation is dying out. A change is coming over people," he told Lowrie. "It's within your power to accelerate that change."[15]

First serialized in 1912, "My Life in Prison" created a stir both statewide and nationally. Older and Lowrie used the exposure to help ex-convicts, establishing an unofficial employment bureau in the offices of the *Bulletin*—a practice that would continue during the run of "A Voice from the Underworld" for the many women who wrote into the paper. Lowrie, flush with newfound fame, began to receive hundreds of letters from those touched by his story, including women of the "underworld" who felt a natural kinship with the stigmatized ex-prisoner. One such woman was contemplating suicide but wrote to Lowrie instead, because he "would understand the misery that had driven her."[16] Other ex-cons, emboldened by the serial, sent their own memoirs into the *Bulletin* with hopes that their voices would be acknowledged. Older, with new-found energy, wanted the experiment to continue.

THE FIGHT FOR RED LIGHT ABATEMENT

In the decades surrounding the publication of "A Voice from the Underworld," prostitution exposés took the country's media by storm and dramatically changed the form and content of U.S. news. Beginning in the 1870s, journalists more often shirked the private-interest pieces that had dominated the pages of the papers, turning instead to muckracking reportage, which aimed to reveal the interconnections between greedy businessmen and corrupt politicians in the country's biggest cities. For the first time, mass distribution allowed papers to gain readerships far from their printing presses, and this provided an opportunity for far-flung activists to unite for common causes. Reform movements grew out of these exposés and vice versa. Although the economic concerns of increasing circulation and advertising revenue were always paramount on the business end, newspapers also made good use of this chance to serve as a public forum, the agora of the nation, both shaping and shaped by public discourse.

Although muckraking is most famously associated with political scandal, the form was realized first and foremost by investigations into "white slavery," which, fueled by racial anxiety, conflated prostitution with sexual enslavement, organized crime, and civic corruption. Beginning with Englishman William Stead's series "The Maiden Tribute of Modern Babylon," published in London's *Pall Mall Gazette* in 1885, the prostitution exposé became a hot new journalistic tack, which quickly spread to the U.S., used at different times and in different ways to either humanize or criminalize sex workers (as well as immigrants, homosexuals, and members of other groups whose existence threatened white Protestant dominance). These exposés often came out of anti-vice reform movements and were written by reformers themselves. Sometimes they even inspired new anti-vice reform movements. Unfortunately, these undertakings rarely bettered the lives of the people they purported to help.

In the "The Maiden Tribute," Stead and his staff gathered a series of interviews with prostitutes, madams, and others involved in the world of ill repute to argue that London's sex trade was based almost entirely upon the kidnapping and abuse of naïve women for the sexual satisfaction of roguish aristocrats. At a time when the interview itself was considered a salacious form, Stead did much to change the public's expectations of journalistic research and objectivity. Despite controversy surrounding the truthfulness of "The Maiden Tribute," the *Gazette*'s circulation increased fivefold over the course of its publication, and stories of its famed editor traveled through England and abroad. "The Maiden Tribute" not only forged new standards for journalism, it also dramatically changed the discussion about prostitution both in England and the United States. The prostitute was no longer just a "fallen woman" filling a necessary but despicable social role; she had become an innocent victim in need of swift rescue. The immediate reaction to "The Maiden Tribute" was the organization of a number of social-purity vigilance groups, who fought to pass and enforce legislation aimed to clean up London's vice districts by expanding police power aimed at prostitutes and brothel owners, supporting laws that would raise the age of consent, and criminalizing male homosexual activity.

This narrative of the "white slave" being rescued by moral reformers would soon dominate the American press and inspire yet another wave of anti-vice reform. From the pamphlets of suffragettes and morality crusaders, the reportage of muckraking journals and yellow newspapers, the pages of novellas, and the pens of playwrights throughout the country, the question of prostitution and white slavery became something of a national obsession. Many of the pieces claimed superior levels of objectivity and authenticity by relying on "interviews," while others simply cashed in on the media frenzy by fabricating sensationalist accounts billed as truth for political and/or monetary gain. Regardless of the sincerity or insincerity of the work, historians have found the great majority of these pieces of media to be compromised; prostitute memoirs and exposés from this era cannot generally be considered primary source documents due to their dubious origins. For example, George Kibbe Turner's exposé "The Daughters of the Poor," published in *McClure's* magazine in 1909, represented the high-water mark of hysteria over the white slavery question in the national media. Turner's piece played upon fears of mass immigration and urbanization, painting a picture of rural white women falling prey to "foreign" pimps in the underbelly of American cities. After being discredited by a New York grand jury trial, the exposé was unmasked as having been largely fabricated.

"The Maiden Tribute" made its way into American papers and into the hands of Frances Willard, president of the national Woman's Christian Temperance Union, who was so moved by the sordid tale that she immediately adopted anti-trafficking and age-of-consent reforms as new tenets of the WCTU's campaign. By 1900 the Woman's Christian Temperance Union was the largest women's organization in the United States, with more than 500,000 members nationwide. Their membership was comprised almost exclusively of white, wealthy, married, and educated Protestant women, and they advocated for suffrage with the belief that women could purify American society through the ballot box. These women, who saw themselves as, by nature, moral, nurturing, and maternal, believed they were endowed with the righteous task of domesticating the sordid world of masculine politics. The WCTU fought not only for suffrage and the eradication of alcohol but also for child labor reform, the eight-hour workday, kindergartens, public parks, and women's vocational education. In California, the WCTU and associated women's groups successfully won the right to vote in 1911, nine years before the Nineteenth Amendment would allow for national women's suffrage, and they quickly got to work pushing their sweeping agenda through the California legislature. State legislators, intimidated by the power of this new, well-organized voting bloc, would pass a critical piece of legislation that would pit social-purity advocates against prostitutes and lead to the eventual demise of California's quasi-legal vice districts.

On the opening day of the legislative session of 1913, California assemblymen and senators found on their desks a piece of paper listing the demands of the Women's Legislative Council of California, an independent group comprising members of the WCTU and other prominent women's clubs. One of the proposed laws, the Red Light Abatement and Injunction Act, aimed to close down all brothels by punishing the property owners. While laws criminalizing prostitution were already in place across California, vice districts were still allowed to flourish due to the graft system in place between prostitutes, madams, property owners, the police, and politicians. Prostitutes gave a portion of their earnings to the madam, who, after taking her own share of the profit, would then pay the police and property owners to turn a blind eye to the illegal happenings inside the house. The graft that protected the vice districts fueled the fervor of Progressive reformers, who would not tolerate the civic corruption that they perceived as a direct result of moral laxity. The Red Light Abatement Act was designed to circumvent the corrupted police force by empowering citizens

—

to charge any owner of a suspected house of prostitution with a public-nuisance complaint; if the allegations were proven true, the property and its possessions could be seized and sold.

These reformers were perhaps naïve in their assumption that they could eradicate prostitution by simply eradicating brothels, and they also failed to recognize the roles brothels played for the sex workers themselves. In cities with recognized vice districts, brothels provided a certain amount of protection to their charges, who were guarded from the violence and police harassment they would undoubtedly face on the streets. The culture of the brothel created a sphere of female interdependence, where social bonds between prostitutes and madams allowed these social outcasts a certain level of camaraderie and safety. The women's clubs insisted that after Red Light Abatement, settlement homes and charities would be created to protect the women displaced from the vice districts, and they pushed on with their moral crusade.

Flexing their newfound political power, members of California's women's clubs embarked on a massive letter-writing campaign to ensure the passage of the Red Light Abatement Act, sending as many as fifty letters a day to each legislator. While there was considerable support within the legislature, several California congressmen feared that the abolition of all vice districts would simply scatter prostitution, making it even more challenging to regulate. Others felt the law overstepped constitutional property rights. Women's clubs targeted these congressmen with letters and telegrams threatening "political annihilation" if they did not vote for the act. Senator John Curtin from Tuolumne County claimed to have received more letters about the Red Light Abatement Act than on any other legislative topic that session, and he eventually voted for the law against his "better judgment."[17] Despite their misgivings, a majority of congressmen voted to snuff out the red light, and the law was signed by Governor Hiram Johnson on April 7, 1913. Notably, only one out of thirteen San Francisco assemblymen and two out of seven San Francisco senators voted in favor of the bill.

San Franciscans were wary of vice abatement for a number of reasons, and the city made various attempts to mitigate some of the negative effects of prostitution while still allowing it to exist. From March 1911 until May 1913, the city ran a Municipal Clinic for the Prevention of Venereal Disease, which regularly tested prostitutes for communicable diseases and offered in exchange certificates to healthy prostitutes that guaranteed their complete protection from police harassment. The women were examined every four days, and they received a new certificate with each passing test. If signs of health issues were detected, the women received free treatment but were forbidden to work until they were well again. Dr. Julius Rosenstirn, the founder of the clinic, believed that it would be impossible to address the problems associated with prostitution if the city were to "close the brothels, to tear down the shelter of the prostitute, to hunt and imprison the street walker," and he believed instead that society could cope with the problems associated with prostitution—namely the spreading of disease—by accepting and regulating the industry.[18] While the Municipal Clinic successfully reduced rates of venereal disease amongst prostitutes by 66 percent,[19] the institution was not joyously received by all of the sex workers it affected. Many of them rightly objected to the fact that, if they were found to be infectious, their photos would be hung in the Hall of Justice, effectively violating their privacy and sabotaging their ability to find work outside of the sex industry.[20] Although Rosenstirn's clinic was controversial amongst reformers and prostitutes alike, his pragmatic attitude toward vice was shared by many of his peers, such as state senator Dominick Beban, who feared that vice abatement would simply "work too much havoc in

[his] district" and asked that reformers study the connections between minimum wage and prostitution before enacting any sweeping legislation.[21]

Adding to San Franciscans' wariness over the Red Light Abatement Act—a wariness that crossed class and ethnic lines—was the fact that it had become closely associated with temperance, due mostly to the two issues' simultaneous introduction to the California State Legislature in 1911. It was their linkage that caused the demise of their respective bills, since even those sensitive to the issue of prostitution gave vice abatement a second thought when it was presented arm in arm with temperance. In particular, restrictions placed on saloons were unpopular with San Francisco's business elite: there were big profits to be made there, and real estate men and Barbary Coast business owners feared a cleanup would impact their revenues. Working-class men and women were also invested in the clubs and saloons of the Barbary Coast as places of employment, relaxation, and social organizing; from the grape harvester and hops farmer, to the cocktail waitress and the traveling minstrel, to the saloon keeper and the distiller, brewer, bottler, transporter, and vendor of alcohol, countless jobs were wrapped up in the vice dens of the Coast, and San Franciscans recognized that laws restricting the sale of booze would not only affect jobs but could potentially destroy the social institution of the saloon, which doubled as a cafeteria, a concert venue, a loan office, and a center of political organizing for much of the city's working class and poor. The women's clubs worked to distance vice abatement from temperance, but the election of 1911 was still too recent in popular memory.

As the Red Light Abatement Act moved through the state legislature, San Franciscans prepared to host the upcoming Panama-Pacific International Exposition of 1915, a world's fair that would bring nearly 19 million visitors from around the globe to celebrate not only the opening of the Panama Canal the previous year but also the successful rebuilding of San Francisco after the earthquake and fire of 1906. The city would be in the spotlight and under the scrutiny of the international community, and the question was, Would the Paris of the West embrace the wide-open legacy of its past or adopt the sterilized image that would transform it into the preeminent city of the future? James "Sunny Jim" Rolph, the wildly popular mayor of San Francisco, came under pressure by reform groups from across the country to do away with San Francisco's brothels or else face international backlash. Church leaders threatened to boycott the PPIE if the Barbary Coast were not closed, and they flooded Rolph's mailbox with inflammatory letters.[22]

Rolph, however, was personally ambivalent to the idea of moral reform and was even known to ride around in his campaign car with Tessie Wall, a notorious madam. Regardless of his shifting take on morality, San Francisco's women's clubs had supported his 1911 campaign against the Union Labor Party candidate, Patrick McCarthy, and Rolph depended upon their continued support. Rolph was certainly under pressure from all sides. Several local businessmen and members of the PPIE planning board, including Frank Burt, the director of concessions, were concerned that if the fair were too wholesome, it would be less profitable; others on the board fully supported the sweeping cleanup. Rolph privately dismissed the idea that vice could ever be eradicated even if they tried, and once the abatement act was signed into law, he shirked his responsibility to uphold it, to the delight of some and the chagrin of others. The Red Light Abatement Act spent four years in legal limbo, but by 1917, sensing a shift in the political winds, Rolph would declare the death of the Barbary Coast and order the closure of every brothel in the city.

Shortly after the passage of the Red Light Abatement Act in April 1913, a group calling themselves the San Francisco

Property Owners Protection Association circulated a petition to place the Red Light Abatement Act on the ballot for referendum, with hopes of defeating the bill. Women's groups and prominent clergymen cried foul, claiming that the petition was full of forged signatures, but nonetheless, the bill was slated for public vote in November 1914. Women's groups, reform politicians, and clergymen redoubled their campaign efforts, and many of these groups strategically targeted Southern California voters, who were notably fonder of vice reform than the more liberal San Franciscans. Newly enfranchised female voters across the state were implored to fulfill their duty as maternal defenders of society by voting to clean up the vice districts, and the *San Francisco Examiner* took up the cause, publishing a series of editorials railing against the culture of corruption on the Barbary Coast. Local clergymen proclaimed November 9, 1913, as "Purity Sunday" and distributed leaflets to their congregations. The outcome of these efforts was that in November 1914, California's Red Light Abatement Act was upheld by 53.2 percent of the popular vote. Not surprisingly, 63.9 percent of San Francisco voters opposed the measure, which failed in every one of the city's voting districts. The referendum fight was not the last hurdle to the passage of the Red Light Abatement Act, which was then taken to the state courts by the San Francisco Property Owners Protection Association. Despite these setbacks, anti-vice reformers continued to organize politically, and by 1917 the Red Light Abatement Act was finally cleared for enforcement. The successful passage of this law in the face of a coordinated backlash reveals the burgeoning power of the anti-vice reform movement and thusly the newly enfranchised women's clubs of California.

During this era, progressive women's clubs were able to influence the passage of a number of moral reform bills by characterizing themselves as representative of the whole of the women of California. Yet certainly not all classes of women were represented; even within San Francisco's WCTU chapters, which were the most ethnically diverse in the state, the vast majority of WCTU members in San Francisco and elsewhere were still wealthy, white, married Protestants. While the Red Light Abatement Act would above all else impact the lives of sex workers, those were the very women who generally held the least political power to steer the lawmaking done in their name.

Marginalized and dehumanized, the prostitutes, dancers, and other women who made their living in the vice districts of the state were not as able to voice their concerns in a public forum for fear that compromising their privacy and the protection of their identities could have disastrous personal consequences, and even, in some cases, mean the difference between life and death. Remarkably, these women soon found an outlet for their demands—on the pages of the *San Francisco Bulletin*. Between the months of June and August 1913, as the referendum fight against vice abatement was building, the pages of the *Bulletin* would feature not only the daily serialized memoirs of "Alice Smith" but also nearly two hundred letters from working-class women and current and former prostitutes. Publishing these suppressed voices alongside letters from clubwomen, clergymen, and state politicians, the paper created an equal playing field for debate, and these women and their stories were granted a previously elusive level of dignity, right there on the black-and-white pages of one of San Francisco's most widely read dailies.

ALICE ARRIVES

"I am going to tell about my life as well as I can. There isn't anything romantic about it. I went into it because I needed money…" So declared the woman called "Alice Smith," introducing herself to the city in the run-up to the publication of her memoirs in June 1913.[23] According to the *Bulletin*, she had been a ghost for several years, flitting between her brothel on Commercial Street and the tall, gray canyon walls of San Francisco's "respectable" downtown, within spitting distance of the Barbary Coast. Just a few short blocks away was broad Market Street and the offices of the *Bulletin*, where a handful of contemporary accounts claim that a woman had indeed been meeting with a small group of the paper's staff to tell her story. Newspaperman John D. Barry was present for one of the meetings:

> There came into the room a girl of medium height, slim and quietly dressed, with refined, rather pretty features and a gentle manner. She slid into a seat, as if afraid. After the introduction she seemed to gain more courage. Already she had had several talks with the two other members of The Bulletin staff who were present. She evidently felt that she knew them fairly well now. In a few moments she had regained her composure and she was talking briskly and smiling. What chiefly impressed me about her was the sincerity of all her remarks and her ways….Occasionally, as was inevitable under the circumstances, the questions would be a little painful. Once[,] the girl lost control and covered her face with her hands and silently cried. In a few minutes she was all right again, and smiling. Already, at these interviews, she had gone pretty far in the course of her life and she was growing used to the ordeal. "At first it was hard," she said. "But now I don't mind nearly so much. It's very interesting. I like to come up." She added, however, that she felt some dread about the appearance of the articles

in the newspaper. She thought perhaps it would be better for her not to look at the paper while they were running.[24]

Fremont Older had led her to his office on her first visit, and he had come out of the meeting visibly moved. Editorialist R. L. Duffus was at his desk that day, and he recalled forty-seven years later, "As I was finishing my afternoon's work, Older came out of his office, through Carl Hoffman's cubbyhole, into the news room. He had been talking, as I learned, with a woman labeled, for purposes of concealment, Alice Smith; and he was crying—not shamefacedly, as men do cry sometimes, but without the slightest embarrassment."[25]

Alice Smith's story impacted Older on an emotional level but also raised important questions for him as an editor. Although he had some understanding of marginalized members of society, having worked closely with several prisoners, he humbly asked himself what did he really know, in the end? If the criminal was not to be abused and shunned, was kicking prostitutes out onto the streets by shutting down the brothels truly moral? Or even practical? In his work with ex-convict Donald Lowrie, Older had learned a great deal that, prior to that experience, he could have only guessed at. Would the same be true for prostitutes? Older turned to Lowrie for help.

Visiting journalist Arthur McFarlane witnessed this collaboration. In a piece for *Collier's* magazine titled "A Friend of Crooks: Fremont Older," McFarlane recounted a scene that had taken place in the *Bulletin* offices:

> The fitting close to this narrative, it seems to me, would be my last glimpse of Donald Lowrie. Recently the "Bulletin" has been telling the story of a woman of the underworld in daily installments as "My Life in Prison" was told. I found Lowrie making shorthand notes, while

across the table from him sat a woman, the smoke of a cigarette curling before her eyes. It was the red sister. She was quarrying out of her memory the material for the next installment of her story. Lowrie looked clean and strong and sympathetic, but anxious. She looked pale and tired, but determined, and also anxious. Both were laboring hard....

That scene dramatizes one of the satisfactions of the editor in his new role as a member of broken lives. He has helped Lowrie, the two-time loser, as prison parlance has it, back to honest living; and Lowrie, in turn, as he helped this wasted woman day by day to untangle the threads of her soul history, is also trying to dig out the trail to the weed-grown, good spot in her heart.[26]

"A Voice from the Underworld" was eventually ghostwritten by a senior journalist at the *Bulletin*, Ernest Hopkins, from notes collected by Lowrie and a few others. The goals of the *Bulletin* were laid out in an editorial on July 2, 1913:

Alice Smith's story, and the remarkable letters from women of the underworld which have been printed with it, will accomplish several things. One end has been attained already. No open-minded reader of the story and the letters will ever look upon prostitutes as he or she once did. They have been seen to be creatures of like motives and like impulses like ourselves, and as much victims of our social system as the children who work in Southern cotton mills, or the exploited...who give up their lives in the bowels of a skyscraper's foundations....

The Bulletin is offering no panacea. It has no remedy to suggest except the remedy of human sympathy and understanding, which must precede any solution. Alice

> Smith's story is a true story. It is being told as the story of
> an ordinary life and not as a vehicle of sensation. Alice
> Smith lived a part of her life within the pale of normal
> womanhood. She lived another part outside.[27]

Unlike other salacious prostitution exposés from the era, "A
Voice from the Underworld" must be read as a continuation of
the prison-reform memoirs Older started with Abe Ruef and
Donald Lowrie and continued with Jack Black in 1916. Older's philosophy, a radical form of Social Christianity he had
embraced as a result of his relationship with Ruef, spurred his
mission to protect those without a voice in society, and he
turned the *Bulletin* toward increasingly controversial waters.
He worked with Clarence Darrow to defend the McNamara
brothers in Los Angeles over the *L.A. Times* bombing in 1910,
and he fought to free Tom Mooney and Warren K. Billings
from prison following their flawed conviction for orchestrating the San Francisco Preparedness Day bombing of 1916. He
formed on his property in the Santa Cruz Mountains a type of
settlement house for ex-convicts, who lived and worked on his
land while on parole. He believed, as he told Donald Lowrie,
that "the old spirit of lifelong condemnation is dying out. A
change is coming over people."[28] He used his newspaper as a
platform to test this experiment, all the while promoting his
belief that, in particular, current and former convicts and current and former prostitutes shared a common social alienation
that had to be challenged.

Before examining the details of Alice Smith's story, it is
important to revisit the question of authenticity. If her story
was ghostwritten, as we know it was, does that also mean she
was a fabrication? After all, the eyewitness accounts to her
presence in the *Bulletin* offices may very well point to a narrative based on the experiences of one or multiple women.

Certain aspects of the "memoir" follow established tropes found in sensationalized exposés of the era, such as her rural origins and her initial deception by an urban pimp...but does that mean they can't have been true in this case?

To address this possibility, it is helpful to look at "A Voice from the Underworld" within the context of the *Bulletin's* history of ghostwritten memoirs. Rose Wilder Lane, a future libertarian theorist and the daughter of *Little House on the Prairie* author Laura Ingalls Wilder, began writing for the *Bulletin* shortly after "A Voice from the Underworld" was published. Hired on as a serial writer, Lane ghostwrote many pieces for the paper between 1914 and 1918. In letters to her mother she explained the process of ghostwriting, and according to her, in some cases, such as with Abe Ruef and Donald Lowrie, the memoirs were not ghostwritten at all—they were edited heavily by the paper for serialization, but they were written by their subjects. In other cases, however, the narratives were ghostwritten by staff writers from interviews. Jack Black, a parolee who became a protégé of Fremont Older's, was interviewed by Rose Wilder Lane, who ghostwrote his first serialized memoir, "The Big Break at Folsom" (1916), until he felt ready to write for himself. His later autobiography, *You Can't Win*, would go on to become an underground classic that heavily influenced William Burroughs and other members of the Beat generation. For some memoirs, Lane said she would use multiple sources to create a single narrative; in "Behind the Headlight," for instance, she used interviews with several train engineers to create a composite engineer whose "life story" she told as a serialized memoir. In another example, she colored the narrative of a police detective with details she had collected from interviews with an ex-con at the paper, most likely Jack Black.[29]

It is possible that Alice Smith's memoirs were a complete fabrication, not simply ghostwritten but a pure piece of fiction, as many exposés of the time were. Considering what we know of Fremont Older and the *Bulletin*, however, this seems improbable. Instead, "A Voice from the Underworld" is most likely the product of interviews with one or several women that were subsequently stylized and heavily edited by Hopkins for mass consumption in a serialized form.

THE VOICES OF THE UNDERWORLD

Despite questions surrounding Alice's true identity, her narrative has an air of authenticity that certainly rang true with the hundreds of other prostitutes and working-class women who read her story. Although Alice herself doesn't appear to advocate for any specific political measures, her narrative is inherently political, as it reveals pointed instances of gender discrimination and economic injustice that shaped the course of her life, and the lives of others like her. That said, the tale does not come across as having a specific agenda, and Alice refrains from summing up her personal views on prostitution until the very end of her narrative. Instead, she focuses on detailing her life as she moves through many jobs and locales across the country.

Beginning as a Midwestern farm girl, Alice moves west to California and spends time variously as a laundry worker in Oakland, a waitress in a small mining town, a "free lance" sex worker, a brothel girl, and a madam. For a time, Alice moves in and out of the world of prostitution, holding down other low-paying jobs to supplement her earnings. Alice's story deals with a number of shockingly revealing topics, including abortion, police abuse, and brothel life, and it does so in a way that is both informative and humanizing. The characters in Alice's story are not caricatures; the women she works alongside are not portrayed as victims to be pitied or beasts to be reviled. Throughout the narrative, we witness Alice's own accounting of the many circumstances in her life that led her to prostitution; contrary to what other members of society had claimed on both sides of the debate over the Red Light Abatement Act, she is neither a woman enslaved nor an entirely free agent.

Over the course of the publication of "A Voice from the Underworld," the *Bulletin* received more than four thousand letters in response, many of which came from other prostitutes inspired to tell their own stories. In some ways, it is the publication of these letters that makes "A Voice from the Underworld" a truly remarkable document. For two months, readers of the *Bulletin* were exposed to narratives detailing the lives, hopes, fears, needs, and desires of a class of women whose voices had previously been largely ignored by reformers and anti-vice activists whose overall aim was to close the brothels and shuffle the prostitutes into settlement homes and employment agencies. These letters are as diverse as they are impassioned. Some express feelings of entrapment and hopelessness, while some beg for assistance; others lambast the reformers for their prejudice and demand the dignity to live without interference. Some call for the development of a workers' state; others proclaim masculine sexuality to be the root of all evil. Some were raped or molested before entering prostitution, some were coerced by pimps, and many others entered "the life" of their own volition. Some of the letters are not from prostitutes but working-class women who felt they may, too, be on the road to sex work. Other letters were written by johns and the husbands of prostitutes, by social scientists, philosophers, novelists, and clergymen, and by politicians both local and far-flung. The varied voices of those published in the pages of the *Bulletin* can be read as a sort of time capsule, a representation of the many arguments placed on the table in California in 1913 in response to one question: What is to be done about the prostitution problem?

Perhaps the most prominent theme that arises again and again, both in "A Voice from the Underworld" and in the letters printed by the *Bulletin*, is that of the plight of the single working-class woman. Alice Smith faced economic adversity that made it next to impossible to support herself without turning to prostitution, a circumstance that is mirrored in letter after letter. A similar desperation is echoed in the missives from women with children or other family members to support. Like many women who turned to sex work, Alice's economic setbacks began in her childhood, when, in her case, she was forced to drop out of school because her family could not afford glasses for her to wear. It is her family's poverty that convinces Alice to leave her Illinois farmhouse for Oakland, California (which she renames "Westville" in the memoir), where she is told she can make $25 per month (compared to the $1.50 per week she earned as a scullery maid in her hometown). Hoping to send money back to her poverty-stricken family, Alice tries out a number of entry-level jobs but soon realizes that $25 means a lot less in the Bay Area. When she lands a job at a laundry working ten-hour days, Alice does some accounting:

> Six dollars a week. Take out two for room rent—that left four a week for eating, clothes, car fare, washing and a good time.
> Cut out car fare. Cut out clothes—for the present. My old shoes would have to do. Cut out washing—I'd do it myself, in my room. Cut out—yes—cut out the good time. I'd need that four dollars just for eating.…
> Well, maybe Sundays I'd go without eating…[30]

Like several of Alice's employers, her boss at the laundry scoffs when she complains about the wage, and advises that she, young and pretty she was, could "pick up lots of easy money on the side."[31]

According to historian Ruth Rosen, these numbers were in no way unusual, but they were certainly substandard. A 1916 U.S. Department of Labor study on the working conditions of women and children concluded that the average female factory or department store worker made about $6.67 a week, but that a fair wage was at least $9 per week, especially if her income wasn't supplemented by a husband or other family member.[32] The assumption that women ought to have a husband or father to help support them was a point of ire for many of the women who wrote in to the *Bulletin*. One letter writer insisted that married women who worked for "pin money," or additional spending cash, were lowering the overall wages paid to women, since they could more easily accept a substandard wage: ✳

> It has been my sad experience that a working woman dependent upon herself cannot compete with girls living at home, and also married women. They work for low wages and can afford to do so, but a woman alone in the world, forced to work for the same wages, cannot exist, although a member of the Women's Political League considered $6 a week ample wage....It is easy enough for members of women's clubs to suggest such a life on a mere pittance, but to put themselves in such a position I hardly think they would find their advice practical. I have tried it.[33]

Another woman who wrote into the *Bulletin* went so far as to say that it should be illegal for any married woman of wealthy enough means to work.[34]

Several letter writers noted the haughty disconnect of many of the clubwomen: "Society women say they will help us and we must reform. I don't want sympathy or a helping hand out of this life. All I ask is a living wage and I will get out of it myself," wrote a woman who signed her name "Driven to Brothel."[35] Bessie C., an ex-prostitute, wrote: "Remember, my dear good women, and religious people who pray for all sinners, that prayers, patronage, or pity have never reformed a prostitute or a convict; only love, and a fighting chance to be on the square."[36] While reflecting upon her first turn to prostitution, Alice Smith also laments that her dilemma could never be truly understood by any woman of financial means. Alice hears of a "good woman, a brainy woman," who had gone out to work in a laundry under a false name in order to better understand the working conditions of the laborers there. But this woman, with her "two weeks of play-laundry-work," would never know what it meant if she had to "work in that laundry or starve."[37]

To starve was no exaggeration, and while Alice for a time moved in and out of prostitution to keep herself afloat, others wrote in about the deplorable conditions they endured in order to avoid the brothel. One woman recounted that the cruel treatment she suffered as a domestic servant "robbed me of two precious girls and almost caused my mind to give way under the strain, depriving me of many years of happiness."[38] Early on in its publication of "A Voice from the Underworld," the *Bulletin* ran a front-page story marketed as a humorous tale of mistaken identity, in which an impoverished girl disguises herself as a boy in order to make a higher wage working as an elevator operator at a hotel.

> I was offered a place [as a girl], but was told the wage would be $20 per month, and I would have to provide my own room and board myself. I said no one can live

on that money, and the agent, leering at me, said: "Ah, you're a good looker. You can do business on the side and make good money"....As a boy they paid me $25 a week and my room and board, and I was happy for a time.[39]

It was not just low pay and poor working conditions that placed single women at a disadvantage. Stringent social codes dictated appropriate gendered behavior and prevented women from enjoying many inexpensive amenities that working men depended upon. While men could enjoy free and cheap lunches served in saloons, women were either barred explicitly from these spaces or stayed out for fear of jeopardizing their reputations. "Nor can she—to be considered respectable—rent a back room in a hotel for $2 a week," wrote one ex-prostitute who signed her name "S.S." "Nor can she get along with 25 cents' worth of laundry a week."[40] These expectations not only divided working-class women from men but further alienated the experience of working-class women from upper-class women, who could afford to dine unescorted in department stores and fine tea rooms without having their reputations called into question. Alice Smith describes the plight of the working girl as an almost inevitable movement from poor wages into prostitution: "from poverty to charity, from charity to drudgery, from drudgery to—this."[41]

How do we analyze these stories and the struggles of the women who wrote into the *Bulletin*? It seems that the paper left this task up to its readers, and many viewpoints abound—from a woman demanding the collectivization of all land,[42] to one defending a universal four-hour work day,[43] to another who begs, "Why not let us have a district where we will bother no one?"[44] While some of these women undoubtedly cast themselves as victims of an unforgiving market, others portray themselves as sensible decision makers, choosing one path out of many laid before them in a world of limited economic options.

Another important theme in "A Voice from the Underworld" is the clash of generations. Alice's grandparents grew up in a different cultural reality than she did, one that held to an even more rigid code of what was considered "appropriate" for members of each sex. According to historian Ruth Rosen,

> Victorians described the male sex drive as strong, passionate, and potentially destructive. They sought to control it because they believed that if excessively indulged, it could weaken and damage mind and body. The female sex drive, by contrast, was in most cases thought to be weak or non-existent.[45]

It was in this context that brothels were seen as emergency valves, releasing dangerous pressure with the help of the already corrupted. As one Victorian-tinged vice report from 1916 put it,

> Vice is one of the weaknesses of men; it cannot be extirpated; if repressed at one point, it will break out more violently and bafflingly elsewhere; a segregated district is really a protection to the morality of the womanhood of the city, for without it rape would be common and clandestine immorality would increase.[46]

The women who did become prostitutes were too often seen as physiologically and psychologically flawed, having had the bad luck of being born sick, as Ruth Rosen notes:

> The prostitute could be the focus of "passions that might have filled the world with shame," servicing men's sexual

needs as other women could not, because a great gulf separated her nature from that of other women. Other women were pure; she was depraved....Her reputation, once lost, was irredeemable...[and] she became capable of any crime.[47]

Any woman who showed hints of sexuality, or even social rebellion, was considered at risk. Poor and ethnic women were thought to be more in danger than white middle-class women; as one muckraking journalist bluntly put it, "The mating instinct comes early to the slum girl."[48] Any sexual conduct, including rape, could trigger such a social stigma in a woman's life that the underworld might seem the only refuge. Over and over in the letters sent into the *Bulletin*, prostitution was the ultimate outcome of women who had been raped, as was the case for Violet Brown, who recounted her horrific story for the *Bulletin*. After being raped in her place of work, she blacked out.

When I became conscious I found myself in a filthy hole of a cellar under the kitchen. The reeking filth of the place was sickening. I was kept locked in this place without food or drink for two days and two nights. And then, in a half-fainting condition hurried through the back yard of the restaurant and into the rear entrance of a house of prostitution. Here I was locked in a room and kept for weeks—how many I do not know. While kept prisoner in this room I was compelled to submit to unspeakable outrages. I was forced, also, to submit to demands of the patrons of the house.

When I was finally released I was too broken in spirit, too outraged and ashamed to want to get away. I stayed in that house for months without so much as stepping outside the door. I ask you, Mr. Fremont Older, how could I have left? I had no money and my people were far away, and I was too ashamed to look an honest woman in the face.

Three years have passed since that time. I have been in most houses in San Jose.[49]

Here we see that, contrary to popular opinion, the existence of brothels didn't protect "pure" women from rape by channeling men's uncontrollable passions into the "underworld"; in fact, it was too often rape itself that drove women into the brothels in the first place.

Alice, before she turns to prostitution, has a near brush with sexual assault, which she relates early in her memoirs. After being propositioned by a Canadian lodger of her aunt's, she wonders aloud why such a thing had happened to her, and whether she could have been to blame:

What had that big Canadian wanted in my room? Well—I knew, all right enough. There was something that always seemed to come into the minds of men whenever I was alone with them.

Was it something about myself alone, I wondered? Was I different in that way from other girls? It worried me.

I got my sister Emma off alone one day and told her about it. She laughed.

"Oh, he's just like the rest of them," she said. "They're always after a girl. By the time you've lived around here a year longer you'll see plenty of that. Men are all the same."

I knew she had spoken the truth. It gave me the queerest feeling—as if I was always going to be sort of hunted; as if I was never going to be safe, never off my guard, always bound to be chased by some man. Emma, too, had known the feeling, it seemed—then was it just the same with all the other girls?...

Was it the same, too, I wondered, with girls who were rich, who had lots of money—girls who weren't just laborers' daughters?[50]

Alice doesn't tell her Grandmother Smith about the incident, fearing that she'll be blamed for the lodger's advances, precisely because of the Victorian code her grandmother kept. Within that narrow worldview, Alice risked a ruined reputation, and possibly much more, and so she kept quiet. But beyond that, she describes her independent streak and innocent desire to have friends and a social life, including chaste friendships with gentleman callers. For that she's branded a bad seed, and she seems to have taken that to heart and developed the attitude that if she was considered bad, why not *be* bad? Ruth Rosen recounts a similar story:

Reflecting society's exaggerated concern about the sexual activity of young, poor, adolescent females, the courts frequently manifested an interventionist, invasive, and punitive attitude toward female sex offenders....In one case...a fifteen-year-old girl, Deborah Horowitz, was brought into court for staying out with boys and "flaunting" her sexual activities. Her probation officer, after ransacking her belongings, found a racy letter that the girl had written to a sailor, along with photos showing her with the top button of her blouse undone and her hat off. Deborah...defiantly insisted that she had never coaxed or invited anyone's sexual attention. Nevertheless, she was committed to the state reformatory for girls.[51]

Further exasperating the clash of generations was the onset of modernization that the Progressive era brought to the early twentieth century. The role of young working-class women in the public sphere reacted to the growth of consumerist culture in the city, shifting their yearnings and aspirations away from the traditions and expectations of their parents and grandparents. In the words of one modern scholar:

> In the early twentieth century in urban areas, men and women of all classes began to appear in public places oriented toward pleasure and consumption—dance halls, amusement parks, and theaters. In the cities young people could often easily meet outside the supervision of their families or neighborhoods, and their activities illustrated the new century's sensual, pleasure-seeking culture, emphasized by mass consumerism on the one hand and individual fulfillment on the other. Nineteenth-century euphemisms faded as, heralded by new fashions and forms of entertainment and glorified by much of the media, sexuality became a major social concern.[52]

Alice Smith, raised not by her parents but her grandparents, felt this cultural divide in a sharp and unforgiving way. When she did what she wanted—for instance, having an innocent "good time" with boys and girls in her grandmother's drawing room—her guardian saw it as one step on the road to perdition when, in fact, Alice was merely behaving like any girl of her age. Caught between these forces, the young girl struggled to keep her head above water in a society that, although becoming increasingly more lenient, was still imposingly rigid toward single working-class women. It is not an exaggeration to argue that had Alice been born ten or fifteen years later, when attitudes had shifted further, she may never have become a prostitute.

Young women pushed the envelope in the bohemian cafés and salons of San Francisco, New York, and other major cities, but they were the exception. For most working-class single girls, maintaining their respectability was a constant source of anxiety. Concerns over social status, coupled with the development of modern advertising, pinched young women of small means into feelings of inadequacy and cycles of desire for better lives they could not afford; advertisements for fine clothes and shoes flanked the pages of the *Bulletin*, right alongside Alice's story. Without the existence of a social net or proper minimum wage, an unmarried working-class woman was truly vulnerable, especially when surrounded by the signs of status wrapped around department store mannequins in shop windows and the well-off women reflected in the glass. As Alice Smith so aptly put it:

> You decent woman who is reading this, haven't you ever stopped in front of one of those lovely windows, and feasted your eyes on the silks, laces, lingerie, costly gowns and jewelry—things that just made your soul seem empty because you didn't have them? Is there any woman anywhere who doesn't love fine clothes? Well—how about the girl who has been poor all her life, and has never had any? How do you suppose she feels?
>
> Well, I'll tell you how it makes her feel. There is a thick, strong plate glass window between the man, standing there, and those diamonds he is looking at; and at that, he only loves the diamonds because he can sell them. That plate glass window protects him from stealing them. But there isn't any protection to hide expensive dresses away from the eyes of the poor girl, who loves

them for their own wonderful beauty; oh, few men realize how much she loves them, or how they reach out and take hold of her, mind and soul.

That plate glass keeps the men from being burglars. But it doesn't keep the girls from going and selling themselves.

Think of that the next time you look into a shop window.[53]

Alma Greene, the twenty-one-year-old prostitute who wrote a series of letters that electrified the *Bulletin* readership, agreed with Alice on this point: "I think, perhaps, the display of fine clothes and hats by women is largely responsible for the downfall of many girls of what you call the underworld. Not that I was particularly weak that way—at that time—but so many girls have told me their lives."[54] Ironically, Alice would eventually sell most of her finery *because it made her look like a prostitute*; working-class single women with expensive clothes were, to the common eye, often easily labeled as sex workers. In yet another irony, by the 1920s the look that had come to be associated with prostitutes had now seeped into popular dress. Respectability for women like Alma and Alice always had a Sisyphean quality.

Another theme that plays an important and slippery role in Alice's story is marriage. At various points in the narrative, finding a husband seems to be the only acceptable fate for a woman, her only means of elevating herself economically and socially. At the same time, however, Alice reflects on the constraining nature of marriage on one's independence. Several letters also illustrate this dichotomy that marriage could be a savior or a shackle—and sometimes both—for any woman. As Alice puts it, "The girl herself didn't have any choice in the matter. She was supposed to take the first man that came along with an offer, whether she loved him or not. Love was one thing, marriage another."[55] Complicated though it was, to Alice and many of her fellow brothel girls marriage was one way to leave behind the life of prostitution. The dream of marriage as escape became a fixation for some, and as close relationships developed between sex workers and their clients, unwritten codes kept the women from engaging with one another's lovers, so as not to steal from another girl a potential way out of the cycle.

This dream became a reality for some women, such as "Jennie," whose story of rescue was related by her husband, "Bob," in a letter published in the *Bulletin* on July 7, 1913. "I saved my wife's life and she saved mine," he recounts after telling of their dramatic meeting "on the seawall at the foot of a San Francisco street." He, an alcoholic, and she, having lost her job as a dance hall girl, were both contemplating suicide at the shoreline when they found one another.[56] But this romantic tale is one of few; several of the letter writers urge their fellow women to forget about their knight-in-shining-armor fantasies.

Alice herself indulges in this daydreaming but, interestingly, she chooses not to marry on a number of occasions. Early on in her youth, Alice had noticed that "as soon as a girl married, she stopped growing, stopped learning, stopped thinking, stopped going ahead any; just gave up and became a drudge."[57] At times Alice blames this independent streak for her own downfall. But this is also one characteristic that gives her narrative its strikingly modern quality. Alice was certainly not alone in questioning the benefits of matrimony; one of the most fascinating series of letters comes from a woman who laments that while she married a man considered to be a model husband, she felt layers of dissatisfaction that she could not explain to herself.

While this woman grappled with the meaning of love in society, others wrote much more blatant critiques of the institution of marriage. Belle Curtis, one of the many eloquent prostitutes to submit a letter, questioned: "Is it worse for a man and woman to live together without having gone through the marriage ceremony, if they love and are true to each other...than for a lawful wife to submit her body to a husband for whom she has absolutely no love? Is not this prostitution?"[58] Another letter writer expresses sorrow for the children born out of sanctified rape—the unwanted sexual relations perpetrated by a husband on his wife.[59] Alice questions the institution of marriage over and over, and while she has many boyfriends and lovers, she never settles down with any of them, even the one who could have potentially saved her from the life of prostitution—the returned sweetheart of her youth, a man named Billy. There are many reasons why Alice refuses to marry: a desire for a life more interesting than those of her hometown housewife counterparts; a cynicism that builds while serving married men in the brothels; a romantic nature that craves passion, not convenience. Only once does Alice want to marry a man, and that is when she finds herself pregnant; she knows that marriage is the only way to save the reputation of her unborn baby. Here in the *Bulletin*, fifty years before the publication of Betty Friedan's groundbreaking book *The Feminine Mystique*, we hear housewives lamenting their loveless relationships and prostitutes declaring marriage a choice, not a necessity.

HOW INCLUSIVE WAS "A VOICE FROM THE UNDERWORLD"?

Whose voices were not included in "A Voice from the Underworld"? Although the editors of the *Bulletin* appear to have made a concerted effort to give space to an array of diverse opinions in the letters they published alongside Alice Smith's memoirs, there is a noticeable gap in the lineup: stories about what it was like specifically to be a woman of color. We cannot identify the race of the women represented in the letters published by the *Bulletin*, and there are only a few brief moments in Alice's story that directly mention race. In one, a madam explains to Alice that the African American prostitutes on their block "don't more'n make their board."[60] Another time race comes up is an unfortunate incident in which Alice says she is uncomfortable when three black prostitutes come to enjoy drinks at the white brothel in which she works. "I didn't like that," she said, "but...it's pretty democratic in those country places."[61]

Black sex workers, as well as Mexican, Japanese, Filipino, South and Central American, and Native American sex workers, were not uncommon in California at this time, and most had turned to sex work out of economic need, not unlike their white contemporaries. Conditions were certainly more challenging for women of color, who had fewer job opportunities outside of the sex market and who would often be compensated less for the same sexual services as their white counterparts. Alice's discomfort in sharing a parlor with black prostitutes could be read as an admission of blatant racism—not uncommon in an era in which eugenical and pseudoscientific philosophizing against racial integration and miscegenation was extremely popular, even amongst many Progressive-era reformers. Due to a lack of material on the subject, however, it is difficult to know with any certainty how Alice, or the *Bulletin*, felt regarding the issue of race and its intersection with class, gender, and sex work. What is apparent is that this is a notable hole in the purported universality of this story and the letters accompanying it.

An even more obvious omission is the lack of any discussion of Chinese prostitution. Chinese sex workers had been common across the state of California since the gold rush, and in 1870, 71 percent of all Chinese women in San Francisco were prostitutes.[62] Most of these women had been kidnapped or coerced into sex slavery, and few lived longer than six years after that due to the deplorable conditions of the "cribs" in which they worked. While "white slavery" was the cause du jour of many U.S. anti-prostitution advocates, white prostitutes in general had a level of freedom that Chinese prostitutes never would. Perhaps this is why many of the former chose to remain in sex work rather than take advantage of the settlement homes and employment agencies set up for them by middle-class reformers. Many of the *Bulletin's* letter writers insisted that not one prostitute would move into a settlement house as an alternative to prostitution, and while that may have been true for many white prostitutes, for Chinese prostitutes the settlement house often offered the only means of escape, other than marriage or suicide. By 1910 the number of Chinese prostitutes had dropped significantly in San Francisco (to only 7 percent of the female Chinese population), in part due to the success of such institutions as the Presbyterian Mission Home and the Donaldina Cameron House. (Another factor was the passage in 1882 of the federal Chinese Exclusion Act, which largely halted the immigration of Chinese women and men until it was repealed in 1943.)[63]

Perhaps a less surprising omission from the *Bulletin's* coverage is that of homosexual and gender-nonconforming voices, despite evidence that male prostitution and gender-bending entertainment was available on the Barbary Coast, not to mention the presence of female homosexual relationships within the brothel system. Although the *Bulletin* was radical in many ways, it, like every other major newspaper in America, was still confined by certain social standards, as well as by laws regulating concepts of "decency." Whether this omission was intentional on behalf of the *Bulletin* is still a question; none of the published letter writers self-identify as being queer or from a community of color, so we just cannot know how inclusive this document is regarding the full range of individuals involved in sex work at the time.

Nevertheless, as "A Voice from the Underworld" developed in the pages of the *Bulletin*, the paper served not just as a forum for public debate but also as a sort of community bulletin board, where women in need of immediate assistance could reach out to philanthropic readers. Fremont Older himself offered assistance to some of the most desperate letter writers, and a number of women took to asking for specific forms of assistance from the *Bulletin's* readers. Women wrote in looking for jobs or safe places to stay. Readers responded with offers of help, and it appears that some women were able to make connections that allowed them to better their lives. Others rebuked offers of assistance, including Alma Greene, who shocked readers when she rejected an offer of charity that had appeared in print. It is in these calls and responses that occur alongside the daily installments of Alice's serial that we see the evolving shape of this piece and the way in which it affected the lives of its readers, both materially and philosophically.

RED EMMA AND THE "VICTIMS OF MORALITY"

On the evening of Sunday, July 20, 1913, seven hundred curious audience members gathered at Jefferson Square Hall in the Western Addition district of San Francisco to hear Emma Goldman, the internationally acclaimed anarchist philosopher, give a speech about "A Voice from the Underworld" and her recently published essay, "Victims of Morality." In her speech, Goldman applauded the *Bulletin* for its fearless portrayal of the life of Alice Smith and spoke freely about her views on morality, sex education, prostitution, and capitalism.

Of course prostitution is one of the symptoms of our terrible economic system, and until we change that system we shall continue to face this and a great many other evils. At the same time[,] I think it is largely augmented by the bringing up of girls in total ignorance of the functions of sex. That is to say girls are raised with the sole idea instilled into their minds that marriage is the reason for existence and the result is that they sooner or later sell themselves to one man, or to more than one. There is altogether too much sordidness in life. Quite often a girl and a man really love each other, but cannot marry for financial reasons. It is natural for them to love, but society says it is unnatural for them to consummate that love save in a prescribed way.[64]

According to Goldman, this speech drew one of the largest audiences of her 1913 West Coast tour. According to the *Bulletin*, Alice Smith herself sat rapt in the audience, beaming as she heard bits of her own story read back to her and the wildly applauding audience.

Having witnessed the effects of anti-vice crusades in New York City years before, Goldman felt an urgent need to combat the wave of reform sweeping the nation. Goldman watched as prostitutes were pushed out of the brothels and forced to ply their trade on the threatening streets of Manhattan's Bowery, a change Goldman attributed to the passage of an anti-liquor law in 1896.[65]

Like all legislation for the elimination of vice, the Raines Law only multiplied the very thing it claimed to abolish….In rain or cold, well or ill, the unfortunates had to hustle for business, glad to take anyone who consented to come, no matter how hideous or decrepit he might be.[66]

Goldman's own relationship with prostitution was complex; while she abhorred the commodification of the body, she had once tried to sell herself on the streets in order to raise money for her radical political campaigns. Modeling herself after Dostoevsky's long-suffering Sonya Marmeladova from *Crime and Punishment*, Goldman put on her best dress and walked up and down Manhattan's Fourteenth Street, hoping to make enough money to buy a gun with which her partner, Alexander Berkman, could shoot Henry Clay Frick, manager of the Carnegie Steel Company, in the wake of the Homestead strike of 1892. (John D. Barry of the *Bulletin* would later use this same Dostoyevskian comparison, describing Alice Smith as a modern Sonya.) Goldman's sympathy for these "unfortunates" grew over the course of her friendship with Ms. Spenser, a madam and morphine addict whom Goldman had helped nurse to health. Goldman also met many sex workers during her stays in county jails and prisons. Overall, Goldman saw prostitution as an obvious consequence of capitalism, and she blamed the stifling social codes of the time for perpetuating the most oppressive forms of prostitution. "It is Morality which condemns woman to the position of a celibate, a prostitute, or a reckless, incessant breeder of children," wrote Goldman in her 1913 essay "The Victims of Morality," and she expounded on what this lack of choice meant for many women:

> Now, as to the prostitute....Who has made her? Whence does she come? Morality, the morality which is merciless in its attitude to women. Once she dared to be herself, to be true to her nature, to life, there is no return: the woman is thrust out from the pale and protection of society. The prostitute becomes the victim of Morality....The prostitute is victimized by still other forces, foremost among them the Property Morality, which

compels woman to sell herself as a sex commodity for a dollar per, out of wedlock, or for fifteen dollars a week, in the sacred fold of matrimony. The latter is no doubt safer, more respected, more recognized, but of the two forms of prostitution the girl of the street is the least hypocritical, the least debased, since her trade lacks the pious mask of hypocrisy; and yet she is hounded, fleeced, outraged, and shunned by the very powers that have made her: the financier, the priest, the moralist, the judge, the jailor, and the detective, not to forget her sheltered, respectably virtuous sister; who is the most relentless and brutal in persecution of the prostitute.[67]

The *Bulletin* certainly was not an anarchist paper, and Alice Smith is not portrayed as a political radical, but many of the themes in her story reflect points made by Goldman in her speeches and writings from 1913. At the very least, the two could agree that society was to blame for the existence of prostitution, not the prostitutes themselves. Alice Smith and Emma Goldman also both make the case that if women were better educated about sex that fewer of them would fall prey to predatory men. Alice may not have agreed with the free-love ethic that Goldman embraced, but she certainly questioned the draconian punishments she suffered for simply socializing with men her age, whether in her parlor at home or at community dances. And while Alice dreamed of a husband and children, she was also disturbed by the loveless and poverty-stricken marriages many of her friends were trapped in, even going so far as to compare marriage to prostitution, an analogy Goldman employed regularly. Would either of these women have supported the Red Light Abatement Act? While Emma Goldman certainly distrusted all legal attempts to regulate morality, Alice never takes a definitive stance on the vice abatement law in her memoir.

THE END OF THE BARBARY COAST

Three and a half years after the final installment of Alice Smith's memoir, the Red Light Abatement Act cleared its final hurdles statewide, opening the way for the closure of the Barbary Coast. Madams Maude Spencer and Reggie Gamble, partners in a high-end brothel in the Uptown Tenderloin, got word of an anti-vice gathering scheduled for January 25, 1917, and decided to act. Facing what was advertised as "a clean-up of the city" but what was in reality a mass eviction of the brothels, Spencer began organizing a march for the morning of the 25th, rallying prostitutes from the city's brothels to join together and let their voices be heard. For help, she turned to Reggie Gamble's friend, Fremont Older. As she told the editor, "I'm going to have them [the women] put it [the issue at hand] up straight...and ask him [crusading anti-vice church leader Rev. Paul Smith], now that he has taken their livelihood away from them, what he is going to do for these hundreds of women, many of them with children and mothers to support."[68] Older agreed to help. Meeting at the *Bulletin's* offices, Gamble wrote (with help from reporters Bessie Beatty and Rose Wilder Lane) the speech to be given to Smith and his congregation the next day. While they planned the speech, Older got the word out with the aid of connections he had made from the publication of Alice Smith's memoirs. He recalled:

> As the women of the underworld were extremely grateful to me for printing their letters during the running of "A Voice from the Underworld" serial, I had no difficulty in gaining their consent to congregate in front of the church at the hour set. I sent a messenger to all of them during the night. In the morning at 8 o'clock I rang up Mrs. Gamble.... She said "I'm already on the job."[69]

By 11 A.M. there were more than two hundred women at the church door. When it opened, Reggie Gamble took the lead, marching straight up to the pulpit and taking her place next to Reverend Smith as an equal. The "fallen women" crowded into the church, challenging the congregation to cast the first stone. Smith was furious but powerless to halt the protest. Reggie Gamble began to address the room:

> We women find it impossible to exist on the wages of $6 or $7 a week that are paid to women in San Francisco. Most of the girls here present came from the poor.... Your sphere is among the well-to-do. These girls are better off in houses of prostitution than they would be as individuals, because at least they get what little protection can be afforded them by the house....
>
> Nearly every one of these women is a mother, or has some one depending on her. They are driven into this life by economic conditions. People on the outside seem oblivious to this fact. One of the girls told me that her brother, a Methodist minister, when she applied for help to him only told her to trust in God.
>
> You can't trust in God when shoes are $10 a pair and wages are $6 dollars a week.
>
> I have the same respect for spiritual faith that any one has. Which of the members of your congregation, Dr. Smith, will take any of these women into their homes, or pay them the proper living wages, or see that they have the care and attention that they need?
>
> You said that you did not want women like this to come to your church. You want this section of the city to be free from their presence. That is quite different from the attitude of the son of Mary to the Magdalene. Jesus did not scorn the Magdalene as you have done.

You want the city cleaned up around your church—but where do you want the women to go? Have you made any arrangement by which they can make their living elsewhere?...

Why don't you go to the big business houses? Why don't you go to the legislature and change the conditions? Men here in San Francisco say they want to eliminate vice. If they do, they had better give up something of their dividends and pay the girls' wages so they can live.

You won't do anything to stop vice by driving us women out of this city to some other city. Has your city and your church a different God, that you drive evil away from your city and your church to other cities and other churches?

If you want to stop prostitution, stop the new girls from coming in here. They are coming into it every day. They will always be coming into it as long as conditions, wages and education are as they are. You don't do any good by attacking us. Why don't you attack those conditions?[70]

Reverend Smith uncomfortably admitted to the economic injustice the women faced, yet unsurprisingly, he remained steadfast in his campaign. Not many who marched expected tangible results from the protest, but there was some satisfaction in just being heard. Such satisfaction was short-lived, however.

On Valentine's Day 1917 a "moral squad" of police officers gathered to storm the gates of the Barbary Coast. They met little resistance. The residents of the Coast had been waiting for weeks for the day to arrive; those who had somewhere to go had already left, leaving the remainder for Police Chief

David White and his boys in blue. The moral squad methodically went street by street, then alley by alley, beginning with the Commercial Street brothels and spreading out until the entire district, ringed by Kearny, Commercial, DuPont (now Grant), and Jackson, had been cleared. No arrests were made even though there was a smattering of protests, "some laughing scornfully, some on the edge of tears." Going door to door, leaving guards at every street entrance, the eviction of some fourteen hundred women had the feeling of a mass lockout.

> Captain of Police Gleason announced that every house of prostitution must be closed before evening, and that tonight a police blockade would be stationed at the entrance to each street and alley where the women have been plying their vocation. No one will be allowed to enter the district tonight, and women who may fail to obey the police injunction will be placed under arrest. The lid is on tighter than ever before in the history of San Francisco.[71]

For those facing the cold February sidewalks, an emergency relief station was erected on nearby Montgomery Street by the City Federation of Women's Clubs for "assistance, shelter, and opportunities to work," though it was clearly stated that no women would be taken into private homes. Temporary work would be furnished by "certain factories and shops," yet there was no mention of wages. Despite best intentions, there was considerable mistrust on the side of the evicted; evidently the bad blood between the clubwomen of the city and their "fallen sisters" hadn't been mended. As the *Bulletin* reported:

> So far but one woman has made application for assistance since the closing of the resorts. This was a girl about 23 years old....The girl was dressed in a solid pink

party dress with no wraps but a fur around her neck, although the night was cold. She told Mrs. Blackburn that 'The Madam had shown her the gate,' and that she was turned out without clothes or money. She withheld the name of the proprietress because, as she told Mrs. Blackburn, the woman had had hard luck and a lot to worry her with the closing of her house.[72]

There had once been many hundreds of brothels in the segregated vice districts of the West, and one by one, city by city, they were being shuttered. Seattle, Portland, and Los Angeles had all pulled the plug on the red light, leaving San Francisco and Reno, Nevada, as the hold-outs. Now, only Reno's few lone brothels were left, and thus came to a close this chapter of the Wild West.

HOW FAR HAVE WE COME?

Just months after the sex worker march and closure of the Barbary Coast, the United States entered World War I. In response, social purity became wrapped up with national security, as reformers feared venereal disease spread by prostitutes would weaken the country's military. A new national social-purity law demanded the arrest of any prostitute found within five miles of an army base, and since essentially the whole of San Francisco fell within five miles of the Presidio, a rash of arrests followed. Today, the pictures of these women, and some men, can be seen lining numerous pages in "Sex Crimes and Muzzlers," a police mug book from 1918 now held in the archives of the San Francisco Main Library's History Center.

As historian Neil Larry Shumsky has noted, the Progressive era failed to eradicate prostitution; it merely scattered it. While the more dangerous industry of streetwalking became much more common, brothels continued to operate illegally in San Francisco and elsewhere. In one of the most dramatic chapters of Alice's narrative, she describes her oppressive fear of streetwalking, and the dangers associated with it, after hearing of the experiences of a friend who had worked the streets in Chicago. Since the 1917 closure of the Barbary Coast and the quasi-legal brothel system, San Francisco's sex workers have had to navigate the criminal underworld through a combination of their own self-organized networks; finding work on the streets and in underground brothels, bars, strip clubs, nightclubs, bathhouses, and massage parlors; and, more and more with the development of the Internet, online. Anti-vice campaigns in San Francisco have likewise continued to flourish and fade periodically based on instances of local and national backlashes against sex work.

The evicted brothel workers of the Barbary Coast had to find and navigate new geographies of sex, and of police harassment, in scattered zones, such as the waterfront, Market Street, the Uptown Tenderloin, and Union Square, and they struggled to find safe places in which to ply their trade. According to historian Nan Alamilla Boyd, the era of Prohibition saw a collapse of the openly licentious culture that had made San Francisco famous and had brought so many to its shores, but after Prohibition's repeal, new zones of sex tourism allowed for a resurgence in the visible sex trade in newly formed vice districts, such as North Beach and South of Market. Bars and nightclubs where liquor ran freely opened again, and bawdy performances by exotic dancers, some of them in drag, created an environment where sex-for-sale could, once again, be easily found.

This began to unravel once the Atherton Report, a' 1935 FBI investigation into civic corruption, revealed widespread systems of graft involving police and underground brothels, and the city was once again bound to clean up its act. By the early 1940s, coinciding again with a world war, national pressure forced city officials to declare yet another end to vice in San Francisco, and brothel sweeps and the harassment of bar and nightclub owners became the de facto law of the land. In the decade that followed, the police teamed up with the Alcoholic Beverage Control Board by penalizing bars that served liquor to known prostitutes and enacting a series of local ordinances that attempted to curb women from socializing in bars, echoing early attempts to restrict women and sex workers from the drinking establishments of the Barbary Coast in 1913. Simultaneously, a tangible nostalgia for the wide-open Barbary Coast filled the cafés and bars of bohemian North Beach, fueling a cultural and sexual revolution that exploded into the 1960s.

While the sixties brought "free love" to the tip of the nation's tongue, a series of police backlashes at San Francisco's Compton Cafeteria and New York's Stonewall Inn simultaneously ignited the nation's gay rights and sex worker rights movements. This broadening of the national dialogue about sex coincides with what is considered to be the beginnings of the contemporary sex worker rights movement. While the 1960s caused a tidal wave of discussion, revolution, and reform about the critical issue of sex worker rights that is, if anything, increasing in momentum today, the forgotten history of the 1917 Prostitute March on the Reverend Paul Smith's Central Methodist Church and the publication of the story of Alice Smith by a sympathetic San Francisco newspaper are necessary links to the history of this continuing movement. In 1913, readers of the *San Francisco Bulletin* were discussing feminism, economic justice, labor rights, prison reform, and the inherent dignity of sex workers as human beings. Alice's story and the accompanying letters serve as a mark of how far we as a society have come—and how far we have left to go.

Notes

1. Reggie Gamble, quoted in Fremont Older, *My Own Story* (Oakland: Post-Enquirer Publishing Co., 1925), 165.

2. Catherine Murphy, "Sex Worker Rights Are Human Rights," Amnesty International, August 14, 2015, https://www.amnesty.org/en/latest/news/2015/08/sex-workers-rights-are-human-rights.

3. Molly Smith, "In this Prostitution Debate, Listen to Sex Workers not Hollywood Stars," August 3, 2015, *Guardian*, http://www.theguardian.com/commentisfree/2015/aug/03/prostitution-sex-workers-amnesty-meryl-streep-lena-dunham.

4. Philip J. Ethington, *The Public City: The Political Construction of Urban Life in San Francisco, 1850–1900* (Berkeley: University of California Press, 1994).

5. Roger W. Lotchin, *San Francisco, 1846–1856: From Hamlet to City* (New York: Oxford University Press, 1974), 254.

6. Evelyn Wells, *Fremont Older* (New York: D. Appleton-Century Company, 1936), 51–52. The self-proclaimed "Emperor" Joshua Norton was a famous San Francisco eccentric who printed political decrees and his own useless bonds, which were, surprisingly, honored by many local merchants who considered him a local treasure.

7. Ibid., 51.

8. Robert Davenport, "Fremont Older in San Francisco Journalism: A Partial Biography, 1856–1918" (Ph.D. diss., University of California, Los Angeles, 1969), 42.

9. Ibid., 60.

10. Pauline Jacobson, "Jerome Bassity, a Study in Depravity," *San Francisco Bulletin*, May 14, 1910.

11. James B. Walsh, "Abe Ruef Was No Boss: Machine Politics, Reform, and San Francisco," *California Historical Quarterly* 51 (Spring 1972): 7–14; and Lotchin, *San Francisco*, 41.

12. Wells, *Fremont Older*, 212–13.

13. Ibid., 244.

14. Donald Lowrie, *My Life Out of Prison* (New York: Mitchell Kennerley, 1915), 44.

15. Ibid.

16. Ibid.

17. Teresa Hurley and Jarrod Harrison, "Awed by the Women's Clubs: Women Voters and Moral Reforms, 1913–1914," in *California Women and Politics: From the Gold Rush to the Great Depression*, ed. Robert W. Cherny, Mary Ann Irwin, and Ann Marie Wilson (University of Nebraska Press, 2011), 243–45.

18. Julius Rosenstirn, *Our Nation's Health Endangered by Poisonous Infection through the Social Malady: The Protective Work of the Municipal Clinic of San Francisco and Its Fight for Existence* (San Francisco: Town Talk Press, 1913), 16–18.

19. Josh Sides, *Erotic City: Sexual Revolutions and the Making of Modern San Francisco* (New York: Oxford University Press, 2009), 21.

20. "Not for Money," *San Francisco Bulletin*, June 26, 1913.

21. Hurley and Harrison, "Awed by the Women's Clubs," 243.

22. James Rolph Jr. Papers, box 56, folder 6, California Historical Society, San Francisco. There are many examples of these letters in the Rolph Papers, but we find J. C. Westenberg's lengthy correspondences with Rolph to be the most illuminating.

23. Alice Smith, "Author's Statement of Reasons that Impelled Her to Tell the Story of Her Life in the Shadows," *San Francisco Bulletin*, June 20, 1913.

24. John D. Barry, "A Woman of the Underworld," *San Francisco Bulletin*, June 20, 1913.

25. R. L. Duffus, *The Tower of Jewels: Memories of San Francisco* (New York: Norton and Company, 1960), 231.

26. Arthur McFarlane, "A Friend of Crooks: Fremont Older," *Collier's*, November 15, 1913, 5–6.

27. "Why the Bulletin Prints the Story of Alice Smith," *San Francisco Bulletin*, July 2, 1913.

28. Lowrie, My *Life Out of Prison*, 44.

29. William Holtz, *The Ghost in the Little House: A Life of Rose Wilder Lane* (Columbia: University of Missouri Press, 1993), 65–66.

30. This volume, 70.

31. Ibid.

32. Rosen, *Lost Sisterhood*, 147.

33. "Life Unattractive, Writes Victim Driven to Brothel," *San Francisco Bulletin*, July 10, 1913.

34. "Girls Tempted by Finery of Richer Women," *San Francisco Bulletin*, June 30, 1913.

35. "Life Unattractive, Writes Victim Driven to Brothel," *San Francisco Bulletin*, July 10, 1913.

36. "Pity, Prayers, or Patronage Do Not Reform," *San Francisco Bulletin*, June 25, 1913.

37. This volume, 111.

38. "Mother's Gratitude," *San Francisco Bulletin*, June 30, 1913.

39. "Dressed as Boy to Keep from Evil," *San Francisco Bulletin*, June 25, 1913.

40. "Womanhood Crushed from Girls' Souls when Once Held in Serpent's Coils," *San Francisco Bulletin*, July 24, 1913.

41. This volume, 27.

42. "Condemns Men Who Champion Social System," *San Francisco Bulletin*, June 24, 1913. See also this volume, 100.

43. "Remedy Found in Economics," *San Francisco Bulletin*, June 23, 1913.

44. "Why Not Let Us Alone? Asks Segregated Woman," *San Francisco Bulletin*, June 20, 1913.

45. Ruth Rosen, *The Lost Sisterhood: Prostitution in America, 1900–1918* (Baltimore: John Hopkins University Press, 1982), 147.

46. Bridgeport Vice Commission, *The Report and Recommendations of the Bridgeport Vice Commission* (1916), as cited in Rosen, *Lost Sisterhood*, 5.

47. William Edward Hartpole Lecky, *History of European Morals from Augustus to Charlemagne*, 3rd ed. (London, 1877), 2:282–83, as cited in Rosen, *Lost Sisterhood*, 5–6.

48. Sarah Cory Rippey, "The Case of Angeline," *Outlook*, January 31, 1914, 255.

49. "Charges Woman Conspired to Bring About Downfall," *San Francisco Bulletin*, August 2, 1913.

50. This volume, 63–64.

51. Rosen, *Lost Sisterhood*, 20.

52. John Whiteclay Chambers II, *The Tyranny of Change: America in the Progressive Era, 1890–1920* (New Brunswick, NJ: Rutgers University Press, 2000), 95.

53. This volume, 118–19.

54. This volume, 190–91.

55. This volume, 10.

56. "Fate Rescues Two Outcasts at Brink of Watery Grave," *San Francisco Bulletin*, July 7, 1913.

57. This volume, 11.

58. "Belle Curtis Again Writes Managing Editor about Horrors of Life," *San Francisco Bulletin*, June 30, 1913.

59. "Always Danger while Women Are Dependent," *San Francisco Bulletin*, June 25, 1913.

60. This volume, 147.

61. This volume, 148.

62. Judy Yung, *Unbound Feet: A Social History of Chinese Women in San Francisco* (Berkeley: University of California Press, 1995), 29.

63. Ibid., 34–35, 72.

64. "'Alice Smith' Lecture Draws Immense Crowd," *San Francisco Bulletin*, July 21, 1913.

65. After the passage of New York's Raines law, which prohibited the sale of alcohol on Sundays unless it was served in a hotel, many saloons started renting rooms, including to sex workers and their clients. Some brothels, including one owned by Goldman's close friend, a Ms. Spenser, converted into "Raines hotels" to avoid the police, and Goldman appears to be saying that the sex workers who had previously worked out of the relative safety of the brothels now had to find clients on the street to take into the hotels.

66. Emma Goldman, *Living My Life, Vol. 1* (New York: Dover Publications, 1970), 356.

67. Emma Goldman, "Victims of Morality," in *Red Emma Speaks*, ed. Alix Kates Shulman (New York: Shocken Books, 1983), 172.

68. Older, *My Own Story*, 163.

69. Ibid., 164.

70. From a speech given by Reggie Gamble, quoted in Older, *My Own Story*, 164–65.

71. "Police Close the Red Light District," *San Francisco Bulletin*, February 14, 1917.

72. "1400 Women Flee before Policemen," *San Francisco Bulletin*, February 15, 1917.

"H m, Let's See; Am I a Waitress or a Candy Girl?"

"But That I Cou..."

Opening installment of San Francisco outcast woman's story of her life and experiences in the shadows cast by the Red Light

BY ALICE SMITH

The following chapter of "A Voice from the Underworld" has been read and approved by committee of clubwomen. The committee is composed of the following:

MRS. JAMES ELLIS TUCKER, president of the Civic Center.
MISS FANNIE McLEAN, head of the English Department of the Berkeley High School.
MISS JULIA GEORGE, secretary of the College Equal Suffrage League.

Chapter I.

(Copyright, 1913, by The San Francisco Bulletin)

[This story will later be published in book form. For this reason it is copyrighted. E. A. Crothers has the property of Alice Smith, to who may have given adequate compensation for this series. Portunately is given to persons the moral work she otherwise to any persons desiring to be about to persons rope. Portunately to about to persons paper, the extracts from the matter provided credit is given. The Bulletin and the copyright line is used.—Editor's Note.]

I HAD eighty dollars. I had earned that money in the usual way.

It was Christmastide—the twentieth of December. I was buying presents. The shops were crowded, and all about me people were spending their money as most of them didn't spend it very often—for the happiness of their friends.

I entered a big department store. Standing by a counter, I reached into my purse and got out a few of the people I was to remember with presents, to remember with presents, of course. There was always more to be made. That particular money had come. It happened, rather easy, and easy it should go.

Eighty dollars. All the girls in my house would remember me—that was certain. I wanted to remember all of them. I wanted to, anyway, and backbiting and all that; but I knew, if ever I got up east I there I could find the best friends in the world, the ones who would care for me most freely and most unconsciously.

Sixteen of them. Four dollars apiece for the girls' presents. Say sixty-five dollars for the bunch. Say, then there was the madam. Of course she costly one. Yet I liked her. She had ability. Yet I liked pick at her sometimes. We girls were too ready to in a position to be bossed around by her, it was nobody's fault—just the fault of circumstances.

All right. Fifteen dollars for the present for madam.

Fifteen dollars left—

Then something happened.

You know that Christmassy feeling that gets over the air during the holidays. It seems as though in those days. Christmas trees and ever saw it in your life were just around the corner, and then all their fragrant smell and sparkling lights and beautiful tinsel and strings of popcorn was sort of floating on the air. You can see floating on the air.

Somehow, things looked different right away.

It had not been yet often; at that particular period of my life, that the thought and memory of my grandfather had a chance to break through. Here it under pretty well. With the aid of the excitement and the smoke and drink—but very much that for the most part very much strain of the wakeful night and the sleepy day, I kept grandpa out of the way. He had little chance. And no use for such memories.

At that time, it was about this further than at any other time, since. The greater part of my dead and hard. All my finer sensibilities were dampened. I was too glad to laugh when things came up that should have troubled and laughter that was false. It was just I had lost. My ambition, the kind of ambition

mind, I was a bit surprised. For a moment I was angry.

Why on earth should I be plagued with I had now? There I had left him before, back in that little Middle Western village; that tiny town of Seven Houses. I hadn't written to him in six months; I had drifted out of the habit of writing; I had to tell too many lies. There was no reason why I should think about grandpa now.

As my anger faded, it seemed as though I became suddenly a little wider awake.

Eighty dollars. When I lived with grandfather, before I left home, I used to do one whole week's drudgery at housework for a dollar and a half a week. Oh, was the money we valued back there. And grandfather, he was a carpenter and painter; he used to get not over two dollars a day. He was an old man too; well over sixty.

Suppose—I didn't want to think it, but I did—suppose I were to send grandfather some money?

Well, that would be a lot of trouble. I had only gold and silver and—I cast one glance toward the money order window—it would take until day after tomorrow to get the money order.

The only way would be to chase down to some bank and get a letter—and how on earth was I to do that? What should I tell him? What had I told him last time I wrote—five months ago? How could I fix up my letter so that he would think I was happy, so that he wouldn't suspect? It would kill him only to let him suspect.

You see, grandpa had raised me and cared for me, from the time my father married my stepmother, when I was a baby of thirteen, nearly fourteen. All my other relatives never more about that later. But grandfather—he was perfect. I would not have had him different for a single thing. There was no bitterness, no hardness, in my thought of him. He was the idol of my girlhood. He was my idol still, in spite of everything.

Standing there in that crowded store and thinking of grandpa, I could not but feel that the thought hurt. And I was glad.

I would send him the whole eighty dollars. No—that would never do. Fifty? No; he would ask how I got so much. No; a laundry worker could send so much. Fifteen dollars; that would be about right.

Fifteen dollars for grandpa, and the same for the madam. Oh, what a life—

I couldn't very well give the madam any less and look friendly, and I could hardly give grandpa more and not be thought mean or odd. I decided it this way. Fifty dollars would do for the girls.

Thinking hard over that letter to my purchase. A big box of stuff for Mabel to send to mother one stack. Something decent for Bessie. What a box and if I had that I wouldn't care to be here today. What's some decent from Tennyson? All right. A volume of Tennyson for Grace; she liked them in her young days; she got them for her young days, alone with her regular showings of two dollars—her a half a day; everything was delivered at the house.

I bought the things for the girls.

But the address—

I reached under—Alice Smith. I reached that note. I reached into the park; We reached the park; not, further out than at a quiet pronoun out, and we came to a roadhouse. We were still dizzy. I had more and more freely, and denly switched to champagne. By that sort of came to its the were all still out of sorts. It was still dizzy. What had I been doing? I stopped hurriedly to see the letter!

Those scraps on the floor—I tore it up, when the furlong, to prevent their getting through my sister that my father was dead.

[We Be Continued]

GIRLHOOD MEMO AWAKENED B

Alice Smith, the Nome de Plume of ... Recalls Happier Days.

I WAS almost startled when I read the name ... be printed under—Alice Smith. It made ... time, years ago, when I sent my grandfather ... first honest money I had earned after I left ho ... favorite daughter named Alice.

When my money came he was sick and ... feeble, and he kept saying, it was Alice who had ... money. They wrote me about it.

So now it's to be Alice Smith who writes this ... ment by Alice Smith.

How much am I getting? Do I like ... note later.

The crowd sped out ...

Am I well? ... prospect of my ... visit? How long ... I enjoy it ... me, and I'll say ... of place. Uncle B'B's. Oh ... old grasper.

Is it right to keep Christmas when ... are better and more merciful in the ... long run—to tell grandfather the ... truth?

"...Dear Grandpa...

No; that isn't possible. I don't ... that for a murderer, as well as a ... money. Yet, I do want to send him the ... Here. I'll carry the job through ... then it's finished, and I was ... go on. I'm a restaurant, and I was ... got a better job soon, as I was thinking ... getting a better job soon, as I was thinking ... rush to get to work, etc., etc., very ... from his law work, etc., etc., very ... love to get that bank note.

I stopped out on the street and ... banker for a minute, trying to set ... An auto came rolling along the ban ... minute, when rolling along the ban ... the curb. It was a big mob ... in—friends of mine and ...

(To Be Continued)

OF NIGHT LIFE AND
RS CRY OUT AGAINST EVIL

LEND HELPING HAND TO WEAK, URGES WOMAN

One Long Acquainted With Outcasts Has Found Many Warm Hearts.

EDITOR BULLETIN: I am one of the underworld ... victims, but there is in my life I have been in business where I have been in touch with them, and I must say, I have found a great many men, that in their hearts and many them, that in the atmosphere, would have developed into noble women. I believe that if at any time, we are in a position to give a helping hand to put we should make an earnest effort to get up as should make an earnest effort to give to Christ, did not give to Christ, did not Mary Magdalene, but said he forgave her, and our only remonstrance to defend the weaker sister is to defend the woman sister. In to defend the evil in the universe is really no better than ours is really no thinketh is really the heart of a man thinketh is his heart?

Let us draw the day and drive for out of the woman can be can find in the ever we can find all that what ... So let me now I who shall also ... For us and her and happiness craves it, knowing very dear tree. I will be more complete in any dear ... I will be more complete in any ... temperament and are all treated ... Blood walk is said that all treated ... a making and helping shall be revived. ... the way. He had little chance ... and no use for such memories ...

A Voice from the Underworld

PART I

I had eighty dollars. I had earned that money in the usual way.

It was Christmastide—just the twentieth of December. I was out buying presents. The shops were crowded, and all about me people were spending their money as most of them didn't spend it very often—for the happiness of their friends. I entered a big department store. Standing by a counter, I reached into my purse and got out a list of people I was to remember with presents. The whole eighty dollars should go, of course. There was always more to be made. That particular money had come, it happened, rather easy; and easy it should go.

Eighty dollars. All the girls in my house would remember me—that was certain. I must remember all of them. I wanted to, anyway. There was a lot of petty quarrelling and backbiting and all of that; but I knew, if ever I got up against it, where I could find the best friends in the world, the ones who would care for me most freely and most consciously.

Sixteen of them. Four dollars apiece for the girls' presents. Say, sixty-five dollars for the bunch.

Then there was the madam. Of course the landlady must have her present—a costly one. Yet I liked her. She had ability. She had tact. We girls were too ready to pick on her at times. If we were in a position to be bossed around by her, it was nobody's fault—just the fault of circumstances.

All right. Fifteen dollars for a present for madam.

Fifteen dollars left—

Then something happened.

You know that Christmassy feeling that gets on the air during the holidays. It seems as though all the Christmas trees you ever saw in your life were just around the corner, and that all their fragrant smell and sparkling lights and beautiful tinsel and strings of popcorn were sort of floating in the air. You can go around among the shops, where that flavor is keenest, with every intention in the world of covering up your feelings; you can't make good.

Right in the middle of my calculations I had thought of my grandfather.

Somehow things looked different right away.

It had not been that often, at that particular period of my life, that the thought and memory of my grandfather had a chance to break through. I kept it under pretty well. With the aid of the excitement and tobacco smoke and drink—not that very much of that for me, but some—and the strain of the wakeful nights and sleepy days, I kept grandpa out of the way.

At that time—it was about five years ago—I seemed to have drifted further than at any time before or since. The greater part of me was dead and hard. All my finer sensibilities were benumbed. I was inclined to laugh when things came up that should have touched me; and there wasn't so much about that laughter that was false. It was just hard. I had lost my ambition, my energy, my standards. I lived in a kind of haze. I could not like the life, I could not hate it; I just didn't care.

When the smell of that holly, or Christmas tree, or whatever it was, brought my grandfather sharply to mind, I was a bit surprised. For a moment I was angry.

Why on earth should I be plagued with that now? Grandpa was living, where I had left him a few years before, back in that little Middle Western village; that tiny town of sixteen houses. I hadn't written to him in six months; I had drifted out of the habit of writing; I had to tell too many lies. There was no reason why I should think about grandpa now.

Eighty dollars. When I lived with grandfather, before I left home, I used to do one whole week's drudgery at housework for a dollar and a half a week. That was the way money was valued back there. And grandfather—he was a carpenter and painter; he used to get not over two dollars a day. He was an old man now, too; well over sixty.

Suppose—I didn't want to think it, but I did—suppose I were to send grandfather some money?

Well, that would be a lot of trouble. I had only gold and silver and—I cast one glance toward the money order window—it would take until the day after tomorrow to get a money order. The only way would be to chase down to some bank and get a treasury note.

Then I would have to write a letter—and how on earth was I to do that? What should I tell him? What had I told him last time I wrote, four or five months ago? How could I fix up my letter so that he would think I was happy, so that he wouldn't suspect?

You see, grandpa had raised me and cared for me, from the time my father married my stepmother, when I was a baby of three, until I was nearly eighteen. There was no bitterness, no hardness, in my thought of him. He was the idol of my girlhood and he was my idol still, in spite of everything.

I would send him the whole eighty dollars. No—that would never do. He would ask how I got so much. Fifty? No; no honest waitress or laundry worker could send so much. Fifteen dollars; that would be about right.

Fifteen dollars for grandpa, and the same for the madam. Oh, what a life—

I couldn't very well give the madam any less and look friendly, and I could hardly give grandpa any more and seem straight. So I decided it that way. Fifty dollars would do for the girls.

Thinking hard over that letter in the back of my head, I went about my purchases. A big box of stationery for Mabel, to write to her mother on—her mother doesn't know that she's in the life. Thinks she's a candy girl. Something decent to read for Bessie—she's got an education, and if I had that I wouldn't be here today. What's some decent poet—Tennyson? All right, a volume of Tennyson for Bessie. A box of fine candies for Grace; she can feed them to her young men, with that regular allowance of two and a half a day. My purchases were soon made. Everything to be delivered at the house.

I bought a fancy little bag of silk, and in it I put the fifteen dollars for the madam and mailed it.

I was getting increasingly doubtful about that letter. Why not try to write it upstairs? There was a woman's waiting room. I climbed the stairs and found a vacant desk.

H'm. Let's see. Am I a waitress or a candy girl? Suppose I say I am in housework? But the address—how much am I getting? Do I like my job? Am I well? Is there any prospect of my coming home for a visit? How long have I been working here? Is my boss kind? Sure he is, and I'll say he has kind blue eyes like

Uncle Ed's. Oh,—poor old grandpa!

Is it right to keep Christmas when one has to lie? Wouldn't it be better—better and more merciful in the long run—to tell grandfather the truth? Suppose I put it down here now,—"Dear Grandpa: I am a prostitute—"

No; that isn't possible. I don't want to be a murderer as well as a liar. Yet, I do want to send him that money. I'll carry the job through—

There. It's finished. I said I was a waitress in a restaurant, and the boss was kind, and I was thinking of getting a better job soon, as I only got seven dollars a week. Was in a rush to get to work, so no more now from his loving Alice.

I stepped out onto the street and paused for a moment, trying to remember which way was the bank. An auto came rolling along the street, close to the curb. It was a big machine, with a bunch of men and girls in it—friends of mine.

"Hello! Why, there's Alice! Wait a moment! Stop!"

The chauffeur drew up alongside the curb.

"Jump right in and come along. We're just going for a little spin out through the park."

They made room for me. I climbed in, smiling. It was too good a chance to be missed. Auto rides were none too frequent. I would get the bank note later.

The crowd sped out along the road. We reached the park; stopped for a time at a quiet beer garden; then out, further out into the country, to a roadhouse. We started buying more and more beer; then we suddenly switched to champagne.

I sort of came to in the morning. We were still out at the roadhouse. The rest of the crowd was drunk. I was still dizzy. I had only a dim remembrance of what had occurred.

What had I been doing? Oh yes: the banknote for grandpa.

I groped hurriedly in my purse. As I thought—I had spent it. It must have gone for champagne.

And the letter? What could have—?

Those scraps on the floor. I had torn it up, when the fun became furious, to prevent their getting a hold of it.

The following April I heard through my sister that my grandfather was dead.

You might think grandpa would get a little dim to me after all these years. But time doesn't touch him. And what I know about other men doesn't touch him, either. Today he seems just as he always did when I was a little girl—about seven miles higher than anybody else in the world; a kind of god.

I was left under grandpa's care and grandma's earlier than I can remember. It was when my father married my stepmother and went away. Grandpa was a carpenter. At first we lived on a farm near a crossroads; then we moved to a little town, seven miles from the railroad, out in the middle of a big farming country.

I wish I could make you see that life as I see it.

It was so simple, so quiet. There was a lot of hard work in it, too, especially for the women. But it was a natural life; that was the greatest thing about it.

I often think today: "Now if I could only get the money, I know what I'd do. I'd buy a little place, out in some pretty country town, and have my friends around me, and go back to the same sort of life I lived when I was a girl." But again, I don't know; maybe I couldn't make a go of it now. The quiet might drive me half-crazy. This life spoils one for anything natural; that's the fearful pity of it.

Grandpa and grandma were my mother's parents. My mother died when I wasn't yet a year old, and papa—my, but that name sounds queer as I say it now!—papa married again. I was three, and my sister, Emma, was five, when he got interested in a young girl, a farmer's daughter, sixteen years old. There was some sort of mixup over it; I never knew exactly what; anyway, he married her and they went West. I never saw papa again until I was seventeen.

Grandma and grandpa kept me, and Emma was sent a little while afterward out to papa's parents, who lived in the same town where papa had gone. It always seemed odd to me to think I had a sister. I used to write to her, maybe once a month; but she never seemed real.

Except for the letters, you see, the only thing I had to go on was one fool memory. It is almost the first thing I remember, and I couldn't have been more than four. There were a lot of people around and considerable noise, and I was playing with some little girl—my sister, though I don't remember how she looked—and in the next room somebody was ringing a bell. As a memory, that didn't amount to much, but it was the best I had for about thirteen years.

Though grandpa and grandma naturally didn't have a whole lot of use for my father, they never said hard things of him before me. That was just like them; they didn't like him, but they had their own ideas about what was fair to him, and about what his daughter ought to think. They weren't going to put anything in my head that oughtn't to be there.

My grandmother was good to me, and all that; but grandpa and I were chums.

We always kept quite a large garden—two or three acres. Every spring grandpa would lay off for a few days to plant his truck. That was the time of my great glory. I would lay off, too— from school—and work with grandpa from sun-up to dark.

He would let me drop the beans and peas, and cut and drop the potatoes, after he had prepared the ground. I never cared how tired I got—that was real work, I thought, and not just housework. I think grandpa got as much fun out of it as I did. "You'll be a man yet," he would say, and I would be proud.

This was grandpa's way; he never talked much, but when he did say something, people stopped still and listened. Whenever he spoke he always said something good; something that meant something.

I wanted to be exactly like him. I was like him, too, in one thing—and that was in being active.

He was never still. He was always doing something, and it was always something that counted. People in that region don't read much; grandma had never learned to read at all, and grandpa never read anything except the Bible and the weekly paper. But once he had a job where he had to walk a mile and a half to work and the same distance back; and he would get up at five, and work around the place until time to go; then he would quit at six o'clock, walk home, and go right at it again after dinner, until it was too dark to see. Nobody in that place stayed up late; sometimes in winter the whole bunch of us would be in bed by seven.

Right up to the day of his death, I've heard, grandpa kept working like that. Except when he was too sick or feeble. Now you can see a little of what I thought of grandpa. If I'd stayed with him, poor or not, and never come West at all, lots of things would never have happened.

Up to the time of my Uncle Ed's marriage, when I was fifteen, we weren't especially poor, as things went. At least if we were I never noticed it. Everyone in that place was poor together. There was food enough, but very little money.

If grandpa was the greatest man alive, Uncle Ed was a good second. He was about five years older than I was. Pretty early in life I made my mind up to one thing: if I couldn't get a man that was exactly like Uncle Ed, I wouldn't have any man at all.

Grandpa himself was ambitious and active, and Uncle Ed

was the brightest young man around. I had ambition bred into me as naturally as I had my health. And the way grandpa and Uncle Ed used to humor me and let me have my own way about things didn't make me any the less ambitious.

I wasn't going to grow up in the same life as the other girls and women I saw around me. As early as the days when I went to the little country school I made up my mind to that.

There wasn't any future for a girl back there except marriage. That was all right in itself; I never objected to that. And I always loved children. But other things about it I did object to.

There were two kinds of young men, and there was a big gap between the two kinds. There were the fine young fellows, and there were the no-accounts. The fine young fellows worked hard, were handy with tools, made all the money there was to be made, and supported their families. The no-account ones used to hang around the grocery store all day and spit into the box of sand that ran around the stove.

Uncle Ed was the best of the hard-working sort. Up to the time of his marriage he was our main support. He was a sort of genius at tools; he learned the carpenter's trade from grandpa, and he picked up blacksmithing, and could repair whatever machinery there was around on any of the farms. People were always calling in Uncle Ed for everything from mending a harvester to curing a sick horse.

Uncle Ed used regularly to spoil me. We were just like brother and sister. He used to take me to all the parties and so I got to go to more parties than almost any of the other girls; and how I did love them!

He knew how to play the fiddle, and I could play the accompaniments on the parlor organ; and we were in demand. He wanted me to look nice when I went with him—there was a little pride in that, I guess—and he bought me a pretty hat and almost the only set of furs around there.

Possibly Uncle Ed's spoiling had something to do with my being so self-willed; or possibly it was just born in me. I wasn't unruly in the least; but I was ambitious. I wanted my life to be different from what I saw around me.

People in that region were strict in their ideas. The lives of the girls especially were all mapped out in advance. You had to follow hard and fast rules, or be thought "queer."

Looking back on it now, I can see that those rules bore harder on the women, by a good deal, than they did on the men. As soon as a girl got through school, at fourteen or fifteen, or maybe less, she was supposed to look out for only one thing—a husband. She was expected to get married as soon as she possibly could, so as not to be a drag on her parents. The parents might be getting old, might not be making a living as easily as they used to: to marry and get out of the way was just a girl's duty. Lots of my chums were wives and mothers by the time they were sixteen.

The girl herself didn't have any choice in the matter. She was supposed to take the first man that came along with an offer, whether she loved him or not. Love was one thing, marriage another.

As I think of it now, I don't recall a single case where a girl turned down the first man who asked to marry her. She would have been thought queer and selfish if she had, I suppose; but anyhow, it never happened. The girls just didn't refuse, that's all.

You see, there were always fully three girls to one man. Most of the young fellows went away to the city.

We'd hear of them now and then, when they wrote to the old folks. One would be a carpenter in the city, maybe, making three dollars a day; or a plumber, or a teamster, or maybe one of them would be keeping a store; and a man who kept a store was way up in the world. Or maybe we'd heard that one of them hadn't caught on, somehow, and was coming back home.

Naturally we girls had to marry what was left. Often a girl's chance would be a widower twice her age, with children as old as she was, and a farm to take care of. This happened pretty often; because there weren't any very good doctors, and what, with the hard work and poor doctoring, an awful number of women, young women, too, died in childbirth.

What used to seem worst to me about it all was this: as soon as a girl married she stopped growing, stopped learning, stopped thinking, stopped going ahead any; just gave up and became a drudge. The work she was expected to do was fearfully hard; her hours would be from about four in the morning until six at night, day after day.

It all used to scare me. I wanted to get married, and to have my own home and everything; but though I had never seen anything different, it was something different that I wanted. I guess I did more thinking for myself than most of them.

Not so very long ago I went back to my old home on a visit. Some of my old schoolmates, girls my own age, seemed like old women, with stooped shoulders and sharp voices and skin a bit yellow—at twenty-five. It made me shudder.

Of all the girls I could see around me as a child, the only ones who had any freedom, any life of the sort I wanted, were the school teachers. They had a little money of their own, and they taught at some distance from their homes, and some of them had been to the city to school.

All right, then, I said to myself. "I'll be a school teacher."

So I went to school and didn't forget to study, with all the fun I had. Then came a disappointment—the first blow in my life.

Nowadays I see little children going around wearing glasses, and I think to myself: "If I'd worn glasses at your age, maybe I wouldn't be where I am today." But grandpa and grandma didn't know about such things as glasses for children.

When I was eleven years old my eyes started to get bad. I had to drop out of school for a while because of headaches.

In the long run it turned out to be pride, more than it was eyes, that ended it. The next year my class was in long division—arithmetic was always hard for me—and I lost about two weeks. When I went back they were way ahead. There were about forty pupils, and the teacher—there was only one—didn't have any extra time to give to me.

I wasn't going to be a burden on the class, not if I knew it. I wasn't going to drag along away behind the rest, or perhaps go back to the grade below. I dropped out of school.

Grandpa and grandma didn't raise any objection. Grandma couldn't read, and grandpa never read much, though he knew how. I suppose they thought the school teacher idea was just child's talk.

Why didn't someone have the sense to make me go? It's no use to say they couldn't look ahead and see what a handicap that lack of education was going to be; it isn't any use saying that now. But what does a headache or two, or a little pride, amount to alongside of—this?

❖❖❖

Not every girl around here had a fellow, because men were so scarce, about one man to three girls. My boy was named Billy, and he was sixteen, or five months and four days older than I was. (We figured out our ages, of course, the first thing.)

It was the regular rule that your "company" could call once a week, on a Sunday night, at first, and not very late. After a while, if he kept coming, he could sandwich in a Wednesday night, making twice a week, and then he could work up until he was allowed to stay as late as eleven. Twice a week to eleven o'clock: that was quite enough, the old folks said.

So Billy started out on this plan. Every Sunday night he would come and make a visit in our parlor. Grandpa and grandma knew him, of course—he was the son of a farmer who lived close by—and they never used to think it necessary to stay around. They knew everything was all right. People there didn't have any strict ideas about chaperones. It was the regular country way to let those things take care of themselves.

Of course we had it all planned out that we were going to be married—someday. He always wanted to buy land and be a farmer, but I wasn't so sure. That was a great point of discussion between us. And the discussion would generally end with me pretending to be mad, and Billy apologizing. That was one thing that got a little bit in the way; my will was stronger than Billy's, and I liked to show it off—to prove my power, you see. And yet I used to wish sometimes that it was the other way around, and that he would take a turn at being the stronger.

Poor Billy! He isn't married yet, right to this very day. That was just a kid love-affair: yet somehow I have hung onto it, clung to it, as though I were afraid to let it go.

It was ten years ago that all this happened, but Billy and I today still correspond.

I have never, in my letters, let him know what life I was leading. I might have gone through many sorts of trouble, known all sorts of men; I have lived in different houses of prostitution, and have been, I suppose, what the world calls a "bad woman," with other "bad women" as my associates. Yet I have never forgotten Billy; never cut the link that binds me to him.

Billy's letters are short and stiff; he doesn't express himself very well on paper. He quit writing "love letters" after I had been away from there a year or two. He isn't a man of any great education; he's only a farm-hand, living at home in the winter, just as he did then, and working when there was work to do. I suppose he has his troubles, his bitter spots, just as I have had mine.

But I write to Billy regularly—filling my letters with lies about how hard I am working as a waitress or a laundry girl—and almost believing, while I write, that I am telling the truth. I'd like to tell Billy the real truth, but I know he couldn't stand it. I get more pain than pleasure out of those letters.

Why do I keep writing to him? I don't know. He seems to stand for something in my life, I guess. Something that isn't Billy at all; something that isn't dead in me, and never will be.

One evening, when I was sixteen, Billy and I made up our minds that we were going to be real reckless.

It was Saturday night, in the spring of the year. There had been parties, and the picnic season was just starting in; and I guess the time of year had something to do with our recklessness.

The previous Wednesday, Billy had been at our house on his regular midweek call, and during the talk—after grandma and grandpa had gone to bed—Billy had mentioned that on the coming Saturday night at a neighbor's house, not far away, there was going to be a dance.

I looked at Billy and Billy looked at me. We both had the same idea.

"Billy," I said, "let's go."

So then we laid our plans. It was pretty easy. People went to bed awful early around those parts. Chances were grandma and grandpa would be sound asleep by half-past seven. The dance began early—maybe a half hour before that—and we would be a bit late; but anyway, as soon as I thought the coast was clear, I was to get out by the window and join Billy, who would be waiting in our back alley, out behind the woodshed. Then we'd go to the dance.

It's hard for anybody who hasn't lived in such a region to realize how reckless that was. People around there were mostly strict church-goers. Dancing was one of the seven deadly sins, and not number seven of them, either. There was more or less drinking at the dances, too; some of the young fellows were likely to go into the next town, a few miles away, where there was a drug store, and get a couple bottles of whisky, and one of them might take too much.

Altogether, girls who went to dances weren't looked upon as being quite respectable.

But my Billy and I didn't bother about that side of the matter. We were just kids, crazy after a good time—and kids of sixteen certainly get crazy that way, sometimes.

If Billy had touched a drop of whisky I would never have walked home with him in the world, and he knew it. So we felt all square about that; and since neither of us had ever been near a dance, we looked on it as a great adventure.

But what if grandma and grandpa should find out? I had the notion that I was too big to whip, being sixteen; but between that Wednesday and Saturday I started to have my doubts. I guess Billy had his, too.

Everything went beautifully when Saturday evening came. I waited in my bedroom until I thought grandpa and grandma must surely be asleep; and it was a long wait. Finally I heard grandpa snore, and decided to take a chance as to grandma.

I raised the window of my bedroom slowly, an inch at a time, braced it up with a stick, and climbed out. It was about the same distance to the ground as it was to the floor inside, and I didn't make any noise. I left the window open.

Billy was waiting behind the woodshed. We put off across the fields in a straight line for the house where they were giving the dance. It was about a mile and a half away.

I'd better explain how much we knew about dancing. I suppose I had heard the word waltz, but that was about all. To divide dancing into waltz, two-step, or any of those things was altogether beyond me. At the parties we never danced round dances, though I fancy we kids would have been willing. But we did have games where they called out the figure, like a quadrille; and we were all sure, we girls, that we could do a regular quadrille if ever the chance came along.

Well, we reached the place, got through the crowd of young fellows around the door, and looked around. I knew everybody there by sight, but they were the bunch I didn't go with especially. A few of the girls I knew pretty well; some of them spoke to me and seemed pretty surprised.

Billy and I took our places in a quadrille.

My, but I had a good time! It was my first dance; and I thought I was in society, sure. I forgot all about grandma or the open window, or anything, and just danced.

An hour went by like ten minutes. We were right in the midst of a quadrille, Billy and I, when I heard some girl behind me calling my name.

"Oh, Alice!" she said, sort of quietly. "There's your grandmother!"

All the dance went right out of me. I got all cold, then I felt as if I was red all over. I couldn't make myself look in Billy's direction, but he saw grandma over my shoulder and stepped across beside me.

Grandma walked right out into the middle of the room, looking neither to right or left; and I guess that was the first and last time in her life she was ever seen at a dance. Just behind her was Billy's father.

"Come along right away, Alice," she said. "It's time to go home."

She didn't seem very mad, by her voice. Maybe she didn't like it very much by herself, shaming me like that before my friends. Billy's father didn't say a word, and he didn't need to; Billy came right along with me.

Most of the people in the room stopped dancing, too, and

stared at us as we marched out. The music kept right on, and I can hear that quadrille tune yet. I kept my head high up in the air and managed to get outside into the dark without crying.

Billy and I never said a word, but just put for home. It was a dark night and we took the roughest way. Poor grandma behind us climbed fences and all without a murmur. She was game. That was a long mile and a half.

We reached our place first. Right at the corner of our lot Billy's father stepped in and saved the day.

"'Tain't but nine o'clock, Billy," he said. "It's not your regular night, but Alice's grandmother says you can go in an' finish your visit til 'leven o'clock, if you want to."

As a matter of fact, I don't think "Alice's grandmother" had said anything of the sort. But most likely she was glad of a peaceful way out. So that was the way it would end; and neither she nor grandpa said anything about it again.

That was my last venture into "society." After that, I was content with the parties. That scrape, which makes me laugh now, was serious enough at the time. It was another link in that chain that has always seemed to hold me to Billy; so that now, even after all these years and after everything I have lived through, I keep on writing to him, though my letters are full of lies.

❖

There was one thing grandpa and grandma did for which I shall always love and respect them, more than for almost anything else.

Grandpa and grandma, in the days when they could afford to have help in the house, used to take in and employ girls who had got into trouble. Three different times, when I was going to school, we had girls doing housework for us that other people in that little town wouldn't have anything to do with. These three girls all had homes a little distance away, but weren't expected to live with their folks.

To me, as a child, they seemed to be just as nice as anybody. But I could see that the gossips in the village felt differently.

I remember times when the old ladies, grandma's friends, used to make remarks, in voices kind of hushed, when one of those girls had come into the room. They couldn't understand, it seemed, how grandma could hire girls such as these were.

Grandma would never argue about it; only she would say something nice about how well that girl did her work.

As to grandpa, he was always as polite and as lovely to those girls as he was to me. And he took care that I was nice to them, too, though I never wanted to be anything else. I felt sorry for them, without knowing why.

It used to bother me a lot, the way those girls were looked upon by the outside people. They were kind of bashful, it seemed, and didn't set themselves forward at all—though usually the girls that did housework in that part of the country weren't regarded at all as servants, but were just one of the family. These girls kept apart, as if they felt they weren't wanted.

It all used to be very puzzling to me as a child. What was wrong? What had they done?

I knew this: that each of these girls who worked for us had become a mother, without being married. But that was all I did know. And I couldn't see anything very dreadful about that. Why should these other women, mothers themselves, treat these girls as outcasts?

Just because I knew what the village thought, I always felt a bit strange in talking to those girls. I had no opinion of my own against them; none at all. But I knew that the other people in the village had put some sort of brand upon them. Exactly what was wrong?

I asked grandma one day point-blank:
"Grandma, what's there about Susie that's so dreadful?"
Grandma didn't answer for a moment. Then she said:
"Susie had a sweetheart."

That was every word I could get out of her. Well, plenty of other girls I knew had sweethearts. I hoped to have one myself, when I was old enough—that was before the days of Billy. There must be something else; but I couldn't make grandma say another word.

And that has always made me feel sorry. After those girls had got into trouble, grandpa and grandma were ready to take them in, and give them a home and a chance to make good; and that was great of them, that was Christian.

But why weren't they just as ready, in a few straight words, to tell me, their granddaughter, a few things that might keep me out of the same trouble later?

That question always seemed so important to me, even as a young girl. Here was something, I felt, that I needed to know; that I ought to know, and I had a right to know. Why couldn't I be told?

But it's just that way. People can be perfectly fine and big, as my grandparents were, in one way, yet be prudish and petty and cruel in another. I was a quick-minded girl; I wanted to know all about everything; and I am perfectly sure my curiosity made those things take up ten times as much of my thoughts as the truth would have done if I had been told straight out.

The other girls, my friends, used to have the same trouble. None of them could get a word out of their parents, or even feel right about asking them. I remember a time or two when we girls got to talking, trying to figure things out by putting together everything we knew; but that didn't get us anywhere. I was always for going to the bottom of those questions; some of the other girls used to get to laughing, and I always hated them for it. So far as I could see there was nothing to laugh about. I wanted the truth.

Could it have been that, even at that early day, I had an instinctive feeling as to what that knowledge might mean to me, some time?

I'm not making any excuses for myself on that basis. I might have ended up here, even if I had been told everything.

But that isn't true of other girls I know, girls who are in this life just because they didn't know. The blame for them is on their parents. There is no other way to it. Such cases aren't the majority by a long way, but there are plenty enough of them.

My grandparents trained me little by little, more by doing things themselves than by preaching at me. And this was the way I came by another of my ideas, that has lasted me all through, and is just as strong today as it ever was.

This is a hatred for divorce. There were no divorces to speak of in that farming region; and though I heard the word and knew what it meant, I grew up to believe it was something fearful. Marriage, with the people there, was for all one's life.

It seems strange, but that idea has worked with me both for good and bad. At one time, if I had been willing to marry a man I didn't love and couldn't stand to live with, I might have kept out of the underworld. But my hatred of divorce and the thought of my Billy, kept me from that.

But today, looking about at the women who are associates, I can see that my grandparents' idea about divorce was right. Do people realize, I wonder, how many divorced women there are in this life?

It seems to me that about half of the women I know in this life are divorced women; who are not getting any money from their former husbands, and who have a child or parent to support.

If I were asked what is the greatest of the many causes that force women into this life, I should say poverty; and the women who are divorced but have to support a child are among the easiest to fall before poverty.

As a girl in that peaceful farm country, I knew nothing of the city and its evils. There was no house of prostitution within many miles of the place where I lived.

It is with a sort of choking feeling in my throat that I think of an answer my grandmother gave once to my innocent question. "Grandma, what is a fancy house?" I had heard the old people use that word, in telling of some sort of scrape that one of the boys from our town had got into in the city. Her reply, as I remember today, showed that she, dear old soul, knew as little about it as I did.

And today I look back on her brave kindness, and the way she and grandpa used to take into their home those poor girls who had fallen; and I think, "If only all good people had the same pity in their hearts, neither I nor a million other women like me would have to stay where we are today."

❖⦂❖

I was standing in front of the mirror in my room, fixing up to go out for a picnic with some friends. I had my arms raised and was just putting the finishing touches to a ribbon around my hair, when I heard a familiar sound from our back yard.

It was the noise of somebody pitching cordwood, two sticks at a time, from a wagon down into our woodshed.

"Grandma," I called out, "Uncle Ed must be getting real good. He's sent us a load of wood."

Uncle Ed had been married for several weeks. What his marriage had meant to us I was just starting to find out. About this wood, for instance—for a couple of weeks lately, we had done our cooking with any old sort of fuel we could pick up about the place. We had even ripped up a board or two off our fences. I could see that grandma was trying to keep down other expenses as low as she could. Even grandpa, who never fretted, had a worried look.

Well, grandma didn't make any answer to me, and I thought to myself she couldn't have heard. The noise of that wood kept right on, and I kept on, too, fixing up for my picnic.

My, what a lot of wood Uncle Ed must have sent up! That one wagon ought to have unloaded long ago. Yet the sound of the falling sticks didn't stop. There must be two wagons.

There must be three! Uncle Ed—why, he was just newly married and he oughtn't afford all of that. Maybe he had been working at some place where he got a lot of wood for pay, and now he was sending us most of it, to show that everything was all right with the family—even if it wasn't.

I walked through the kitchen out into the back yard, all dressed up nice for that picnic with the ribbon in my hair. Grandma was leaning with her face pressed close against the kitchen window, looking out into the yard. I didn't see her face, but walked right past.

Why, there were four—five—six wagons, different sizes, all lined up. And what a crowd of men! Must be about everybody in the whole village.

All of the sudden my heart stopped still, then gave a jump. I faced around and tried to see grandma's eyes through the window pane.

Grandma was bent way over. She was crying. Then I knew for certain. We were "objects of charity."

I turned my back on that crowd of men and boys—I had seen my Billy among them—and made for the house. I had the feeling that I wanted to hide. I ran past grandma and into my room, not knowing where to go or what to do. It was too dreadful to think of.

"Objects of charity." Then we were really poor—as poor as the poorest of the village. Uncle Ed's marriage had taken away our support. And now the neighbors had come to the rescue. All our troubles, that we wanted to keep to ourselves, were public property.

Then I cried. I could never hold my head up again.

I knew the way of the town. They meant it for generous, and it was. People in larger cities don't do things like that. The plan had been all cooked up last night. Early this morning they had gone out and cut the wood and loaded up the wagons. Fellows had swung an ax—for charity—who hadn't done a lick of work in three months.

Charity—that was the word that hurt. I couldn't seem to get rid of that word ringing through my head.

Have you ever been an "object of charity"? It takes all the strength out of you.

You feel ashamed of yourself—horribly ashamed—and you feel angry that other people should know about your poverty, and you know how they must hold you in contempt. And you hold yourself in contempt, too; and that makes you angry, and when you are angry you hate the people who are trying to help you. You hate them like mad, but you are afraid to face them or look them in the eye, because they might see your hate, and think you ungrateful. But you've got to thank them, and cringe and crawl before them. You would die gladly, you think, sooner or later than say, "Thank You."

That is about the way I felt then, and have felt since when people have tried to help me—not from friendship, but from plain charity. I'll tell more about that when I write my ideas on that charitable home where we women are to come and be reformed.

On the street the other day I saw a well-dressed man give a quarter to a hobo that asked him; and from the way the well-dressed one said, "Here, my man," I knew as well as could be what the hobo was calling him, to himself. It's the same proposition with us women, and would be with anybody.

Well, one thing was certain about our fix: that sort of business couldn't go on. Something would have to be done about it quick. I would go to work.

I slipped out into the kitchen. Grandma was still standing there by the window crying and looking at the pile of wood.

"Grandma, is it true?" said I. "Are we so poor?"

She nodded.

"But didn't grandpa have a bank account once? What became of that? He had five hundred dollars, you said."

Grandma just managed to jerk out—

"There's twenty-six left."

Only twenty-six dollars!

A person can go through a lot without changing in the main things. Here I am today in the same fix I was then—no money, no special skill, and casting around to find some place in the world where I can be of use. That very fix is the commonest sort of thing, in this life.

But whether one is a young, proud girl of sixteen or seventeen, as I was then, or whether one has seen life on the roughest side, one thing stays the same—the hatred of charity.

I don't believe the most broken-down woman in this life is much different that way from the proudest lady that ever lived. The only charity anyone can take is the kind that comes from a real friend, out of real friendship and big-heartedness, and not out of scorn.

I could hardly wait to go to work.

Every time I glanced out into the back yard and saw that big woodpile, I could hardly stand it—I felt so ashamed.

My Aunt Susan, my father's sister—I didn't know her very well—lived a few miles away, in a fine big white house, that stood back from the road behind a bunch of trees. She had lots of money, for around there. I liked the thought of living in a house as grand as that; I could see myself driving around that turn in the road, and my friends coming to see me in that house.

Well, I packed up all my things in one of those old-fashioned straw baskets with two handles. I left early in the morning, before grandpa was awake, and grandma didn't say much of anything. I told her I was going up to Aunt Susan's to work, and then just skipped out with my basket, feeling real daring and adventurous.

Aunt Susan was just getting into her phaeton in the curved driveway, when I marched in with my baggage. She seemed a bit surprised to see me. She was going out for the day, she said, but I was to go inside and make myself at home. She didn't ask what I had come for or how long I was going to stay, and I could see those were hard questions to ask. I felt uncomfortable.

I spent that whole day doing nothing. I tried once or twice to break into the work, but she had help already in the kitchen and it seemed as if there wasn't anything to do that wasn't already the job of somebody else.

I wandered around the house, staring at the furniture—which was awful hard to dust, and must have cost a lot—wondering whose room was which, and what they were going to do with me, and maybe feeling a bit sorry I had come there.

It was pretty late in the afternoon that I saw the housegirl go outside to the garden to get the vegetables for dinner. At any rate, here was something I could do; so I went out and started in to help her. Just then my aunt drove up that curved driveway.

I looked at her and she looked back. Then she went into the house. In about a minute she came outside with an apron on and sent the girl inside, saying she would get the vegetables herself.

We worked along for a minute or two, and I never felt worse embarrassed in my life. I couldn't figure things out at all. Finally my aunt spoke, in a funny, flat sort of voice that showed how hard it was for her to say it:

"What was you meaning t' do, Alice? Did you want to work, or what?"

"Yeh, I want to work," I said. "Kind o' got to."

"Well, there ain't any place for you here right now," she said. "You can stay a while, if you want, but we got help."

"Well, then, do you know anybody that does want help?" I asked.

"The Harrises need a girl," she said. "Sarah Harris, you know, is dying of consumption, and all the relatives are there. I don't know if you are big enough to do that heavy work" (she looked me over critically—the first time in my life I was ever looked over that way), "but you can try it if you like. I'll take you around there this evening."

So after supper we went around to the Harrises, whom I knew only slightly. Mrs. Harris also looked me over and seemed doubtful, but she had a houseful of people, and needed help.

"Well, Alice, you can try it," she said finally. "Do the regular work, and I'll give you a dollar and a half a week."

That was perfectly fine. A dollar and a half a week! What more could anyone expect? I accepted right off.

You see, that was the way wages were around there. No girl ever got more than two dollars a week. Oftener they got a dollar or a dollar and a quarter. Those were regular rates.

I wasn't long in finding out what work I was supposed to do for that dollar and a half.

According to a good old custom of that region, all the relatives of the Harrises were camping there, sort of waiting for poor Sarah to die. There were plenty of relatives, too. We had fourteen at table three times a day, and on that first Sunday we must have had twenty or more. It was a regular hotel.

This was the first time I met with real drudgery. I was supposed to do all the work.

My day started at half-past four when I got up. At six there was a big breakfast—meat and eggs and pie and all of that. Then dishes—for fourteen. Then cleaning up the kitchen—I shall never forget that kitchen, as big as four ordinary rooms, and all that width of floor to be mopped.

Then sweeping and dusting and bed-making; then the churning. Then dinner—another big meal with different kinds of meat, and vegetables that had to be got out of the garden. Then more dishes. Then, in the afternoon, the laundry. There was a lot of extra laundry, of course, because of the sick girl and those fourteen relatives. Then supper, just like dinner, another big husky meal. Then dishes again, then bed.

You would have thought that big crowd of relatives would pitch in and make light work of it all. But the only thing they did was to help clean off the table and scrape up the dishes—because they didn't want me breaking any of that nice china. I did the rest.

As my aunt had hinted, I wasn't a very big nor heavy girl—I only weighed about a hundred and ten. But I had agreed to do that work, and I was going to do it if it killed me.

Mrs. Harris saw pretty early in the week that that huge laundry was a bit too much for me. So she took some of her best things and sent them out to be done.

But I kept up my courage. I was working, anyhow, and that meant a lot. No more charity for me.

Do you see the step I had taken? I had traded charity for drudgery—just as a girl must do if she has any pride. Later on, as you shall see, the drudgery got too much for me, and I took the next step—traded drudgery for this other life. And that step seemed just as needful as the first one did. But once I had taken it, I could never trade back. Practically every girl I know in this life has gone through that same mill—from poverty to charity, from charity to drudgery, from drudgery to—this.

I don't know how you are going to stop it, unless people do something that will lessen the drudgery.

The thought of that dollar and a half a week kept me up during those first hard days in the Harris kitchen. But by the end of a week I was worn out. From half-past four in the morning to seven at night, day after day, I drudged ahead, and not one of that crowd of relatives lifted a hand.

I got to hate those people, though really I didn't get acquainted with any of them except Mrs. Harris herself.

On Sunday afternoon I felt just awful. It was Sunday evening that Billy always came to see me; and this night he wouldn't be there. Uncle Ed was married, too, and wouldn't care anything about my happiness anymore. And grandpa—poor grandpa—was sick and feeble. There wasn't a ray of light. The whole world seemed dark.

I was tired to death, of course, or I wouldn't have felt so blue. It was all I could do to keep from crying. I didn't see how I was to stand that work any longer. But I made up my mind to stick to it if it killed me.

Late in the afternoon I had a few minutes to myself and strolled around the yard. All the crowd of Harris relatives were on the front porch, having a fine time and making a lot of noise. I heard one of the girls holler out—

"Oh, look at that fellow with the funny walk! Ain't he the bow-legged one, though."

Naturally I craned my neck to see who it was they were laughing at.

Crossing the trestle, just a little way off, making toward the house, was Uncle Ed.

I was never gladder to see anyone in my life. Just when I was all forgotten by the whole world, here came my dearest uncle, who was just like my big brother. I was so relieved, and so tired, and so worn-out, and so wild with anger because these people had made fun of Uncle Ed's walk, that I just sank back into the shrubbery and burst out crying.

Uncle Ed strode right up to the house. The Harris crowd stopped tittering.

He had spied me, around the corner, and came right around without saying a word to anybody.

"What's the matter, Alice?" he said. My, his voice sounded good!

I managed to get out some of my troubles.

"You come right back with me to your grandmother's," he commanded. "I'm not going to have you work another day in any such place as this. You come right along."

It seemed good for somebody else to take the reins for a while. I didn't even hesitate. I would have done anything anybody had told me to, just then.

I went upstairs and got my things and found Mrs. Harris. I could see she was a bit sore, but I didn't care.

"Here's your money, Alice," she said. She handed me a dollar.

"I—I thought it was to be a dollar and a half a week," I said. I was still half-crying.

"Well, you see," she explained, "there was that fifty cents for laundry that I had to send out because you couldn't do it."

I took my dollar and got out of that place. That was the meanest trick ever I had played on me. It stings me yet to think of it.

I only had to stay with grandma and grandpa for a few days. The mail-carrier who brought the mail everyday from X——, seven miles away, told me that a girl was wanted as a companion to old Mrs. Drew, a widow about eighty who lived by herself in a house along the railroad track.

For two-bits fare, the same mail carrier took me the next day to Mrs. Drew's house. I soon found out that if I wanted to talk business with her, I would have to talk loud, for she was real deaf. It only took a minute to fix it up; I was to do whatever work there was, and she would pay me a dollar and a quarter a week.

At first she said a dollar; then I did my first stroke of business and held out for an extra quarter. She used to pay me regularly every Saturday evening, making as much over it as though it were a thousand dollars, and she never failed to remark:

"That's twenty-five cents too much."

I used to like old Mrs. Drew, but the life there was awful quiet. I was supposed to stay around the place the whole time. Billy couldn't come to see me, it was so far.

The only part of the work I didn't like was reading the Bible in the evenings. We had an arrangement, by which I'd read one chapter to her, and then she would read one to me, every night. I didn't enjoy it, because when I read I'd have to holler at the top of my lungs to make her hear; and when she read, her voice was sort of husky. It kept me clearing my own throat, out of sympathy, every ten seconds, and wishing she would clear hers. But she never did.

Old Mrs. Drew was as spry as anybody, for all her age. But she had a sort of hatred for anybody else's having a good time. Now, I was seventeen, and just full of high spirits, and as crazy about a good time as could be—a picnic, to me, was just meat and drink. It was a good deal like a prison around there.

I wanted to see my Billy especially. I had been going with him for two years, and I missed him awfully. Finally, after several weeks, Billy got restless himself, and one Saturday I got a note from him saying he was coming that very Sunday evening.

I was all excited. It seemed years since I had had a sight of Billy. But I wasn't at all sure how Mrs. Drew would like it. I was sort of scared to say anything to her about his coming.

Sunday evening we got through supper early, and I went after that Bible reading like a good one, with one ear listening sharp for the click of the gate.

I had finished my shouting and Mrs. Drew was reading along in her husky voice when the gate clicked. I heard steps—Billy's steps—and there was a knock on the door—loud enough so the old lady heard it.

"That must be Mrs. Grover," she said. "She told me she might come over."

I knew perfectly well it wasn't Mrs. Grover, but that spry old lady beat me to the door and opened it. Billy used to have a way of popping in awful sudden when a door was opened, and getting clear into the middle of the room before you had a chance to see who it was. I used to joke with him about that trick of his. Well, he got clear past Mrs. Drew. She had barely time to turn around before I said, "Good evening, right this way, please," and led Billy into that little sitting-room.

It sure was good to see my boy again. I forgot all about the old lady. Just as the clock struck eleven she opened the door of the room, looked at me for half a minute without speaking, and passed on. That was all we heard from her; and Billy stayed late that night.

There was one other time when she wasn't quite so good-natured about it. It was about a couple of months later.

One Saturday morning I was out in the back yard raking up the leaves, and I felt simply awful. Earlier that morning I had lifted a heavy washtub, and my back ached, and I ached all over. It seemed as if I hadn't the strength to swing that wooden rake.

A buggy drove up the road and a couple of my girl friends were in it. They waved to me. I didn't understand that they wanted to speak to me, so I didn't go out in front. They passed out of my sight on the other side of the house, and as I learned afterward, stopped at the front gate.

Old Mrs. Drew was out in the front yard. They asked to see Alice, I later found out, and she told them I was busy doing my work and mustn't be interrupted.

I saw them going and I figured they must have stopped, because they had taken so long to pass. All of a sudden I began to suspect there was something in the wind. A party!

I knew right away it wouldn't do any good to ask Mrs. Drew. Seeing she had turned them away, it wasn't likely she would tell me anything. But I began to forget about my tiredness, and had my head full of plans as I went about that raking.

No sooner was lunch over than I made to the post office. Sure enough, there was a letter for me. I tore it open. It was an invitation to go to a party at a house about three miles off, that very evening.

And that was when I forgot all about the rest of my tiredness. It would be like coming back to life to go to that party.

I did my share of the Bible-reading at top speed that night. As soon as I was through I made for my room. I could see that Mrs. Drew had her eye on me.

Presently, she opened the door of my room. There was I, in the act of putting on my nice blue-and-white polka-dotted shirtwaist—with a black skirt, the regular finery for such occasions.

"Where are you going?"

"Going to a party," I mumbled, with my mouth full of pins.

"H'm," said the old lady. "You haven't got my permission, nor your grandmother's, to go."

"I don't care," I fired back. I had forgotten I was tired, but I must still have been short-tempered.

She went away, and I made for my party. Fun? It was like getting out of jail. I never had quite an evening in my life.

The very next morning, before she had any time to bring the matter up, Uncle Ed came for me. Grandmother was sick, he said, and I was needed at home. I went right along with him.

It was one of my girl chums that got the place with Mrs. Drew; and she told me afterward that the old lady said—

"Alice is a fine hand at the work, all right, but she's awful fond of a good time!"

Grandma's illness didn't last long. Soon I got a place in the kitchen of a restaurant, over at X——. Though I didn't know it, I was on the very brink of one of the greatest changes of my whole life.

CE FROM THE DERWORLD

STORY OF "ALICE SMITH" APPEALS TO MRS. PINCHOT

MRS. AMOS PINCHOT.

WHIT

BY WILLIAM

TH," whose life story, "A Voice From the Underworld," will make, in tomorrow's issue, a pre-ished in The Bulletin. her reasons for giving the stirring tale of her experiences onday's issue the first chapter of this remarkable serial will

JESUS sat in
Answering
Questions o

Thither a woma
In the act of
Worthy of dea

Knowing that
Love and mer
Asked him wh

FAULT," ASKS THIS WOMAN, WE ARE THE WORLD'S MISFITS?"

Stooping, Jes
Something th
Hid from th

I have read the letters
"A Voice from the Under-
like to say something on

halls, your lodges, picnics, etc., do not reach all
men; and there is a large class of these men
everywhere to be found. Big cities have thousands of them. Decent girls, decent society do not
care to meet them, so we are the only women that
are in the reach of their pocketbook and their
leisure. We often know them very intimately in character,
many of them are splendid fellows in character,
but the stigma that society has cast against us
prevents them from forming a marriage bond.
Society will not abolish prostitution as long as
some of its members are in such a strange fix.
Men are cowards and will not openly acknowledge
this fact.

'He that
May be the
At the wo

This is th
Thence the
Neither h

he good people who try to
agree with the people who
seems alive to see what we
we do not fit in their
We are the misfits in the
must recast the molds before
roblem. You like to have us
not save the factory girl, who
twelve hours a day for a
ruins herself as quickly—I
do. Many of us here have
rial brothels and prefer not to
here is miserable, but we have
in the underworld individually
to fear unemployment and

Afer a s
"Whithe
Hath n

But not all prostitution is caused by economic,
social or moral defects. Many belong to the realm
of psychology and cases of such kind can hardly
ever be treated with the crude instruments that
law, morality and religion puts into the hands of
its chosen practitioners.

Answere
"Cease
Neithe

a menace. Why does not
is surely a greater problem than
us society wash us now—after
sh the mill—to return to the
scale, compete with our sisters,
eir virtue dream and wear calico

They are all good people, but they do not understand. They are like the supporters of capital
punishment—they do not know how to cure.
Therefore, they kill.

Nathe
Lifte
Gazi

Let us alone as long as you do not want us.
Let us live our lives as best we can. We were not
always inmates of the red light district. Society
drove us here and it is not Christian to inflict on
us more punishment for society's crime. Society's
constant persecution forces us to bribe officials,
preachers, etc., we are forced to do this—society
forces us to do it. Self-preservation is the supreme
law. Why does society condemn us when, through
its clumsy methods, it forces us to apply this law?
Life is life and, in self-defense, all methods are
fair.

"De
I tl
Go

the men who patronize us.
not all bad. Many of them are not
t calls successful. They would not
society as "fit to marry my daugh-
a girl has met here afterward the
ace rejected. Some of these men
strangely isolated from all feminine
I know many who do not know—
chance to meet a single decent woman
their life. They perforce come to us.
or companionship and we earn quite
rs in this way—strange as it seems
ot take this as a mere guess. I know
bsolute, undisputed fact. Your dance

D
ve
"Whith
Hath n

I hope these lines will help the outworld to
understand the underworld. It is seldom that we
make an outcry to deaf ears, but perhaps the
Voice will not be lost this time.

I do not sign a name. I too have prejudices, and
"WHAT'S IN A NAME?"

HER UNFORTUNATE RAISES HER VOICE

BULLETIN—Reading some
stories of those poor unfor-
victims of the underworld,
sympathize and although
may I take great pleas-
ing these few lines, hop-
will act as a lesson to
ard their lives from the
lls of the Great White Way.
writing my story as told
nderworld and can tell of as
of my present as well as of

I was not a young girl I ca
near by college of business for
could in course of a few year
ssed. The I first found out what

it meant to make my own living,
agencies were open to me and the world
was as free as the air we breathe. I
came to San Francisco, when I entered
—realize that a well known business man
of our city today, only to find that my
great sorrow in the course of a year or
two that I was at the threshold of
shame, brought upon me through the circumstances of this very business accident. My first experience was to be invited
to a very well known club in this city
clubhouse for men only. But there
I found a very neat room set aside for
lady visitors at the club, and just like
it from me, lady visitors were allowed
to enter any day of the week they had
a mind to. Next I found myself taken

All
drinks and later to be intoxicated in
places very strange to me indeed.

Oh, had I not seen this great city of
San Francisco I might perhaps again
have the pleasure of talking to my dear
old mother, who has died of a broken
heart through pure grief of my ill-
spent life. I firmly believe that had I
received a loving pledge to start with I
would have led a better life.

If I could only change my life, or
if I could only live over again I would
could live my life over again while
away, as they were my ruin in life.

In a state of despondency, I am writ-
ing this, so I close with regards.
MISS BESSIE M'LOUGHLIN.
San Francisco, June 1½

and, strange to say, we even
the British embassy were some-
volved in this obscure and name ini-
unsavory incident which in April 1901
drove the culture-revelation of the present war
And that outbreak of the present war
until the outbreak of the war had not
(of which, in some way, we had magnifi-
cent information), when the magnifi-
cent diplomacy of Sir Edward Gray
himself revealed to be relied upon by
England could still be relied upon the
hour of their misfortune.

Noted Society Woman Thinks Idea of Its Publication Is Excellent.

THE APPEAL of "A Voice from the Underworld" is being heard in far
places. Already the announcement of The Bulletin that it was about
to publish the life story of Alice Smith has struck sympathetic
chords in the East, and the editor is receiving many telegrams felicitating
him upon the opportunity to set before the world, in the words of one of
its outcast women, the true problem of the submerged. The keenness of
enlightened, sympathetic opinion is that the publication of this biography
will do more toward solving this great problem than any other effort that
has been made.

As an indication of the appeal in "A Voice from the Underworld," a
telegram received today from Mrs. Amos Pinchot is significant. It reads:

MILFORD, PA., June 26, 1913.
Fremont Older, Managing Editor Bulletin, San Francisco:
cellent. Please send me installments of The Underworld's b s.
GERTRUDE PINCHOT.

Mrs. Pinchot is one of the foremost women in the United States in the
effort to better social conditions. She is a warm friend of Colonel and
Mrs. Roosevelt, and is in the exclusive Astor set of New York and Newport.

"WHY NOT LET US ALONE?" ASKS SEGREGATED WOMAN

FREMONT OLDER:
I would like to say a few words
on "A Voice from the Underworld." I am a resident of the negro-
world district and therefore speak from
experience.

I notice one of your subscribers suggests a segregated district from the
fence and utter abolition from the
outside world. Why not? In some
day a week not to let some color or
open our dress to deck other people.
I notice you would know why we do
not let us alone. That is just one that
be secured by all. And is there a place
because we cannot get a place is so
we are scorned.

It is true that men, that some are
human. It is a true saying that a
woman is a woman's worst enemy—
That is so. It is so hard for a woman
to leave this life. Any woman who
are not sufficient for a girl away from
home to clothe herself properly and have
the pleasures that a girl craves without
depending upon some "gentlemen friends"
a part of their living, as I myself have
done in the past.

But this evil cannot be done away with
high fences and seclusion, as the
girls would revolt against such treatment and would go on the streets and con-
sequently be scattered all over.

Why not let us have a decent
We will better our lives? No, we do why
not let us alone? Other people do. why
must we be hounded? The scattered al over
gated district, or the scattered all over
more wanted, we had our reference.
so what are we for? Some of the
girls have little or no education, or to
better but would fall to be servant girls
And the women do want children—we are
home, around them.

If some of us were willing
to leave this life? And by the women who
to take us that their homes are so good
they put not want us; we are good
enough for them, what is there for us
but this life. Some other woman comes to be so narrow
minded and will have this life, but we
will eventually have to live this life, but
women who don't understand us should
ONE WHO KNOWS.
San Francisco.

GES TEACHING OF HOUSEWORK AS A SYSTEM

conomic Science Essential
to Success, Declares
Clubwoman

PHILADELPHIA, June 2—House-
ing as a profession is the idea advocated by Miss Mary Urner, president
of the Limited annual Franchise League
of this city. Although domestic science

schools in addition to courses in cooking and baking. When the work itself
becomes reputable and those who engage in this occupation receive a thorough education, housework will become as dignified a profession as
teaching or any other so called lady-
occupation.

SAYS SIR GERALD LOWTHER FAILED AS AMBASSADOR

London Newspaper Asserts
Diplomat's Retirement
Was Forced

of "gee, haw" and "k'yup" have very
significant meaning to the white horse
that strain existed on Washington

All able bodied citizens a mile of
avenue for years within a mile of two of
the progress locomotive works
road, because the Pennsylvania Railroad Company has cost reason down
would be costly to clear a crossing, would be the

MULE POWER TO SEE LAST DAYS ON THE PENNSY

Electric Tractor Replaces the
Long-Eared Sort in
Philadelphia

found on the Pennsylvania lines.
With the passing of the mule came
from Wesahuncer avenue on the mechanism
to the city. There was a tract
means in the city has a tram
also an annoyance to work it
that was a tram locomotive works
that was out of the get related mule ma
locomotive stood on Market gre
sewed the tracks, ran across the suburbst d
To run across the suburban of

SELECTED LETTERS
TO THE EDITOR

FREQUENTLY TEMPTED

I have been reading the letters from the underworld with great interest. I am not of the underworld, but when I was a young girl I had to make my own way and I want to say to the women who have never had to get out and work for a few dollars a week, that they don't know what a great temptation it is for a young girl when some smooth-tongued man comes to her and proposes a release from such conditions.

When I was seventeen years old a young man I was keeping company with deceived me, and after he got me into trouble, when I went to him and asked him to marry me, he laughed in my face, and told me he never had any intention of marrying me. Well, I worked as long as I could, and I went to a place where I had a friend. She took me in, and if she had been my own mother she could not have been better to me. When my baby came, it only lived two days, but I still stayed with this old lady. She took in washing for a living, and she wanted me to stay and help. After I had been there a short time, some of the good Christian women came to her and told her if she kept me they would quit coming to her house, and Mrs. W. told them if that was Christianity, she didn't want to be a Christian.

But please don't think all men are the same. I am married to a man that always gives the girl all the credit that is due her. He says a girl has to fight her own passions as well as the man's, and sometimes it is a hard job, for some men are nothing more nor less than brutes. I say this thing of prostitution will never stop until more women will help. As for myself, my sympathy is with the ones of the underworld.

A Friend

Girl Kept from Work by Immoral Employers Seeks Help to Escape Brothel

It is very doubtful whether a letter written by one who has not fallen will be read with as much interest as from one who has, no matter how close the writer is to the brink.

When one goes to bed hungry many times the demarcation between right and wrong becomes much less in evidence and it requires some rubbing of the eyes to distinguish it at all...

I have tried so hard to obtain employment, without success. I have only done bookkeeping and other lines of office work, and have had to give up positions because of my employer wanting to become familiar.

If I worked I did not feel that I wanted to do something else, and if I did something else I most assuredly would not

work. One of the last few positions was in the office of a professional man who, when I gave him to understand that he
was not doing right, informed me that he would be pleased
to give me a good recommendation should I want another
position.

Naturally, I took the "hint" and when leaving he told me
that if I had done the right thing I would not need to work.
He always allowed $100 a month for his "friend" for clothes
and entertainment.

One of the times when he attempted to be familiar I
asked him if that was the way he treated my predecessor,
and his reply was that she had a husband and he would not
think of it. This shows that man regards a woman alone and
unprotected legitimate prey...

Perhaps I was foolish, but it always provokes me when a
man imagines that it is a compliment to be insulted by him.

Another great factor in keeping women in my fix out
of employment is the fact that married women whose husbands are able to support them are working in offices for
smaller salaries than one can live on. The women need the
money, or at least earn that money in order to have a good
time or for extras. Then, another thing, employers...paying
such small salaries...discriminate against one who is alone.
If those women who are married like working so much why
did they marry, depriving another woman of a husband?

Now, tell me candidly what do you expect me to do—
what is there I can do? My money is almost gone. I can
cheat my stomach, I can wash at night, but to be without
a place to sleep? No matter what else you do, you must pay
your rent or get out. So if you will tell me of any possible
solution of my trouble I shall very much appreciate it and

there will be one less to reform. Yours very truly,

ALICE A. MAXWELL

[If the writer of the above letter will communicate with Mr. Older he will arrange to have her meet sympathetic women who are anxious to help.]

KEEP UP GOOD WORK, WRITES HOPELESS ONE

Hearing my friends of the underworld speaking of the chance you have given us to tell you of our life (being one of them myself), I can't help writing, as the good people on the outside don't understand us, as they think they do.

The State has passed a redlight bill, but it will never do the good they expect it to do, and as for building a home for us, they will never fill it, because there is not a woman among us that will accept it unless we are forced to. We feel that if we do so, and some good home is found for us after we have been there the required length of time, there will always be someone to point the finger of scorn at us, no matter how good we tried to be. I am a girl from a good family, but poor, and had to go out and work to make ends meet.

I must say I was led into this life by my boss, who had a wife but no children. The child from our friendship is the reason I am in this place, trying to keep it in school. I feel that I am doing what a lot of mothers are doing. I could not expose him, because everyone would have gone against me, and would have said I should have known better, even if I was but 13 years old at the time. I am 30 now.

When I went to work for this man I received $1.50 a week. This may seem strange, and you may say impossible, but you can find girls and even women in the South working for that kind of money. In the state of Georgia, where I came from, they are glad to get that much...

We send you thanks from the bottom of our hearts for giving us a chance to be heard.

If my letter is not good, put it in the waste-basket, as I feel better for having written, anyway. Thanks.

Georgia G.

"Is It Our Fault," Asks This Woman, "That We Are the World's Misfits?"

I have read the letters and articles about "A Voice from the Underworld" and would like to say something on it, as a member of it.

I do not agree with the good people who try to help us without knowing anything about our conditions; and I do not agree with the people who condemn us. Society seems always to kick about us. Is it our fault that we do not fit in their ready-made molds? We are the misfits in the world and I think you must recast the molds before trying to solve the problem. You like to save us—pray, why do you not save the factory girl, who works from eight to twelve hours a day for a mere pittance? She ruins herself as quickly—I mean in body—as we do. Many of us have escaped the industrial brothels and prefer not to return. True, life here is miserable, but we have solved our problem in the underworld individually and do not have to fear unemployment and hunger.

Unemployment is a menace. Why does not society solve it? It is surely a greater problem than prostitution. Does society want us now—after putting us through the mill—to return to the five-dollar per week scale, compete with our sisters, who cling to their virtue dream and wear calico dresses?

Do not condemn the men who patronize us. They, too, are not all bad. Many are not what the world calls successful. They would not be accepted by society as "fit to marry my daughter." Many a girl has met here afterward the fellow she once rejected. Some of these men seem to be so strangely isolated from all feminine acquaintance. I know many who do not know, never had a chance to meet a single decent woman or girl in all their life. They perforce come to us. They long for companionship and we earn quite a few dollars in this way, strange as it seems. Please do not take this as a mere guess. I know it as an absolute, undisputed fact. Your dance halls, your lodges, picnics, etc., do not reach all men; and there is a large class of these men everywhere to be found. Big cities have thousands of them. Decent girls, decent society do not care to meet them, so we are the only women that are in the reach of their pocketbook and their leisure. We often know them very intimately and many of them are splendid fellows in character, but the stigma that society has cast against us prevents them from forming a marriage bond.

Let us alone as long as you do not want us. Let us live our lives as best we can. We are not always inmates of the red light district. Society drove us here and it is not Christian to inflict on us more punishment for society's crime. Society's constant persecution forces us to bribe officials, preachers, etc. We are forced to do this—society forces us to do it. Self-preservation is the supreme law. Why does society condemn us when, through its clumsy methods, it forces us to apply this law? Life is life and, in self-defense, all methods are fair.

I hope these lines will help the outworld to understand the underworld. It is seldom that we make an outcry to deaf ears, but perhaps the Voice will not be lost this time.

I do not sign a name. I too have prejudices, and

"WHAT'S IN A NAME?"

WHAT IS FEMINISM? HERE IS

Ellen Key ✸ Dora Marsden ✸ Rose Mayreder ✸ Olive Schreiner ✸ Charlotte Perkin

INTRODUCTION ON ✸✸✸ By Mrs. Elwyn Stebbins

MRS. ELWYN STEBBINS OF

MAYREDER

rman Psychologist and
Author, says:

ans capable of combating the
have arisen out of a high
ilization must be sought in
elf. The chief objective en-
eavor is how to overcome
of the intermediate stages
nilication of civilization
at we behold the changes
hose new conditions for
she may be enabled to
uties of a higher spirit-
ning her duties as an
tions which will dower
mph of all civilisation
redestination of the
roblem of obtaining a
men in the social
must be solved by
at which forms the
very woman who,
as risen above the

the typical femi-
e family and to
ng that, accord-
was capable of
pect that in the
ancipation will
re of woman
the sense of
degree of an
mmon good.
ly feminine
ions of its
the inter-
reat power
progeny,
woman,
is—in-
y which
emands
al than

LIBERTY FOR WOMEN! This is the
'core of Feminism. There are as many
interpretations of the term, however, as
there are leaders in this world-wide, rev-
olutionary movement. But on the essen-
tial question of freedom from the shackles of legal,
political and social convention all are agreed. The
fundamental difference appears as soon as we look
for the purpose which animates this demand for
liberty.

Until within the last ten years every great
feminist has insisted that freedom for woman to
realize her possibilities as a human being meant a
service to the race such as she has not been able to
render for many hundred years. The leaders of
this "social" feminism, Ellen Key, Olive Schreiner,
Selma Lagerlof, Charlotte Perkins Gilman, however,
emphasize each a different aspect of freedom and
its probable effect on woman.

Olive Schreiner in her brilliant and ardent book,
"Woman and Labor," shows convincingly the
economic and religious causes which have led to the
"parasitism" of woman, and the peril to any
people whose women exist for their sex functions
alone. Her plea is for the opportunity to work—to
be a productive factor in the economic world. With
a full sense of the supreme importance of Motherhood, she yet believes that Motherhood alone cannot fill the heart and brain and hands of Woman,
and that a sturdier, nobler race will be the children
of women who do their part in the actual work of
the world.

Less inspired and inspiring, perhaps, but ani-
mated by the same conviction of the necessity for
economic independence for women, Mrs. Charlotte
Perkins Gilman offers a solution for the practical
difficulties of the situation. Inseparable from her
carefully worked out plan, which seeks to harmon-
ize woman's function as child-bearer and rearer
with her activity as an industrial factor, is the additional feature of collective living and education.
Physical motherhood, ordinarily requires no pro-
longed absence from one's occupation, whether
domestic or industrial. It is the rearing of the
child which presents the problem. For this great
task the individual mother is usually, she thinks,
entirely unfitted, and the condition of the private
home ill-adapted to its successful accomplishment.
The training of the child should be done by special-
ists in the various stages of child education, who
would deal with children in groups. She would
abolish also the cumbersome domestic machinery of
the individual home and make a co-operative
kitchen the basis of a more sensible living. Thus
would individual housekeeping and care of children
cease to be the tremendous obstacles they have
always seemed to woman's productive activity outside the home, and thus would be brought about a
desirable, as Mrs. Gilman fervently believes, social-
ization of all our domestic and industrial activities.

The third great member of this "social" feminist
group, Ellen Key, resembles Mrs. Gilman and Olive
Schreiner only in the necessity she, too, sees for
woman's economic independence. She differs from
them in the immensely greater emphasis she places
on the importance of "Motherliness." Ill-fitted as
are the majority of individual homes and individual
mothers for the rearing of their children, and individual
as, she believes, incomparably better than that of
nstitutional or collective education, such as Mrs
Gilman advocates. She protests against the attitude
hich considers equally laborious and monotonous
ndustrial occupations so greatly superior to home-
and domestic work. The home and the
d are woman's primary concern, and while free
from the necessity of "support" by men in
ential to true human dignity, and the beauty and
of love, economic independence can be
ed, she thinks, without the destruction of
and individual "motherliness." To this
suggests various expedients, such as the
sation of domestic labor, where the mother
as the work of the home; a subsidy from the
the care of mothers, and the

CHARLOTTE PERKINS GILMAN

Editor of The Forerunner, says:

THE economic independence of woman
will change all these conditions as naturally and inevitably as her dependence
has introduced them. In her dependence
industry she will develop more specialization in
less sexuality, and this will lower the pressure
on this one relation in both women and men.
And, in our social intercourse the new character and new method of living will allow of
broad and beautiful developments in human
association. As the private home becomes a
private home, indeed, and no longer the
woman's social and industrial horizon; as the
workshops of the world, woman's sphere as
well as man's, become homelike and beautiful
under her influence, and as men and women
move freely together in the exercise of common racial functions, we shall have new chan-
nels for the flow of human life.

We shall not move from the isolated home
to the sordid shop, and back again, in a world
torn and diseased by the selfish production
of one sex and the selfish consumption of the
other, but we shall live in a world of men and
women, humanly related, working together as
they were meant to do, for the common good
of all. The home will be no longer an economic
entity with its cumbrous industrial machinery
huddled vulgarly behind it, but a peaceful and
permanent expression of personal life as with-
drawn from social contact, and that social contact will be provided for by the many common
meeting places necessitated by the organization of domestic industries.

OLIVE SCHREINER

Author of "The Story of an African Farm," says:

WE have called the woman's movement
of our age an endeavor on the part of
women among civilised races to find
new fields of labor as the old slips from them,
an an attempt to escape from parasitism and
an inactive dependence upon sex function
alone; but, viewed from the other side, the
woman's movement might not less justly be
called a part of a great movement of the sexes
towards each other, a movement toward common occupations, common interests, common
ideals, and an emotional tenderness and sympathy between the sexes more deeply founded
and more indestructible than any the world
has yet known.

during the period necessary to bear the child and
care for it through infancy; greatly modified marriage and divorce laws, including absolute control
by the woman of her own property and person, etc.
Sharp, indeed, is the line of cleavage between
these leaders, whose various contributions to the
ideal of service to the race—and the smaller group
of more radical feminists which has sprung up in
the last few years. These ardent spirits deny any
obligation to society, exalt the ideal of self-realisa-
tion and call on woman to readjust fundamentally
her point of view. Women must learn to judge
themselves, as is their text, as individuals, not
as wives, mothers, daughters, nor
Marsden "creature are not

ELLEN KEY

Author of "Love and Marriage," "The Century of the Child," etc., says:

AS motherliness has been sung more than
it has been understood, we have had
in the illusion not only that it was in-
exhaustible, but that its instinct was infallible
—that for this sacred feeling Nature had done
everything and no culture was needed. Hence
motherliness has remained until this day un-
educated. This sentimental view of motherliness as the ever holy, ever infallible power,
must be abandoned; and even this province of
Nature brought under the sway of culture.
Motherliness must be cultivated by the acqui-
sition of the principles of heredity of race-
hygiene, child-hygiene, child-psychology.
Motherliness must revolt against giving the
race too low, too many, or degenerate children.
Motherliness must exact all the legal rights
without which woman cannot, in the fullest
sense of the word, be either child-mother or
community-mother. Motherliness must cause
women to demand all the training for the home
duties and community duties, which the majority of women now lack, as well as the State
en medically equipped, without which at
the same time self-support

EDNA

*Noted Ame
Aut*

THAT women sho
be servants to n
eyes of Nature;
their energies, must b
the development of thei
advancement of their pe
should, taking into acc
need for a new freedom
only not regard society, b
set about the task of chang
tion upon and opposition
mands—all this tends towar
ing of something new in th
not be left unrecognized. We
to define the Woman as a
as a political movement, a
movement, or a divorce
economic, or sex

A Voice from the Underworld

PART II

My Grandmother Smith, whom I had never seen, had come on a visit from the West.

It didn't excite me very much when I first heard that. There was nothing to indicate that I was nearing my life's greatest turning-point. That is the way the biggest things come to us—they don't give any notice in advance. They just arrive, and later on we look back and see how big they were.

Poor grandpa couldn't seem to get over the blow of Uncle Ed's marriage. He was able to get around the place as well as ever; but his mind was wandering now and then, as old people's minds do—he was seeming to live in scenes that had happened long ago, and mixing all of us up with people that had lived in those days.

It all made me so eager to help them! I was getting two dollars a week in my restaurant; and it was the dream of my life to save every cent and give it to grandma and grandpa.

When I heard that my Grandmother Smith was in the neighborhood, it only meant one thing—a chance to hear some real news about my father and my sister, Emma. My father, you will remember, had married again, when I was a baby, shortly after my own mother had died; and he had gone West. Emma had been taken by Grandmother and Grandfather Smith, just as I had been taken by my mother's parents. They had all lived in the same Western town, a small city, which I might as well call Westville.

So I was curious to talk with this new grandmother and find out about my sister and father. But I had to keep down my curiosity for a whole month, while she visited first one group of relatives and then another, in a circle of thirty miles. Half these relatives I didn't know; I had always had a sort of dislike for my father's people.

A person from the Pacific Coast, who had traveled and all that, seemed very grand to me. I dressed myself in my best, but I felt like a green country girl in my shirtwaist and skirt, and I wondered what my sister Emma's clothes were like. I felt sort of as if I was going to call on the Queen of England.

Grandmother Smith was younger than my other grandma, I noticed, by a good ten years. She had a sort of narrow, pinched face. I hardly had time to sit down opposite her, in the parlor, before she said—

"Alice, why don't you come West?"

I was so surprised that I couldn't say a word. Come West! It had never occurred to me that I could ever come West. It didn't seem possible. I got my voice back and answered—

"I'm working."

"Where?"

"In a restaurant here."

"A restaurant! And living by yourself?"

"Yes, I have a room over the restaurant."

I wondered if this was a dreadful thing, as Grandmother Smith's voice seemed to show such horror. It did sound bad, I supposed, to say that I worked in a restaurant; but it really wasn't bad, because my job was helping in the kitchen, and I never had to wait on men; besides, the work wasn't hard and I was getting two dollars a week. But maybe, after all, it wasn't quite respectable; Grandmother Smith seemed to think it wasn't, and she must know.

"Why don't you live with your grandparents?"

"They are old, and can't afford to keep me," I said. "It's to help them that I'm working."

"How much are you earning?"

"Two dollars a week."

It sounded awful small as I said it to her.

"Your sister Emma," replied Grandmother Smith, "is making twenty-five dollars a month."

"My!"

Twenty-five dollars a month! I never knew girls got so much pay anywhere in the world.

And then the thought came to me—

"Why, if I only could get West somehow, maybe I could make twenty-five dollars a month, too; and help grandma and grandpa!"

"I was just thinking," went on Grandmother Smith, "that if you came West you could work, just like Emma is doing, and not be so far away from your real family. At least your own father would be nearby. I don't think it is safe for a girl to be off from her folks like this."

I would have laughed at that, if I hadn't been too busy thinking of that twenty-five dollars a month. The idea that X—— wasn't "safe" was funny enough. I couldn't quite see what she was driving at; but I didn't care. I was wondering about going West.

"Well," she said, "you go and think it over and give me your answer before night. I'm leaving day after tomorrow. I guess we can borrow the fare somewhere, and you can pay it back later. It's only thirty-five dollars, this time of year."

I got out of that house, my head fairly buzzing with the new plans. The first thing I must do was to talk it over with my Billy. Billy wasn't living at home either, but was driving a delivery wagon in X——, and we saw a lot of each other. He was eighteen, and I was five months and four days younger, and we were planning to get married in a year or two, just as soon as we could make a little money.

I left word at Billy's store that he was to come around and see me the first minute he had. He came at lunch time.

"Oh Billy," I told him, when he arrived. "I'm going West."

"Huh?" said Billy. "You goin' away from me, Alice?"

I hadn't really thought very much about that side of it. I didn't like that idea at all. But I went on excitedly:

"Girls out there make twenty-five dollars a month when they work, and I'm only making eight. I can get a job like that out there, and send lots of money back to grandma and grandpa. I can send them maybe fifteen dollars a month; why, they can live on that, and ten ought to be lots for me to live on. Don't you see what a wonderful chance it is, Billy? Don't you see?"

"Billy, I'll come back in a year or two," I said.

"Will you, sure?" said Billy, brightening up. Then we started to make plans. Maybe Billy could save the thirty-five dollars himself and come out there; and maybe, then, we could both save enough to get back on, and we would return together and get married; but we would be great people in that region, because we had traveled so. I had never had the slightest idea but that I'd come back again, and I could see the way people would look.

As to where I would live out West, I never gave a thought. It was easy to find places to live. I supposed, in a general sort of way, that I would make my headquarters with my Grandmother Smith, seeing she had invited me to come out there, and that I would spend most of my time working. I wasn't going to waste my time, but was going to work hard and save all the money I could; maybe, besides the fifteen dollars for grandpa,

I could put aside a dollar or two to help Billy and me later on. There wasn't anything I couldn't do, with all that wealth.

That very afternoon I went back to Grandmother Smith, and told her that I would come West.

"You said you were going day after tomorrow" I said. "So I will quit my job at the restaurant tonight, and just run over tomorrow and say 'good-by' to grandma and grandpa. They'll be so glad!"

"They'll be nothing of the sort," said Grandmother Smith.

"Why—what—don't you think they'll want me to go?"

"Of course they won't. They never traveled. They don't know how it is out there. There's no use spilling your plans. It's better for them to have you off their hands and in the West, and you know it."

Well, that was true, of course—I was going West mainly so I could send more money back to the dear old folks who had done everything for me all my life. And yet if they knew I was going it would probably cause trouble. It would be too hard for us all.

"Can I write them a note?"

"Yes—after you are safely on the train. Write them, then, telling them you have gone West. By the time they get the note you'll be well on your way. Then they can't have you brought back—you ain't eighteen, you know. And, then, there won't be any trouble over parting and all that."

It was a cruel plan, and you can see I must have been half crazy to follow it. But I was dead set on going West. I twisted it all around in my head until I made myself believe that my going West was really the best thing for grandpa and grandma, and that if I saw them before leaving it would be worse for them.

So that very evening I quit my job in the restaurant, and had a long parting session with my Billy, at the close of which I was just about ready to tell my Grandmother Smith that she could go back West by herself. But I didn't. Early the next morning my new grandmother and I drove out to a farm owned by another relative, a man, from whom she borrowed the thirty-five dollars for my tourist ticket.

After another day and night, during which I was too excited to eat or sleep, we climbed aboard the train—for fairyland, I thought, though the ticket read Westville. For all my excitement, I hadn't been able to get my poor grandpa and grandma out of my head. And now, on the train, I sat down and wrote the hardest letter I have ever written in my life. It sounded so cruel, the bald, blunt truth—"Dear Grandpa,—I am aboard a train going West. I am going to make twenty-five dollars a month and send you and grandma fifteen. I am going to live with Emma and Grandmother Smith. I will come back to you soon."

I heard afterward that when grandpa got that letter at the post office he fainted, and they had to carry him home.

Poor old folks! I never saw either of them again.

From the moment I set foot aboard the train for the West, I was like a bit of wood set adrift.

When my Grandmother Smith had said, "Alice, why don't you come West?" I had thought it was an invitation, and that I naturally would live with her, when I wasn't working. When I found out differently, I hadn't any strength in myself to fall back on. I was too young.

So here I was, a bit of wood drifting in a stream, and the stream was going to carry me—just where it did.

I was naturally all excitement to get to Westville, on the Pacific coast, and see my sister Emma. I hadn't ever seen her in my life, so far as I remembered. It was great to feel the train bringing me closer to her all the time.

I didn't have so much curiosity to see my father, somehow. I guess I felt a little bit as if he hadn't quite done the right thing by me, nor by my grandparents, in letting them raise me.

It bothered me so much to think of poor old grandpa and grandma, and that letter of mine dropping out of a clear sky. But I didn't do much thinking. In all my life I hadn't been thirty miles from home; and now I couldn't get enough of looking out of that car-window.

I never had thought there was anything in the world so wonderful as the mountains. We went through a few cities too, among them St. Louis, where I saw my first street car; and I hoped Westville would be something like St. Louis.

As to Grandmother Smith and the rest of my new relatives on that train, I missed something in them—I couldn't tell exactly what.

I remembered how grandpa and grandma, my mother's parents, had taken in girls that had "got into trouble," and given them good positions; well, I was certain my Grandmother Smith would never do a thing like that. She didn't seem so broad, somehow.

She questioned me a lot as to how I had been raised; and she wasn't slow in letting me see that she didn't think much of "those people" who had brought me up. When I told her about my Billy, and how he used to call twice a week, she seemed sort of scandalized; and that made me angry, because she put the worst interpretation on it.

"Your sister Emma doesn't have any such friends coming to see her at night," she said, pursing up her mouth.

We came through the last mountains and down a beautiful fertile valley, and when we finally reached Westville it was night. Westville, I found, wasn't as large as St. Louis, and it wasn't even the largest city on the Pacific coast; but it was a good-sized town. I'm not going to give it any other name than Westville, because even if my relatives did figure in a way in making me what I am, there's no use hurting them about it now.

I got more and more excited as we got near Grandmother Smith's house. To think I was actually going to see my sister at last!

I knew Emma would be just splendid, and I expected to feel like a green country jay alongside of her; but anyway, I made up my mind to play up as well as I knew how. I wanted her to get the best first impression of me.

It was real late when we got to the house. My sister Emma had gone to bed.

"Oh, Emma," my grandmother called out. "Get up! Come out here! Here's Alice!"

She left me there waiting in that strange room.

And just as she slammed that door I got busy. I had on a coat I had bought back in X——, it had cost me six dollars. I never liked that coat; had the idea it didn't look well on me. I tore it off as quick as I could, bundled it up into a ball, and sent it flying into a corner, behind a davenport. It hit the wall and dropped out of sight.

Then I yanked out the pins that held my hideous hat. It wasn't my own hat—it was borrowed from a cousin because Grandmother Smith thought my own was too old. This was a nice enough hat, but I just knew I looked like a fright in it. I sent it flying after the coat.

And just as it disappeared my sister Emma came in and kissed me.

My, but was my sister pretty! I had seen pretty girls before, I thought in that instant, but never one that looked like that.

I stood back and took stock.

Emma was smaller than I was, and she had great big blue eyes. She had blonde hair that curled close all over her head, and a tiny mouth and red cheeks like a doll. She was dainty and pretty beyond anything I ever thought lived in this world. But I didn't feel she was really my sister. She was beautiful and I loved her, and we would be great friends; but there wasn't any sisterly feeling in it at all.

Just then Grandmother Smith's nervous system had a shock. "Why, what on earth has been happening to this parlor?" she said, staring all around. "Who's been fixing this room all up?"

My sister Emma's cheeks got redder than ever.

Grandmother Smith turned on her.

"Did you buy them curtains and that sofa? Where'd you get them pictures? What have you been doing all this month I've been away?"

"Well, it didn't look very decent before," my sister answered. I could see she wasn't used to answering back—she was the quiet kind. "I just got a few things. I bought them with my own money."

"Yes, but who'd you get 'em for?" said Grandmother Smith. She lit into Emma and gave her a regular raking over the coals.

But I was waiting for Emma and me to get off together, so she could tell me more about that parlor. It was a pretty little room now, with nice curtains and pictures and a new daven-port. I wondered what Emma's young man was like—and—yes, I wondered whether he would have any friends to bring with him when he came to call. Not that I wasn't true to Billy—nothing like that, yet. But I was just a kid, and everything in the world was new, and there might be something new in that direction, too. I had started to drift already, you see.

I slept that night with my new sister, and we talked a long time. She told me about her young man—he was the son of a liquor dealer, and he had lots of friends, and among them was a young fellow named Sam, in the upholstery business, who was a nice chap.

Then she told me about her job. She was a telephone girl on the private exchange in the Westerner building, a big newspaper plant. She got $25 a month.

That was the part I was waiting for. I told her all about how I had gone away from grandpa and grandma without sending them any word until I was on the train, and about how poor they were, and how I was going to get a job, too, and send them the money. Out of a twenty-five dollar salary, I said, I surely would be able to send them ten or fifteen.

"Why, you can't do that, you little silly," she said. "It isn't possible to hardly support yourself on that, much less send any money back home. Lots of girls here have to make money in— other ways."

I didn't stop to ask her what ways. My heart sank like a stone.

"Hardly support yourself? Why, that's awful big pay, ain't it? Back home they only pay two dollars a week, and that's lots!" I was about ready to cry.

"Maybe it's a lot back there, but it costs more out here just to live," said Emma, and I knew she told me the truth. All the hope went out of me. I burst out crying.

What was the use of my coming West, then? What was I here for, anyway, if I couldn't help grandpa and grandma? Why wasn't I still back in that restaurant in X——, making two dollars a week and seeing lots of my Billy?

Where was I drifting to, then? What was in the future, now I had made this great change?

I didn't know, but I was scared.

❧∗❧

I was on my way to pay my first call upon my father. So far as I could remember, I had never seen him.

What a strange new world I had dropped into! I thought,

as I walked along in the direction Grandmother Smith had pointed out to me. It was just five days ago that a strange woman, whom I had never seen before, had got me to leave my own home and come West with her. Then last night they had shown me a lovely girl, a little older than I was, and told me this was my sister, Emma.

And now here I was going to call on a strange man, who was my own father. I was walking through the streets of a strange city. My whole life was strange. It didn't seem to be real.

I could see it was awful crowded at Grandmother Smith's. At breakfast that morning there had been too many people for the room. And I hadn't slept well, because, besides crying myself to sleep, I was used to having a bed to myself. My clothes were going to be in the way, too; they wouldn't go into Emma's wardrobe.

If there was one thing I hated, it was being in the way. I wouldn't stand it, that was all. I'd go.

And just as I thought that, that queer feeling came back again—the feeling that I was drifting—torn loose from everything I had been tied to, and just drifting.

I reached the house where my father and stepmother lived. It was a little affair, only three rooms.

"Are you Alice? Come right in," said my stepmother, Annie. I took a look at Annie to size her up.

I could see at first glance that Annie was hard-worked and poor; and at second glance, that she fretted about it. She was a young woman—not over thirty-five—but she looked kind of worn-out and discontented.

I could see she wasn't dying with joy to see me, either, and I could guess the reason. She was worried because she might have to support me. But she and I got to talking all right after the first few minutes, and I was telling her all about people at home that she used to know, and the way I had come West.

Pretty soon Annie said, just as she probably had been told to say—

"If Grandma Smith don't find it right convenient to keep you, Alice, you could come over here, while you are looking for a place. Only we're awful crowded, with the two children and all."

I thanked her for the invitation. But it wasn't a very cordial one. I thought to myself that a good deal would have to happen before I would accept it.

At noon-time there was a heavy step outside, and a short, dark-haired man, with deep lines in his face, wearing dirty working clothes, came in.

"Here's Alice, Fred," said Annie.

I stood there and stared into the air, as awkward and embarrassed as I ever felt in my life. And my father stood there and stared, and felt sort of queer himself, I guess.

Pretty soon the thought came to me that maybe I ought to shake hands, like I did when I was introduced to other people. I was trying to get up the courage to make the break, when he sort of found his voice.

"How do you do, Alice?" he said, and I answered, "How do you do, papa?" I felt as if I ought to add, "I'm pleased to meet you"; but I thought maybe that would be too funny, and I didn't.

Then he stepped forward and kissed me. For the first time in my life I knew what it was like to kiss a strange man.

We all sat down to lunch, and while we were all in the room, Annie and the two children and papa and myself, it wasn't so bad. But right afterwards they all went away and left papa and me alone.

It was awful. We couldn't find a word to say to each other. I didn't dare open my mouth, because the thought came into my head that if I did I might ask him something about my own mother, who had died when I was eleven months old.

On his part, I guess, he may have felt ashamed for not doing more for me; or maybe he felt that I thought he ought to be ashamed, and was sore at me for thinking so. Anyhow, it was awful. It just froze my tongue.

That was the first of many such times. I have never been able to talk to my father, all my life since then. Something comes up between us. That word, "papa," has always had a funny sound to me.

As I walked back to Grandmother Smith's, somehow I felt a long way from home. Alongside of Annie's poorly-kept three rooms, that nice parlor Emma had fixed up looked fine to me. But I was lonesome.

It was in the same parlor that I was sitting a little while later, when Grandmother Smith came in. She looked at me a moment, hesitated, then said—

"Well, Alice, did Annie ask you to come over and live with them?"

"What?" I sort of gasped. I had supposed all along that I was to live with the person that brought me West, except when I was working.

I stared back, feeling further from home than ever, then I answered, sort of hard—

"Yes. Annie said something about my coming there—if I wanted."

Grandmother Smith seemed relieved.

"Well, you'd better do that, then. You can move over there any time you want to. Then we won't be so crowded here."

"I would sooner die than stay with you another minute after that," I thought, as I stared at the door after she had gone out. It was a hard blow, and I wanted to cry.

I got my things together and moved over to the stepmother's the next morning.

After that, I had three weeks that were real hard. I couldn't stand it at my stepmother's. There was my father around, stiff and embarrassed, as if I was always going to accuse him of something. Annie, I guess, made an effort to be nice to me; but she was a natural scold, and worried over money; and, anyhow, we just couldn't get along.

I knew all the time that I was in the way.

I kept remembering, too, that I wasn't paying any board. Annie had lots of little ways of letting me know about it, too. I made up my mind that the very first thing that came along I would get out of there.

"Alice, while you're sitting around, I wish you'd run down to the grocery and get me four bits worth of sugar," Annie said to me one afternoon.

She handed me the fifty cents.

I went to the grocery store. "Send up twenty-five cents worth of sugar to this address right away, will you?" I asked. Then: "Give me an evening paper."

I turned to the advertisements, found the column of "Female Help Wanted," and read:

"Wanted—A girl for housework in the country; $15 a month and found. Apply 364 Sanford Street."

I asked one person and another until I came upon that address. A lady answered the door.

"But where is your baggage?" she asked, after she had explained to me that the position was at a little railroad depot back in the hills, working for herself and her husband, who was the station-agent.

"My baggage? It's—it's at my father's," I started in, then seeing that she looked suspicious, I told her the whole story.

"Where are you going to stay tonight?" she asked. "I'm not going out to our place until tomorrow."

"I—I can stay with you, can't I?"

I wasn't a bit shy about making that proposition. I was just from the Middle West, where that was the regular way of doing things.

She looked at me, smiling.

"You—you're not a Westville girl, I can see that," she said.

"No, ma'am, I'm just from—home," and then, because she looked kind, I told her about my coming West.

She took me in and kept me all that night; and the next morning she gave a boy twenty-five cents to go around and get my clothes from Annie. And then we took the train, and I was happy once more. I was working, at last, even if two sets of relatives had practically turned me out.

The bit of driftwood downstream sometimes gets behind a rock and stops drifting for a while. That was the way with me; and the rock was this job at the station-agent's, in the little country town near Westville.

That family left me to myself a good deal. I could arrange the furniture to suit myself—they liked it. I had to sleep downstairs, on a cot, in the ticket-office; and I liked that, too, because I had lots of room. You know how those little depots are—all windows; I used to undress in the dark. One night a hobo, walking along the railroad, put his face to the glass and stared inside for a while, and I didn't sleep very much that night.

That station-agent kept a little store behind the depot. I needed a good many things, and during that first month I got them on account. When the end of the month came, and he paid me, there was just five dollars and fifty cents left.

My, but was I proud! Here was the first money I had earned since I came West. It began to look as if it might have been the right thing for me to come West, after all.

What should I do with it? Why, there was only one thing to do—send it to poor old grandpa back home.

I hunted around till I found a piece of cardboard off an old box; and I cut it out to just the shape of an envelope. Then I took my new gold-piece, and sewed it to the cardboard with black thread.

Anybody feeling of that envelope would surely have been tempted to help himself.

Well, I heard later on what became of that money. Grandpa had gone down to the mail one day—he was a feeble old man now—and they had given him my letter. He opened it right there in the store; and poor old dear, he just broke down and cried.

After I had been at that place about five months, a new station-agent was appointed; the people I was working for went away, and I was out of a job. I know I wasn't wanted at my Grandmother Smith's, because there was no room; and I knew my stepmother didn't want me—I would almost have died sooner than go there; but what was I to do? I had no other home.

I put my pride in my pocket—for once—and meekly went back to Westville.

Annie, my stepmother, greeted me with a sour face; and right away I had the same old feeling back again—that terrible thought of being in the way. It drove me pretty near crazy. Annie was crosser than ever, after the way I had run off before; and she kept saying things to me that hurt. It was very clear I wasn't wanted.

I was getting a bit hardened. A new sort of feeling began to grow up in my heart—a kind of desperate, don't-care attitude. That was the result of the way I had been greeted out West. It seemed nobody cared what I did or what became of me, anyhow.

I started to see a good deal of my sister Emma now. We had some real nice times together, and once or twice I was in her parlor on Sunday nights when her young man called and brought a friend.

The four of us one night went to church together. After the service, we stepped into a negro church which was almost next-door to ours. The preacher was warmed up in great shape, and before he got through it was eleven o'clock.

I knew, as we walked home, that Annie would surely give me fits for staying out so late; and I wished Emma would think to ask me home to stay with her.

I was by myself when I reached my father's house. I went to the front door—it was locked.

Without ringing the bell, I worked around quietly to the back yard, thinking to get in without waking anybody. The back door, which was almost never locked at night, was fastened tight.

I stayed out there in the dark, in that back yard, for a long time thinking about things. This hurt my pride worse than anything that had happened. To be locked out at night, as if it was a disgrace, and all for a visit to a negro church! I didn't mind catching it so much; it was just that there wasn't anybody who cared enough about me to make a few allowances, even for little things. It was that old feeling of taking charity.

Finally I went around again to the front and rang the bell. Papa got up and opened the door. No sooner did he see me than he started in to scold me.

"Alice, what do you mean by coming in so late? Didn't Annie tell you"—

Well, that was all the start Annie needed. She broke in and talked to me worse than ever I was talked to in my life. It seemed as if she had just been piling it all up, and now that she got her chance, she was going to make the most of it. At last papa had to stop her by saying, "There; that's enough Annie."

It was only a few days after that, when Emma said—

"Alice, the night exchange girl down at the Westerner is going to quit. Come down and learn the switch-board, and maybe I can get you the job. She's got another place."

That job looked fine to me, even if the hours were hard—

four o'clock in the afternoon to eleven at night. I learned the board all right—there were five trunk lines and twenty department phones—and a couple of nights later, when the night girl quit, Emma introduced me to the boss. I was told I could have the place.

I went right out to Annie's house.

"I've got the job at the Westerner building," I told her. "Going to start work this afternoon."

"What time do you get home?" asked Annie.

"Eleven o'clock at night," I said, "but"—

"Well, you can't stay here anymore, then," said my stepmother, decidedly. "Your father works hard all day, and I ain't going to have him disturbed by your coming in every night at no such hour. You'll have to move, that's all there is to it."

"Can't I have a latch-key?" I asked.

"There ain't no key," said Annie.

"I'll pay you $15 a month board," I said.

"I don't care," said Annie. "I wouldn't bother with you for the whole twenty-five."

That desperate, don't-care feeling came up inside of me then, stronger than ever. If I had known everything at that time that I knew a few months later, I know what my answer would have been. But I was too new to the city. All I knew was, I had been turned out, first by Grandmother Smith, and now again by Annie.

The bit of wood hadn't yet drifted quite far enough down the stream. I went back and told Emma and started to work; and she fixed it up with Grandmother Smith that I could come there for a little while at any rate, and pay the $15 a month board to her. I went there that very night; and it was the same old crowded state of affairs with Emma again.

This business of turning girls out-of-doors just because they might be a little trouble, or because you don't think you ought to be responsible to them, is something I have heard of in other quarters. It seems to be a favorite trick of a certain sort of people to say to a girl, when they are a bit irritated, "Then you can go away from here. I don't want you around."

But can't people understand that they are all responsible for each other, in lots of ways? And don't they see the thing that is always ready and waiting for a young girl—for every young girl, no matter how good her family—just as soon as the home ties get a little bit weak?

It's none of my business to preach; but I have seen what harm has been done by such little things as that. Every girl that is locked out at night, or that is made to feel she isn't wanted at home, is just that much nearer the brothel—nearer than people suppose.

Back at Grandmother Smith's again, it wasn't long before the old crowded feeling came on me.

Living in the same apartment house was a huge man, a Canadian, who made his living heaving big blocks of ice onto wagons. He was a widower, with a daughter eleven years old. Always, when I remember that man, I think of what I have heard about the "Cave Men." He was one of them.

Now, that little daughter was a bit too bright for her age. She knew a lot of things she didn't need to know; and she spent most of her time teaching those things to the children of the neighbors. Naturally, the neighbors kicked.

So the Canadian "cave man" wanted a girl to come over and take care of that child in the daytime while he was at work, and to do the regular housework. He offered $15 a month, board, and a place to sleep. So that was how I began to hold two jobs at a time.

Well, it made me pretty sleepy, working from seven in the morning to eleven at night; and sometimes I used to go to sleep over the Westerner switchboard. But it was pleasant otherwise, except for one thing. That huge, clumsy Canadian got the idea he wanted to marry me.

Not that he ever proposed. I never gave him the chance. He just used to sit and stare at me, and when I saw a certain expression come over his face I used to quietly go out and pay a short visit to grandma's.

He got worse and worse. His eyes would get a sort of gloating, brutal look to them, and he would sit there staring at me and licking his lips and seldom saying a word. I have seen that same look since then, in the eyes of other men that weren't supposed to be "cave men," but respectable husbands and fathers; but this was the first time I met it. It doesn't add to your respect for the world of men.

When the thing at last came to a head, I didn't cover myself with glory. In fact, that little eleven-year-old girl, who was always the bane of my life, seemed for the moment older and wiser than I was.

I had come home, as usual, at eleven o'clock, and had gone to bed right away. I slept with that little girl. I don't know how long I had been asleep; but suddenly the creaking of the door gave me an awful start.

"Burglars!" popped into my mind, and then a cold shiver ran all down me so I couldn't move or hardly breathe. Then the soft footsteps of a man came nearer, and I heard his breath sort of hissing through his lips. So I knew it wasn't burglars, but something that might easily be worse—that Canadian.

He came over and stood by the bed for what seemed like hours. I couldn't even get breath enough to scream. At last he put out one hand, bent way down and pressed my shoulder— not shaking it, but just pressing it sort of heavy.

That brought me to myself a bit. I gasped out—

"What are you doing in here?"

The big, stupid fellow just leaned there for a minute while

my question was sinking in. His breathing was louder than ever. Then he did a strange thing. He reached down into his pocket, and then held out his huge hand to me. I heard the clink of money.

"Don't you want this?" he whispered. "Here—take this."

I was broad awake now. It flashed through my mind that it was his payday. Was he drunk? I couldn't smell any liquor, though he was close enough to me.

I tried to answer him calmly, but my heart was bumping so the words wouldn't come right.

"No—no—you go away from here—go away!" It seemed as if I was afraid to talk loud, and I have often wondered why that was. I whispered as if my fix was the same as his.

He just crowded up a little closer to the bed.

Just then the little girl sleeping next to me woke up. She must have got the same shock I did, but she was wide awake all at once, and seemed to understand the whole thing.

"Daddy," she said, "you go right out of this room and don't bother Alice anymore. Go right out, now."

There was decision in her voice. She didn't sound like an eleven-year-old kid at all. That big Canadian straightened up, turned around sort of jerky, and marched out the door.

"Now, Alice," said the child, "he might come back. So you get here on the inside of the bed, and I'll trade places with you." And, then, now it was all over, I had to get worse scared than ever, and broke down and cried as if I couldn't ever quit.

Little fool as I was, I was afraid to tell Grandmother Smith about my night's adventure with that big Canadian. She would scold, and tell me it was all my fault. She always liked to put the worst interpretation on everything.

But it made me think a lot. Remember, I was still green from the country.

What had that big Canadian wanted in my room? Well—I

knew, all right enough. There was something that always seemed to come into the minds of men whenever I was alone with them.

Was it something about myself alone, I wondered? Was I different in that way from other girls? It worried me.

I got my sister Emma off alone one day and told her about it. She laughed.

"Oh, he's just like all the rest of them," she said. "They're always after a girl. By the time you've lived around here a year longer you'll see plenty of that. Men are all the same."

I knew she had spoken the truth. It gave me the queerest feeling—as if I was always going to be sort of hunted; as if I was never going to be safe, never off my guard, always bound to be chased by some man. Emma, too, had known the feeling, it seemed—then was it just the same with all the other girls?

"Of course it is, you little silly," Emma said, when I asked her. "It's always that way. Men are all crazy on the subject. A girl has to be mighty careful. My, you're green."

As she said it, it seemed as though I knew it already—had always known it, in fact. But never before had I had it put to me so square. Was it the same, too, I wondered, with girls who were rich, who had lots of money—girls who weren't just laborers' daughters?

That talk stuck in my mind. I couldn't get rid of that awful idea. And the more I thought about it, the worse it all got.

What could a girl do? Could she keep away from men altogether, never see them or talk to them or have them come to the house? No, no; that wasn't possible; besides, it wouldn't make any difference. The only thing to do was, keep my head and play the game, just the same as all the rest of the girls—the same as every girl in the world. It was just fate.

After that night, the Canadian "cave man" didn't bother me. He hardly said anything to me at all. He sort of got onto himself. And only a little while afterward that horrible little girl of his, who had seemed so grown-up that night, lost me my job.

My work had been going wrong one day, and I was getting sort of worn out and sleepy, I guess, with the long hours. I was putting out the cold supper that I always left for the Canadian and his little girl, when I heard her laughing in the next room.

"Come, now, and look at the bedroom, Alice," she called. "I've fixed it all up nice for you. You can't go to work until you've cleaned it all up."

I stared through the doorway. That bedroom was regularly "stacked." That child had stripped the bed, yanked out the bureau drawers, taken down the pictures and curtains, and pitched everything all over the floor. How she had ever managed it by herself, I don't know.

I lost my temper. It meant a good hour's work, and I was already late down at the Westerner.

The first thing I grabbed was a piece of rope she had hauled in there. She was a big girl, and put up a fight; but I tied her to the foot of the brass bed, and then I gave her the whipping of her life.

"Now, you fix this room up again yourself," I ordered her. "I ain't going to do it for you." Then I went to work.

I knew perfectly well what this meant about my job. I didn't even wait to get fired. I just took my things that night, and moved over to Grandmother Smith's.

But in a few days I was back again. The Canadian had come over and told grandma that he couldn't get along without help. And so she took pity on him, and said I would come back.

He promised me a raise to $20 a month, if I could put in my whole day and not stop off at four o'clock. Now, just to explain what a tiny bit of money means to a working-girl, let me show you how I figured it out.

To begin with, I couldn't stand it much longer to hold both jobs. It was wearing me out; besides, I wanted my evenings.

At the Westerner I was getting $25 a month; and if I lived at Grandmother Smith's, I would have to pay fifteen of that for board and room, besides being crowded. I would have $10 clear.

But if I gave up the telephone work, and put in all my time at the Canadian's, then I could send grandpa and grandma $5 a month, and still have $15 clear for clothes and washing. That difference of $5 a month was the winning argument.

If people who have a dollar or two to waste could only know, just for a little while, what it means to figure that close on money—the awful deadness of the future—I just know people wouldn't be so ready to blame the girl who gives in, has her "good time," and lands—here.

❖

I had my evenings free at last; and now that little parlor Emma had fixed up started to be of use.

Emma, in spite of all Grandmother Smith's scolding, had several young fellows coming around to the house regularly. There was the boy she was engaged to, son of a wholesale liquor man; and there was his chum, a young upholsterer, and some others.

That young upholsterer, Sam, picked me out right away. He was a nice enough fellow in some ways—only I still remembered my Billy, and was writing to him regularly.

My scare from the Canadian was still fresh in my mind, with all that it meant—the fear and everything. One night in our parlor the four of us kids got into a sort of roughhouse—just a kind of wrestling match—and this young Sam let drop some remark, a word or two, that I can't remember now—that let me know what he was thinking.

Sam, too! Oh, were all men alike? Couldn't a girl ever walk, or run, or rough-house a little, or anything, without bringing up a certain sort of thoughts in a man's mind?

And that brought up again that same feeling as if I was drifting—drifting away from everything I had once known, into new and dangerous things that I didn't know how to face.

"Alice," said my Grandmother Smith, "your Aunt Eleanor hasn't any girl now. Why don't you move over there, and take that job?"

I was glad enough to do it. I didn't love the idea of being employed by relatives, especially, but I liked it better than I liked being out of work. The Canadian was going away that week.

Aunt Eleanor seemed to like the idea, too. Her little daughter was thought to be dying, and there was a raft of relatives there—this family had brought out that same old custom with them, from my first home in the Middle West.

They gave me a cot in the dining room to sleep on, and I started in to do the kitchen work, just the same as any hired girl.

But it had been so friendly that nothing at all was said about pay. Just at that time all of my clothes were wearing out, all at once. I needed new things from head to foot; and especially I needed new shoes. My old ones weren't fit to be seen. They were worn right through.

I had been four or five weeks at Aunt Eleanor's, when one day the thought popped into my head—

"Say, I wonder if Auntie isn't ever going to pay me anything for all this? Does she think she's letting me work here out of charity? Good heavens!"

For I had been going on the belief that I was a regular hired girl. And so had that bunch of relatives—they hadn't been making it any easier. It was the sort of household where anybody eats any time of day, and people were always running out into the kitchen; they didn't have regular hours for meals or anything else.

That charity idea stuck in my head. I couldn't get it out. A couple more weeks went by, without anything said about any pay; and my shoes were getting worse and worse.

Finally I went up to Grandmother Smith.

"Does Aunt Eleanor think I'm doing all that work free of charge?" I asked her.

"Why, ain't you the ungrateful thing!" Grandma lost her temper right off. "Here's your auntie doing you a kindness—keeping you off the streets, you might say, when you was out of a job; and now you want pay! I never heard of such ungratefulness."

Ungrateful! That put a different face on things. My grandmother didn't seem to see that if I hadn't taken that job with Aunt Eleanor, I would have gotten one where they paid me.

One thing was sure. I would quit right away. I walked back to Aunt Eleanor's, thinking hard. What could I do next? Where was I to live?

I was passing along a street, when a girl came out of a big doorway and pretty near ran into me. I looked up. The place was a steam laundry.

"Do you work in that laundry?" She nodded. "Is there any chance for a job there now? Do they need any girls?"

"I don't know for certain," the girl answered, "but it wouldn't hurt a bit to try. They're always taking on new girls; only they don't pay you much."

Down on the block next to the laundry I happened to see a sign—

"Rooms for rent. Steady or transient."

I hadn't ever been in a rooming house before. I climbed up the stairway and rang the bell by the desk. A woman answered.

"How much do you charge for a small room?" I said. "Steady?"

She looked me over kind of funny. I guess my greenness sort of stuck out, and she wondered what was my game.

"Two dollars a week," she replied.

I didn't make any answer, but just walked out and went right on to my Aunt Eleanor's.

"Auntie," said I, "I'm going to leave here. I've got another job." I hadn't, but I had to break away somehow.

She looked surprised, and I could see her thinking the same that grandma had thought—that I was ungrateful. It made me madder than ever.

"I don't know whether you ever meant to pay me anything for all the work I've done," I said, thoroughly mad. "But if you did, I wish you'd do it now. My feet are just on the ground."

Well, after a little side-stepping, she paid me, making as much over it as if she was doing me the greatest favor of my life. And what do you think she gave me?

Three dollars. For two months' work.

"Thank you, aunt," I said, trying to hold my temper. "I'll try to remember this."

Feeling as if I had cut loose from one of my last holds on the world, I went downstairs and walked over to the laundry.

❧⋮❧

"Any experience?" asked the boss of the laundry.

He was a tall man with a black mustache, and he grinned at me in a way I didn't quite like.

"Not in this work," I answered.

"Well," he replied, "you're a good-looking girl. I can take you on, I guess."

"What pay?" I asked.

"Six dollars a week," he said, grinning again.

"But I can't live on that!" My heart sank.

"Oh, that's all right," said the man, grinning worse than ever. "Didn't I say you was a good-looking girl? You can pick up lots of easy money on the side."

He winked over my head at some other girl who was passing by.

Money on the side! Well, here was something new. What did he mean? Then I knew. That same old fear again.

"All right, I'll take the job," I said. "I guess, as you say, I can get along."

He laughed at that, as if it was a real good joke. I had just said it to be sassy, because he might not want to give me the job otherwise. He told me to come around seven the next morning.

I went back to my new two-dollar room, turned on the light, sat down on the hard bed, and figured things out. I had a sort of feeling as if I was hanging by a thin rope over a volcano.

Six dollars a week. Take out two for room rent—that left four a week for eating, clothes, car fare, washing and a good time.

Cut out car fare. Cut out clothes—for the present. My old shoes would have to do. Cut out washing—I'd do it myself, in my room. Cut out—yes—cut out the good time. I'd need that four dollars just for eating. Divide it by seven. That meant sixty cents a day. Ten cents for breakfast, twenty for lunch, thirty for supper. That would make four-twenty a week—I'd be twenty cents short.

Well, maybe Sundays I'd go without eating, only twenty cents' worth.

Or maybe—there was that easy money to be made "on the side." No; not for me. That didn't attract me at all. I wasn't far enough along for that. But the idea stayed with me, and bothered me.

I soon found life wasn't quite a path of roses, even if I was out in "the world." Have you ever done laundry work? Then you know what it is like.

Ten hours a day, and on my feet shaking out clothes the whole time—that was part of it. Heat and steam all around—that was another part. Ten-cent breakfasts, twenty-cent lunches, thirty-cent dinners—that was another. No clothes; that was another. And my shoes all worn out.

I wasn't a very big girl, though strong for my size. But I had come from a country where there was always a huge lot of food put on the table for every meal. It wasn't long before I found myself starting to get weak with that sort of feeding. At that time, of course, there were cafeterias and a girl couldn't go to the real cheap restaurants.

I would go to bed at night so tired I could hardly walk, and I would get up in the morning pretty near as tired—with all the time that empty gnawing feeling at my stomach. But I knew that if I once should cut loose and feed myself a big satisfactory meal, there would be one day toward the end of the week when I wouldn't have anything to eat at all.

I made up my mind to get used to it if it killed me. And sometimes I thought it would.

The other girls in that laundry were most of them living just the same sort of lives—fighting with might and main to make both ends meet. Lots of them had a harder time than I did, not being so strong. If they gave up, they knew where they would land.

There was one of them I felt so sorry for that I took to bringing her a ten-cent egg sandwich every noon-time. It cut a dime from my supper money, but it was worth it to see her eyes.

These were the first Western girls I had got acquainted with. Looking back now, I can see they had a lot to do with "putting me wise," as the saying goes.

We would eat our lunches together, and sort of talk things over.

What did we talk about? Well, there were three or four girls who seemed to have lots and lots of clothes. They came to work wearing hats with big feathers, silk petticoats and all that sort of thing. And they were forever rubbing it into us girls in one way and another. They seemed to take joy in making the rest of us feel cheap.

They would talk up sharp to the boss, and the boss would talk back to them, in a way the rest of us couldn't seem to do. And they took their meals at a little better restaurant, and when they talked to us they were always joking about things that girls don't usually joke about. Yet they didn't seem happy; their eyes were sort of hard.

So the rest of us girls found plenty to talk about, in the way those girls acted. And that was where I fully understood the real meaning of what the boss had said to me, when I got the job. "You're a good-looking girl; you can always make money on the side."

These were the girls who did that.

"But why do girls who do that have to work at all?" I asked once. "What do they want to stay around the laundry for, and kill themselves with working? Why don't they just go where they belong?"

I was hard-hearted then. I'd never wish that for any girl now.

Well, one of the older girls explained to me that they probably lived at home with their folks, and didn't want their parents to know how they were doing. So they held onto the laundry job. They would make their extra money in the evenings, making believe they were staying at a "friend's house," or were "out to supper" or "going to the theater."

And that just added to that awful idea, that all around me everybody was doing these things, and that a girl who kept straight was doomed to be sort of "out of it."

I got to thinking to myself, sometimes, when I would get up in the morning all aching from the work of the day before, and drag off to work without much breakfast—

"Just, suppose, now, that I did as those other girls do. Wouldn't it be easier for me?"

Those are risky things to be thinking. But I thought them, just the same, and they didn't seem to be "bad" thoughts so much as just tired thoughts, desperate thoughts, hopeless thoughts.

And I know those other working girls had the same thoughts, day in and day out; they always had those other girls before their eyes, rubbing it in about their better meals and their fine clothes; and there wasn't a girl there, no matter how "straight" she was, that didn't feel sort of envious of those other girls.

Grandmother Smith, of course, learned that I had left Aunt Eleanor's. She was in a great fuss and stew when she found out I was living somewhere else. When she heard I was rooming by myself downtown she regularly went up into the air.

She stormed around at first and talked to me as if I was lost beyond all hope. Then, when I stayed right on, she changed her tone, little by little, until at last she was fairly pleading with me to come home again and room with Emma.

I got off my high horse when she had been sort of pleading long enough. After a good two months at that rooming-house, I finally moved back to Grandmother Smith's. I was never so glad to get anywhere in my life, crowded as it was.

I kept on, however, with my work in the laundry, and took my meals downtown; but I had a little more money to spend on them, now, because Grandmother Smith wouldn't charge room rent.

But it was Grandmother Smith herself, with all her prudish ideas, that gave me the hardest blow of all.

❖❖❖

Emma and I started out to have a "good time."

We were living together and both having our evenings off, for almost the first time since I had come West. That little parlor came into demand now. She had fixed up that parlor, you remember, out of her own money, and had started in to have her young men friends call in the evenings. And now that she had made the start, and I was there with her, we two girls sort of went in for a good time. Not in any bad way; we were perfectly "straight," and in our parlor the young fellows behaved themselves, but we had lots of friends, and they kept coming around.

Grandmother Smith didn't like this idea. In her day, she used to say, things weren't so free—and I guess they weren't. She was prudish, and was always getting shocked at the most innocent things.

If she had stopped to think, she would have seen that our parlor was the safest place for us girls, especially since we had so many young men friends. There couldn't be anything harmful going on right in that parlor, under her very eyes. But just the same it shocked her prudishness.

I have studied a good deal over this. It always seems to me that it is the natural thing for young folks to jolly around and see lots of each other; the only thing is their mothers ought to sort of know about it, and be in on the fun, or else it isn't quite safe. Mothers ought to understand.

My grandmother never even tried to understand. She just set herself against us; and nagged and scolded and forbade.

Lots of good it did her to forbid! She couldn't stop our having our friends come to the house. She was sort of setting herself against something nobody can ever stop.

Well, finally it came to a climax.

One night we gave a party, with some other girls and quite a crowd of fellows in. They stayed till after midnight, playing games and having a real good time.

As Emma and I were going to our rooms, here came Grandmother Smith in her nightgown.

She started to scold; and we started in to answer back. It got worse and worse, until I guess there must have been considerable noise. It made us angry to think she thought we were bad.

The very next day, when I came home from work, I found Emma crying.

On the wall where the telephone had been, there was a blank space. I looked into our parlor. The pictures were down, the curtains were gone, the davenport was gone, there was no carpet on the floor.

Right or wrong, Emma and I made up our minds right then that we would not be bossed like that. It had come to an open show-down between us and grandmother.

From the very night that Grandmother Smith closed our own home parlor to us, my sister Emma and I started to meet our "company" on the streets.

Grandmother had accused us of being "bad." If you call a person a sneak or a liar enough, he generally becomes one. All right, then, we said; if she wants us to be bad, we'll just show her.

It was easy. All the boys knew that Emma worked on the telephone switchboard at the Westerner, and if there wasn't a phone at the house, there was a whole switchboard there. I could always be found at the laundry, at quitting-time.

And, because we liked our friends and wanted to "show" our prudish grandmother, we began to make dates right along. The boys were always ready enough to take us to shows or for walks, or to candy-stores, and once in a while we had a buggy ride.

We got more and more used to hearing a certain brand of talk, and to resisting a certain sort of persuasion. I know I got so I didn't think any less of a fellow if he said things to me that I wouldn't have let anybody say a couple of months before.

I had the taste of beer once in a while, too, although I didn't like it, but only took it because the boys would laugh if I didn't. I hated to be laughed at. And, like any kid, I got the notion that it was lots of fun to be "real fast," and that I was being very grown-up in going around the way I did; also that I was getting a fine revenge on grandma.

A cousin of mine had a sweetheart, and they used to go out with our bunch once in a while. One night the girl invited us all to come up into her parlor; and that was how we made our first visit at Mrs. Trent's.

Mrs. Trent was a woman about thirty-five, the wife of a saloon-keeper. The first time I saw her I liked her very much; I thought I had never seen anybody who understood young people so well, or liked to have them around so much.

But I was kind of shocked, I remember, that first night I went up there, when a young fellow and a girl I knew came in, and the young fellow sat down on a chair and pulled the girl down on his lap. Everybody laughed and seemed to think it was a good joke, so I didn't see why I ought to object. I thought if Mrs. Trent didn't mind, I hadn't any business to.

Mrs. Trent herself had peculiar ideas. She seemed to like to have the young people cut up all they wanted to. There would be sandwiches, and most probably beer, and in the course of the evening somebody might tell a story or two that was quite a bit off color. But I thought it was all splendid and what they call "Bohemian," and I sat there and took it all in.

Still, I remember I was really startled when one night a young man came up there, and one of the girls whispered to me that he was Mrs. Trent's lover. It was a new idea to me that a married woman should have a lover. I had always considered that once a woman was married, she was settled for life so far as a man was concerned.

Then there was her son. He was living at home, and his young sweetheart was living there, too—with him. Both were under twenty. One night somebody made a remark to Mrs. Trent about that queer situation, and she replied with a laugh—

"Well, I'd sooner have them right at home here, open and above-board, than to have them living somewhere else on the sly."

That was just the way she felt about such things. Now, I suppose I have gone lower than Mrs. Trent ever went in her life; but I have still kept to my old-fashioned ideas in some ways. I never could agree with her on any such proposition as that.

I never could make out whether her husband, the saloon-keeper, knew her relations with the young fellow who was her lover. I sort of think he did know about it, at least in part. He used to come up there once in a while, and once I saw him when this young man was there, and he shook hands with him just as if everything was all right. I shouldn't wonder if his ideas were as queer as his wife's.

And so it was here, in Mrs. Trent's parlor, that I first came to look with any enjoyment on the idea of "being bad." There had never been any attraction to the notion before. But now that "Bohemian" idea started to lure me.

One night up in Mrs. Trent's parlor there was quite a big crowd of us young people. The room wasn't so very big, and as it happened there weren't chairs enough.

We had been pretty gay that night. I was standing out in the middle of the floor, when suddenly I felt someone throw his arms around me and start to drag me backwards.

I couldn't see who it was. He sort of carried me back a few feet, and then I found myself sitting on his knee. Naturally, I twisted around to see who it was.

It was Mrs. Trent's lover.

Just then I glanced around again, and here was Mrs. Trent standing in the doorway. I met her eye square. I didn't like her young man, especially—he was too fresh, sometimes—but I could see that she was half-crazy.

She took a step or two forward, and reached out her hands with the fingers apart, like she was going to get me by the hair. The fellow let go of me, and I naturally got over to the other side of the room.

Then Mrs. Trent ran forward and threw her arms around the young fellow, put her head down on his shoulder, and burst out crying.

I started to go, feeling pretty uncomfortable. Everybody in the room stopped talking and stared at her as she sat there sobbing. As I passed by, she caught sight of me; then she broke out swearing and calling me vile names. I went down the stairs with her still yelling things after me.

That ended my visits to Mrs. Trent's. I never had the desire to go there again. But the few times I had been there had got in their work with me. I was more used to a good many things than I had been before. I wasn't ready for the street or the brothel—not by a good deal. I hadn't yet met the man who finally put me there. But I was to meet him very soon.

The first thing that happened to me was that I lost my job in the steam laundry.

❧✦❧

Whether you are a man or a woman that is reading this, I want you to stop right here and go back over your own life. Whatever you are today—rich man, poor man, beggar man, thief—wasn't there some "one man" or one woman in your life, that played a big part in making you what you are?

If you are good, wasn't it some one person that made you feel good? If you are bad, wasn't it some "one man" or "one woman" who was the turning-point?

So, when you hear us women talk about the "one man" who put us where we are, you needn't just say, "Oh, she's making excuses for herself." Instead, just go back over your own life. You will see the "one man" there, too, for good or bad. Then you will understand.

I believe, or think I believe, that one's whole life, right from the start to finish, is just a proposition of "one man," many times over. First you meet one person, then you meet another; and each person stands for some special thing—and stamps you with that thing.

Often they don't stamp you very hard, and it doesn't stick. But sometimes, once or twice in each life, a person comes along who is right in line with everything else that is working on you at the time. When this happens, it is a turning-point.

Really, when you think of it, how much did you, yourself, have to do with shaping your own life? Mighty little. It was shaped for you. You aren't to be praised for it; and you aren't to be blamed. It's almost a joke to speak of it as "your" life. It's everybody's life.

The "one man" in my own life wasn't an easy man to understand.

He wasn't my lover, like so many of the girls I know had. He wasn't just a plain passionate brute, such as some of my friends tell of—a beast fit for the gallows if ever any man is fit for them. I know some fearful stories of that sort.

No; the man that was my "one man" was twice my age, and I thought he was just grand. He seemed to me to know the world through and through; though I can see now that he was a pretty ordinary sort. But he was clever, in a certain way, and he dressed well—just the sort of man to trip up a foolish girl of eighteen.

His name, so far as this story is concerned, was Henry Marsh. He kept a cigar store. I used to wonder why he stayed a cigar-dealer, since he had unusual brains, I thought, and I could only explain it because he was a man who seemed to have lost his dreams—sort of disillusioned. The only thing he cared about now was making a little money; as to social position or standing in the world, he sort of laughed at such things.

I used to think his way of laughing at them was kind of bitter. But I couldn't be sure; he was a big mystery.

My sister Emma and I were in the thick of our "good time." I never did get sleep enough those days; and I started to find it harder and harder to be on time to the laundry.

For three or four mornings I was late; then one morning I was good and late. That boss—the man who had once told me to "make money on the side"—fired me.

I found a new job, just the sort I liked, except it was only for a short time—out in the country, picking apples.

I don't know anything that shows better how I had changed, since coming West, than the way I took this new job. I had been born and raised in the country, and loved it; but now I had had my taste of "life." I found it a bit stupid at that apple orchard; the evenings dragged.

The person there that interested me most was the boss, Mrs. Jackson.

Mrs. Jackson was separated from her husband. She took care of their two children—little dears they were, too. She was a little bit what they call "fast"; she had men ringing her up over the farmers' line telephone all hours of the day; and once in a while some man would call for her in an auto, and it was whispered around that they went to a roadhouse.

I got to be real good friends with Mrs. Jackson. She suited me fine—fitted in with my new ideas of life.

One afternoon, just at the close of the season, I was inside Mrs. Jackson's house, playing with the children. She was taking a nap, upstairs, when the phone bell rang.

"Hello," said a man's deep voice. "Is Jessie there?"

"She's lying down just now," I answered. "Wait a moment.

I'll call her."

I started to put the receiver down, when I heard the man's voice buzzing inside of it.

"Hold on, there, hold on!" he was calling. I put it back to my ear in time to hear him say—

"Whose sweet little voice is this, coming over the line?"

"Oh, it's mine—just mine," I answered.

"'Mine,' huh? Well it's a nice little voice. What do you look like, 'Mine'? I bet you've got pretty eyes."

"Sure, my eyes are pretty; they're a deep hazel," I answered. "Be real good and maybe you'll see them some day. I'll call Jessie." I heard his voice still calling through the receiver as I went away.

I met Jessie after she had hung up. She seemed a bit upset.

"Who was it?" I asked.

"That's my husband," she replied. "He wants me to bring the children into town tomorrow; he's going to buy their clothes for winter."

She took the children, next day, and went into town. Along toward the late part of the afternoon, when it was about time for her to get back, the phone rang again. I answered.

"Hello; are you the same little girl I was talking to yesterday?"

"I guess I am," I replied. His voice sounded quite serious this time.

"Well, I'm Jessie's husband, as you know," he said. "Now, tell me; is there anybody in the room there, that can hear what you're saying? I don't want anybody to hear."

"It's all safe," I answered, glancing around.

"Well; I want to see you and have a talk with you—private. I've got something I want to tell you. It's very important."

I was kid enough to be fooled by that. What could it be about?

"Now, you're coming into town tomorrow. When you get in, will you call up Parker 238—room sixteen? Then we can make an appointment."

I promised, quite impressed with this new affair, and my curiosity all worked up.

I called up Parker 238 first thing after I got to grandma's, next day. We fixed to meet at the postoffice at two o'clock that afternoon; he told me to look by the radiator for a man wearing a gray suit and blue necktie.

I was promptly on hand; and because I was still a bit bashful, I walked to the general delivery window, hunting for that radiator out of the corner of my eye.

Standing by it I saw a tall man, very fine looking, smooth-shaven, dressed in what seemed to me the height of elegance. He caught my glance, came forward, and heard my name as I asked for my mail.

"So you're the little girl I'm looking for," he said, as I stepped back. I was scared because he looked so elegant and rich. But his manners were nice.

"Now, I want to tell you the truth," he said, "What I did want to see you about was this: you've been working out at that ranch, and you know how my two children are looked after. I wanted to ask you all about them."

He meant this, I could see; and I told him all I knew about them, and answered about a hundred questions. Only one thing he said I must mention:

"I've got some photograph enlargements of those two children up in my room—regular beauties. I'll show you them some day."

He was careful to bring that first walk to a close early.

"We won't go any further now; your grandmother mightn't like it if she saw us," he said; and I was thankful, and thought what a fine gentleman he was.

After that I saw Mr. Jackson often. He used to take me to ice cream parlors, and was always perfectly lovely to me; and I felt flattered, because he was twice my age. Emma met him, and the three of us went to a show together once in a while.

One evening, when he was going to take Emma and me to the theater, he remarked—

"Alice, you remember I said I had some beautiful enlarged photos of my two children up in my room? Well, you two girls just come up there with me, and I'll show them to you."

It wasn't time for the theater; so up we went. I had never been in a man's room before, and that sounded sort of risky and "Bohemian," so I liked it. Emma and I followed him up the stairs of a nice rooming-house.

"Excuse me, while I see if everything is all right," he said, and went ahead of us into his room.

I heard him say, "Why, hello, Henry," then he opened the door to us and called, "Come right in. Here's my roommate, Mr. Marsh."

I caught a glimpse of a tall, broad-shouldered man, fully thirty-five years old, dressed as finely as Mr. Jackson himself, with deep lines in his face. He was just rising from a chair as I entered.

I was looking into the eyes of the "one man."

"Henry," said Mr. Jackson, "we're going to the show. Won't you make it four?"

"Why, thanks—I'd like it very much, if the young ladies"— he gave me a look I couldn't understand at all—"don't mind the company of an old man."

He laughed; I liked him.

Henry Marsh and I, little by little, became great friends. I got so I used to tell him all my troubles—every time grandma scolded, or every time anything went wrong in the laundry— where I got my old job back. I was overawed by his manners and his age and what seemed to be his knowledge of life; and then, that little touch of sadness about him, as if he had lived a lot, and left lots of experience behind him!

It all fascinated me, and made me think I was the most remarkable girl in the world, just to attract a second glance from such a man.

The more I saw of Henry Marsh, the less I got to know of him. He was a puzzle; and it was as a puzzle he fascinated me.

He came just at the right moment—or the wrong one. Here was I, drifting and weak; stubborn, headstrong, foolish, but not really "bad"; poor, all but homeless, snatching at every little thing that offered some fun. And above all, I had that idea that all around me the world was bad, and men and women were all sunk. I knew the constant demand men made on women; and I had got used to that demand; it was one of the big facts.

Then came this man; twice my age, with a suggestion of a "past" about him, a "man-of-the-world," as I told myself.

Henry Marsh and his room-mate, Mr. Jackson, just about spoiled our old friends for us. We had no more time for those green kids. These older men made them look small and young. These two older men had the air of knowing the world through and through; yet they never tired us out with their persuading. They didn't seem to be chasing us.

We tried with all our might, Emma and I, to "play up." And it was so grand to be going around with men who dressed fine—men you had to call "Mister!"

Grandmother Smith was getting crosser and crosser. I couldn't do a single thing that didn't shock her.

Little by little, Grandmother Smith came to believe that I was doing things I oughtn't to do. Long before I had any real idea that I might be "bad," I was getting what you might call suggestions from her. She got so, after a while, she would name the men she suspected. They were all too absurd—fellows I would never have looked at.

Emma might ask to go downtown, or some little thing, and Grandmother Smith would start in—

"See there, now, Alice, what you've made out of your sister, with your goings-on and everything. You've ruined Emma, that's what you've done, with your sneaky ways and your talk and all. You ain't decent and fit to go with a pure girl, you ain't. If Emma's ever on the streets, it'll be your fault."

She used to feel real bad, when she said things like that; and lots of times I have seen her with tears in her eyes. I guess she really thought them. She had said them so often that she believed them.

Then I would flounce out of the house, in a fit of anger, go to some telephone booth, and call up Henry Marsh. It was good to have somebody to talk to; and he always seemed to understand.

Whether he ever really cared a rap I couldn't make out. I used to wonder a lot about it.

"Let's go to the show tomorrow night, Alice; there's a good play," Henry Marsh said one evening.

I accepted gladly. Those evenings at the theater were the joys of my life. I loved the plays and the music; they made me forget I was tired and everything. And then, I knew it was a little risky.

I met him on the street-corner as usual. It was a little early for the play.

"Let's have a little walk," he said. "There's no hurry."

I was willing enough to take a walk. I didn't notice which way he was going. First thing I knew, we stopped in front of the rooming-house where he lived.

Mr. Marsh stopped.

"Just wait here a moment, will you, Alice?" he said, in a natural manner. "I've got to go upstairs and get a handkerchief."

"Sure," I said. "I'll wait. Hurry up."

He skipped half-way up the stairs, then stopped and called back—

"Say, you might just as well come on up. No use to wait there. Come right along."

Well—there was persuasion in his voice, and naturalness. He did it well. And I had climbed those stairs before, with Emma and Mr. Jackson—why not with Mr. Marsh? I didn't offer any objection—hardly felt any.

"Take a seat on that lounge," said Mr. Marsh. "Make yourself comfortable." His manner was easy, as if it was perfectly all right, and I took my tone from him.

"We might as well be sitting here and talking, instead of hiking around until that show starts, don't you think? I'm a bit tired. Say, Alice, here's a bunch of nice photos I took last year, up on the Columbia River. Look 'em over—you'll like 'em."

He brought his photograph album over and sat down beside me on the lounge.

I turned over the leaves of the album. They were good photos; they showed him in a new character, too—the out-of-door sportsman, dressed in rough clothes. He looked different, somehow—not so attractive.

I was just wondering if it wasn't time to go to that theater when he spoke up:

"Say, Alice,"—he seemed sort of embarrassed—"would you mind if we didn't go to that show tonight, after all? I'm kind of tired, and I think it would be nice just to sit here and visit. What do you say?"

Gee! That scared me for a minute. That was going further than ever I had gone in my life—to sit alone with a man, in his room, and "visit." Then I thought, "Well, I enjoy his company; if I go home there's just grandma's scolding; and besides—it's cheaper to sit here. He won't have to spend so much money."

"All right," I said, feeling a bit disappointed, because I really had wanted to see that show. "Just as you say. I'll stay a while, anyhow."

"I tell you," he said, brightening up, "I'll go out and get some stuff to eat. We can sit here and have a little feed." He put on his hat and went out.

As I sat there on his lounge, waiting for him to get back, I amused myself by looking around his room—at his silver brush and comb, a picture of a chorus-girl on the wall, and on his bureau a photograph of a handsome, tall, beautifully-dressed woman; a woman a good deal older than I, with a look of having seen the world.

I wondered about that woman.

I was still wondering about her when he returned.

"Here's the supper," he said, gaily. "Here's a box of bonbons. Here's a basket of fruit—apples, peaches, plums, apricots. Here's some cookies; and here"—he took a bottle out of his pocket—"here's something to drink. Now, we can have a good time."

I wasn't going to seem green, even if I wasn't used to this sort of thing. I wasn't going to let that woman on the bureau outshine me—not if I could help it.

We laughed and chatted along, over the fruit and the cookies. Presently he rummaged in a drawer, got out a couple of glasses and a corkscrew, and opened the bottle. It was some sort of red wine—port, I think.

"Here's luck," he said, filling a glass and giving it to me.

Then I got a little scared. I had been brought up to be afraid of wine; even when I went out to dinner I never had any.

"Oh, don't be afraid of it; it isn't strong. It won't do anything to you," he laughed.

Just then my eye happened to fall again on the photograph on the bureau.

"That woman would have emptied this glass at a single gulp," I thought to myself.

I raised the glass, held my breath and swallowed hard. It wasn't so bad as I thought—only strong; it made me blink.

"I—I don't like it very well," I said, laughing. It made me feel sort of good.

He laughed back.

"Oh, that's all right," he said. "You'll get used to it. Have some more."

But I wouldn't. I decided I'd had enough. And I had.

We sat and talked for a long time. Grandma had been acting worse than usual that day, and I got to telling him about it. It all came over me so hard—and I suppose the wine had a good deal to do with that—that I found myself crying, and Henry Marsh trying to comfort me, and listening to my troubles.

Henry Marsh let go of me—he had his arm around me—and stepped across the room to a side door. What was he going to do now, I wondered? I stopped crying a moment, out of curiosity.

He turned the key and opened that side door. There was another room beyond, just about the same size and shape as the one we were in.

"Do you see that room?" he said. "How do you like that? Well,"—his voice became very serious and earnest, and he looked straight at me—"Alice, you haven't had a fair deal at home. Now, girlie, if your grandmother turns you out—you just come down and live in here—with me."

I looked back at him, as steady as he was himself.

"All right," said I. "I'll remember that."

I got up too late to get any breakfast, if I was to get to the laundry by seven o'clock. The night before, Emma and I had had a date to go out to dinner with Henry Marsh and his friend, Mr. Jackson, who was going away. Emma had a headache and stayed home; but I went with those two men, all dressed up in my best clothes. It was the first time I had ever been to a big swell restaurant; I didn't know just how to act. Over at the next table I heard a man give his order to the waiter—"Fried oysters!" So when the waiter came to me, I sat up real straight and gave my order, too, "Fried oysters!"

After dinner, Henry Marsh had taken me to a show, and I hadn't got home until late. I hated to get up and go to work; and that black day started sleepily.

Over at the laundry, the boss called me down for coming in five minutes behind time. He had a perfect right to; but I got sulky about it, and went to shaking out clothes with a sour face.

"Anyhow," Henry Marsh said, "if things get too bad, girlie, you come and live with me. You haven't had a fair deal at home."

It had been a week now since he had made that proposition. Not a day had gone by but what it had come to my mind—had been there a good part of the time. It just fitted in with that hard, reckless feeling that was growing stronger and stronger inside of me. Because it offered a way out it probably helped that reckless feeling to grow.

What if I should do that—just kick out from Grandmother Smith's, quit the laundry, make the break once and for all? While my hands were busy, my mind was busy, too, picturing how it would happen. I would just pack my clothes into that straw basket, get them out of the house when grandma wasn't looking, walk into Mr. Marsh's room, and say, "Well, I've come!" He would open that door into the next room, just like he had done that night, and say, "That's fine, girlie; here's your new home."

I glanced up from my pile of clothes.

A girl I hated was standing right across from me, staring at me. Her name was Evelyn. She was the particular favorite of the boss. He was a married man, with a family; but that didn't prevent him from taking Evelyn out to dinner and to the shows, buying her fine clothes and silk petticoats, and giving her money and everything.

Evelyn was pretty, in a cheap, brassy sort of way. And she just thought she owned that laundry. She would boss us girls around as sassy as you please, and we knew it would be worth our job to talk back to her.

But this particular morning I was sore.

"Well, what do you want? See anything green?" I burst out at her.

"No, Squinty," she said, turning away.

That didn't add to my good temper any. I hated to have that brazen thing, who wasn't "straight" and who sort of gloried in the fact, rub it into me as if she owned the earth. I wanted to get even with her some way; and it sounds foolish, but somehow or other the thought came to me—

"If I was as crooked as she is, then I could get back at her once in a while."

Something hateful happened to spoil every hour of that long day. When six o'clock came, I was ready to bite the head off anybody that said a word to me.

"I suppose it's Grandma Smith's turn now," I muttered to myself as I dragged up the stairs. I was so sure she was going to scold at me, that I started it myself.

"I'm going downtown tonight, and it won't do you any good to say I can't," I began, just about as soon as I got inside the house.

"You ain't going to do no such a thing!" she screamed back, and the fight was on.

All through supper we kept it up. It was far and away the

worst quarrel we ever had. Generally, when she tore into me,
I didn't answer back. I loved old people, and had strong ideas
about talking back to them. But this night I cut loose and said
anything that came to mind. I felt awful bad the whole time,
too, as if I was just about ready to die of lonesomeness and that
hurt feeling. If anybody had spoken a kind word, it would have
broken me all up.

"It's no use you talking; I'm going downtown, and if Emma
wants to, she's going with me," I yelled finally, rising from the
supper-table.

Then raising her voice to the loudest I ever heard it, grandma
shouted—

"I just tell you, now—if you go downtown tonight, you can
stay!"

Into my head like a thunder-clap rushed the thought of
Henry Marsh.

"All right, grandma," I said, so quietly I guess she was sort of
scared. "I'll just do that."

I walked into my room and started to put on my hat. Emma
was lying on the bed, crying. I went to the wardrobe and fished
out that straw basket; and it seemed strange, because I had pic-
tured that same thing to myself earlier in the day, and now it
wasn't like that at all. I felt as if it wasn't real—I was a little
bit dizzy, I guess—and I had the queerest feeling as if it all had
happened just that same way before, if only I could remember
when.

I began to throw my things into the basket.

Just then grandma came in, almost running.

"Now, see here, Alice, it's no use for you to pack them
clothes. I ain't going to let you take them. That's all there is
to it."

Then all my own anger, and that hurt feeling, and her saying I was "bad," and my thoughts of Henry Marsh, all came

up inside of me at once. I said just one thing, and I guess that branded me forever in her eyes. It seemed as if it really wasn't I that said it at all.

"All right, grandma. The less clothes I have, the faster I can go." Then I went out of the house and slammed the door.

I hurried along through the streets with my head down, crying and fighting not to cry at the same time. I wouldn't let myself think a single thought. I guess a person that is going to commit suicide feels the same way. I didn't watch where I was going, and I turned the corners by instinct. I came to the rooming-house where Henry Marsh lived, and ran up the stairs.

I guess Henry Marsh, man-of-the-world as he seemed to be, got the big surprise of his life a moment later. He was taking a nap on that lounge when I gave one hard bang on the door and, without waiting for an answer, rushed into the room.

I was crying hard now. Without saying a word I stood in front of the mirror, with the photograph of that woman staring me in the face, and started to take off my hat.

"Why, Alice, what on earth's the matter?" His voice—for once—showed sincere surprise and concern.

"G-grandma t-turned me out, th-that's what's the m-matter," I sobbed. Then facing him square, I said, "And I've come to accept your invitation."

Marsh was on his feet right away.

"Why, you poor little girl," he said, "of course you can stay, just as I said. Of course you can." I clung to him and poured out my troubles.

"A-and I can have that next room, like you said, can't I?" I finished up.

"Why—why—" he was almost embarrassed now, but not quite—"the truth is, girlie, that next room is rented."

Then I took the very last step; it was so easy to do.

"I don't care." I started to cry harder than ever. "I don't care.

It's all the same anyhow. I don't care."

So that night I stayed with Henry Marsh.

The bit of wood, drifting down the stream, had got to deep water at last.

Never again, after that night, was I to lift up my head among pure women; never again to hold clean talk with men; never to be anything but what I am now—a branded creature, childless, facing night after night the horror of this painful, dirty life; shut off from purity, my longing for purity still eager and alive.

Is it any wonder I look back to that day and wish—just as I wished in the early hours of that next morning—that the sun had somehow forgot to rise?

But the sun did rise. The sun doesn't care for such things as lost women or girls. It rises anyhow, just to show up our shame all the redder in the light of day. We are never at ease again until the sun is out of sight and everything is in the half-dark—where "human nature," that lying phrase Henry Marsh quieted my fears with that night, seems really the soiled, passionate thing these men would make it out to be.

I cannot forget that night. He promised to marry me—how many times that promise had been made to girls by men who knew they never would keep it! He used that old cry of "human nature," and I accepted it. I was so bitter in my heart, and I felt so young—so pitifully young, while Henry Marsh seemed old and wise and experienced in the world; surely I could take his word, that "everything would be all right!"

In some ways, as I woke up that morning, I felt like the oldest and wisest person in the world. In other ways I felt like a little young child. Surely it was a great bit of wisdom that made me say to myself—

"Anyhow, I can't go back now. It ain't possible. People don't take backward steps. I've got to go on."

But should I give up my job in the laundry? Was Henry

Marsh going to support me altogether? How was I to make my living?

Henry Marsh himself answered that question.

"Now, see here, Alice," he said, early that morning. "You'd better show up to work in the laundry, just the same as ever. And you mustn't let your grandmother or anybody else know where you're living. They're apt to get up some sort of a search for you—there might be trouble."

"Do you think I ought to keep right on at the laundry?" My heart sank. I was hoping I could get rid of that.

"Yes, I do. For one thing—you'll need the money. I—I'm not a rich man, you know." He laughed. "I've got my cigar-store, and that's all. I can take care of your room-rent, and some clothes, and some of your meals, but to be comfortable you'll have to work, too. You haven't any other way of making money—yet."

I was sort of changeable and moody that morning, besides being tired and sick. At moments I had a bigger feeling of reck-lessness than I ever had before. So long as I had a tight hold on being "respectable," I had been sort of cautious. There was always a limit in my mind then, and I wouldn't go past it. But at times, this morning, I had the feeling that the limit had been taken off. I had cut loose now; I would show them I wasn't afraid to go the whole way. But even while I was thinking that, I didn't let myself say exactly what "the whole way" was.

Once that day I had a little spat with that Evelyn, the boss' "favorite." For once in my life, I answered her back. I wasn't going to be afraid of her any more. I was just as wise as she was.

But at the end of that day, as I walked to Henry Marsh's room, I was half ready to go back to grandma's, tell her where I had been and the whole truth about everything, and face the music. Maybe she would believe, if I did that, that I hadn't been really "bad" before; and maybe she would be sorry she had turned me out last night.

Henry Marsh came in, with a smile on his face, and called me his "little girl"; then I knew, of course, that I wouldn't ever go back to grandma's. There was a queer way about that man. He made believe to be cold and perfectly fair about everything, and it always seemed as if he really put things before you, and gave you your free choice; but at the same time you always did what you knew he wanted.

I found out about that handsome woman whose picture was on the bureau.

"Was she your wife?" I asked him, point-blank.

"No," he answered, with a queer smile. "I never had a wife."

"Then you lived together," I exclaimed. I was going to find out.

"Yes," he smiled more queerly than ever, "yes, I guess we did. She was a clever woman," he added after a pause. And that was all I ever learned about her—almost.

most Beyond Her.

After Securing a Position as Waitress She Finds the Scars of the Underworld Too Deep to Be Hidden.

By Alice Smith.

XXVI

"I had heard of men who had been heavy drinkers and who had tried to quit."

"...with the other he gripped my wrist tight."

NOTICE

Because of the limited quantity of these dresses they will be on sale in the San Francisco store only, and not in the Oakland establishment. Transbay customers please note this.

SELECTED LETTERS TO THE EDITOR

Points Finger at Woman Who Marries Money

The letters you have received from those you call women of the "underworld" are as different as human faces, but they all amount to the same thing, and that is, that there is in this world a separate class of women given up by society to the uses of men who claim that they have a natural right to do things which they deny to women of all other classes. These men say it is necessary for them to have this privilege because they are physically different from women and have greater needs. This is pure humbug. Women and men have the same natural tendencies in these matters. Women do not yield to their impulses because from their childhood they have been told they "must not," whereas men from their childhood have been told that they "may"; and men, having control, have punished women who have claimed for themselves the same privilege that men have exercised.

Why do you speak of us as belonging to the "underworld?"

Who, then, constitutes the "upper world?" Is it the men who come to visit us? And why are they in any respect above us?

Is the woman who marries for money or for social station any better than we are? Does she not sell herself as we do? Is there any difference in selling one's self to one man for a year or for several years and selling oneself to several men for a shorter or longer time? If there be, then I do not understand the meaning of the word morality.

Eva Wilkins

Dismisses Her Sweetheart When He Denounces Effort to Save Unfortunate Girls

In your paper of June 24 "Eva Wilkins" wrote a letter that I think is the best I have read, but I know the men do not think so. I agree with her that the men who go there are no better than the woman they are with.

Since reading her letter, I have broken my engagement with the man I was to marry in two months. We had a heated argument over her letter, and he said they were trying to hatch up a lot of lies on the men, so these women would get sympathy. We were not mad at one another; but we debated that question thoroughly. I asked him if he did not think it would do any good, and he thinks it is all silly. I then asked him if he found out that I had ever gone wrong in my life, would he marry me? "Certainly not," he said. Then I asked him if he ever went there, and he said he did sometimes, and then he owned up to all he had known since he was old enough to think for himself. Well, it amounted to over twenty, and he is twenty-eight. Now mind you, if I had ever done wrong once, he said, I would not be good enough for him. I denounced him and told him I hated him and that I would not marry him if I died grieving over losing him; but I am not going to do that. I am glad I spurned him.

I have been a decent girl all my life, and he knows it, too; but that don't matter, he would be good enough for me. I know there are good men that do not think as he does; but they are all narrow on the woman subject regarding morality.

I think it is all right, but just let the men be decent, too. If I ever have a son I will certainly drill his brain on the right road.

Personally I think "A Voice from the Underworld" is going to do a lot of good; in fact, I know of one case where it has. A girl had a date with a young man to take in the Coast, but after reading all those awful heartbreaking letters she called him up and gave him the mischief for asking her to go; and then he came back at her and said: "Why didn't you refuse in the beginning?"

If a man sees a girl is weak in any of these respects it is his duty to talk her out of it; he claims to be the stronger sex, but I can't see it that way.

I am so glad nothing has ever happened to me, as I believe my conscience would kill me. I get the paper to read as soon as I get home and read every word these women have to say.

I do not care whether you publish this letter or not; I did not write it for that. I only wanted you to know that your paper is doing good on that score.

A Sincere Reader and Admirer of Your Paper

Condemns Men Who
Champion Social System

You deserve great credit for opening your columns for a discussion of the "Social Evil" and will you kindly permit an "unfortunate girl," a prostitute born in San Francisco, to say a few words, based on bitter experience.

The worst prostitutes this world knows are of the male gender, and in the main are found in editorial chairs and in pulpits misnamed "Christian," defending a system of society which they know is rotten—a system which makes a decent living, especially for women, very difficult.

The "segregated" district as run at present is not only a "delusion and a snare," but it is a fraud. It is a source of graft and was instituted for purposes of graft, and graft only.

I have talked with hundreds of my class, watched them closely and know that but few of them are naturally and inherently bad. Quite a few, say 12 or 15 percent of the women leading lives of prostitution were at the beginning unusually healthy and strongly sexed. They loved, were deceived, and deserted, as in my case, and finding the struggle for bread a hard one, they yielded to the sale of their sex favors, and as their charms faded, drifted into common prostitutes.

No, Mr. Editor, we are not prostitutes because we love the life. Most of us would love to be real wives and feel the clasp of baby arms about our necks. But if as virtuous girls men could not marry us because of the uncertainty of being able to support us in decency, we cannot expect it now. And why cannot men, thousands of them in California, support wives? I'll tell you why. For ten years, since I was a girl twenty years old, I have been traveling up and down California and have followed my calling from Marysville to San Diego. My heart has gone out many, many times to poor working men as I've seen them trudging along packing their blankets over fertile, but barren, soil, millions of acres of it, held for speculation. Under a just system these acres would be cut up into small farms and their owners and tillers would support wives, not prostitutes.

There is but one remedy for prostitution. Make it possible for everybody to be employed at some useful labor and hold the man or woman not working, if healthy, in disgrace. As things are now, I, a woman of the town, am shown more consideration and get kinder treatment than I would were I working in somebody's kitchen. I once had a beautiful place in Piedmont. I was to get $30 a month. As I stood on the front porch and took in the grand view before me I felt proud that I had made the resolve to lead a decent life. But the reception I got from the mistress chilled me to the marrow. I was given the poorest room in the house and treated as if I were a thing without feeling, a creature not fit to sit with or to talk to. Of course I went back to the red lights.

To the good people who are really interested in us I say you cannot save us unless you overthrow the system of society that made us what we are. If you save me today, someone else will take my place tomorrow. All you can do is to make it a little easier for us. Stop hounding us. Give us a district all our own. Keep the police from grafting on us and the saloon from poisoning us. Many saloons would go out of business if not run in connection with prostitution. Sterilize all the vile creatures found living off us. If prostitution is necessary, then we are useful members of society and are entitled to protection.

Build your proposed home, but not for fallen women. Build it for fallen men, for men who have fallen through the prostituting greed for gold and who in their frenzy for it forget the common instincts of humanity.

One of Society's Victims

Give Us a District and We Won't Bother You

Having read so much about women from the underworld let me say a few words as one who knows.

When 15 years old I was thrown on the world to make my own way. Raised of a good and loving mother and not knowing the ways of the world, I entered into the night life. I found out it was not what it seemed, so I quit and went to work. I worked awhile and it became known that I had been what the world calls a "sporting" woman. I was promptly discharged.

Discouraged and sick, I tried to find more work, but I must have references, and where was I to get them? Well, what was there left for me but to go back; and back there is always a glad hand to help the girl that is down. They will even lend you their clothes until you can "get on your feet," as they call it.

You, the good people, don't want us; you don't want us to mix and mingle with your sons and daughters, do you? No!

Then give us a district and we won't bother you.

I know hundreds of girls who have tried to reform, but they can't. No; once a prostitute, always one.

God knows I tried to do so dozens of times, but was thrown back farther away every time.

I myself would work and be glad to get it, but I can't get work to do. I even went to the Associated Charities once for work and they asked for references.

Now what am I to do? Readers, I could tell you a story that would make every mother in the United States shed tears, but what's the use? You can't help us, because in your heart you don't want us.

If we get off of the line the police hound us and send us back.

So just let us alone, and when that Mighty One calls us all before the bar of God we will tell Him all and plead to Him for mercy.

CECIL LINDEN, OF THE UNDERWORLD

ME SARAHS CEASE TO

R. OLDER: When you told me about your great underw... enthusiasm I felt. You gave as your warrant for such a venture in frequent usu... ...d classes of our people. (That word "classes" is getting into frequent...) You do not need such a warrant. The fact that you are going to do something... s warrant enough, and that something! To give the first hearing at the judgment bar of... the woman stoned. It thrills all lovers of justice everywhere. Let us hope the Sarahs will cease to drive forth the ...gnant of results will this course be! They are too many to enumerate, but just this one will alone make ...e. It will prove the attitude of the "good" woman. The energy that has been spent in condemnation ...the deserts of life and then go on living with Abraham.
...ned to solution of the evil.

MARGARET E. MORE.

Alamos, California, June 23, 1913.

VICE NOT NEEDED FOR PROTECTION OF WOMEN.

EDITOR BULLETIN:—Now that the old belief of the ...given way to one of strength, ...our ability we are learning of the inescapable horrors of prostitution and the far-reaching and frightful consequences...

BEGIN EARLY AND TRAIN AT HOME

Woman of Years Suggests That Mothers Are Following the Fatal Course in Keeping Daughters Ignorant of the Pitfalls of the World.

EDITOR BULLETIN: Keep up your good work. Let the few narrow-minded citizens who go kicking against your publicity of the true conditions of life. Every time you print your paper there is a boost. Let them stop for every knock being in their home if they wish; let them hide the truth from their daughters; but, after all their efforts, will they be able to stop their daughters from satisfying their awakening curiosity?

Will you tell me why mothers and fathers permit their daughters to grow up in total ignorance of the true facts of life? I know of more than one home where they would not let "their daughter read about the underworld, and yet, through sheer ignorance they are exposing their own daughters to such a fate. They do not tell them the right way; they let them find out by others, because they wish to keep them innocent and so-called "pure." I venture to say that if a mother would talk over freely and candidly the evils of men and how to guard against their flattering, yet poisonous tongues—they are today...

Believes in Segregation.

I HAVE read the many different letters from the girls of the underworld, also the two chapters from Alice Smith...

Hope Is Not Left Behind Is Belief of This Symp...

EDITOR BULLETIN:—The opening of your paper to the social evil is a sturdy step in the right direction...

HERE'S A CHANCE FOR SOME GIRL TO MAKE GOOD

EDITOR BULLETIN: I have read with interest the different letters published in your paper...

Tempted Woman Believes Safety Lies in Mother's Teaching

EDITOR BULLETIN:—Your letters published concerning this moral affair interest me immensely...

Socialism Only Hope

agrees With Preacher

FRUITVALE

A Voice from the Underworld

PART III

Three or four nights after I went to live with him, Henry Marsh sat down by me on the lounge.

"Alice, how much are you getting at your laundry?" he asked.

"Six dollars a week."

"H'm. That isn't very much, is it? You need clothes, don't you?"

"You bet I need clothes. Needed 'em all my life."

"Well—now listen, Alice." Henry Marsh's voice became more serious. "You can make better money than that, just as well as not. You're free from your family, now. And you've got a room downtown—a very convenient location. And then—you're young and reckless. Now, here's the proposition: Down at my cigar-shop I see lots of my friends who have money to spend. They're going to spend that money—on women. Women are in demand." He looked at me hard. "I don't see why you shouldn't get that money."

His voice was cheerful, strong—not at all as if he was suggesting anything bad.

"No—no," I managed to say. "I'm not—not"—

"Not in the market?" He laughed. "I don't see what's the difference, kid? You've gone the whole way already—with me.

If you're that far along, why not with others? And you might as well get that money as anybody."

Just one idea flashed into my head—a jealous idea, I guess, though I wasn't exactly in love with Henry Marsh.

"Did—did that other woman, the one you lived with, do that way?"

He colored, and tried to laugh.

"I guess she did, Alice, but I didn't know it till—afterward."

Then he left me to think it over. It made my head buzz worse than ever. What sort of a girl did he think I was, anyhow?

I groped around, wondering what could have made him willing to make such a proposition; and the only explanation I could find was that he had loved that other woman very much; and when he found out she did these things, he had just decided they were right. He had just made a business proposal to help me along; that was all. When I put it that way, I could see that maybe Henry Marsh's life had been shaped by other people, the same as mine; and I didn't blame him.

When the reckless mood was on me, good and hard, after a few days, I was ready a dozen times to say, "Go ahead, Henry; send along your friends!" But when the other side of me was on top, I would tell myself, "No; I'll work in this laundry all my life if I have to; but I won't be one of those women. I won't." And all the time I sort of knew how it would end, and dreaded it.

Like everything else, it settled itself.

One morning I got up feeling pretty bad; all nervous and ill. It was just the way I had been living—all day the laundry, and at night this new life to face, and I had been drinking a good deal, to keep me going.

"Gee, I'm sick this morning," I grumbled over the table to the girl that worked opposite me in the laundry. One of the girls I always suspected of "making money on the side" overheard me.

"Alice is sick this morning—ahem!" she told the whole laundry. It seemed to amuse several of the girls, and they started to laugh.

"Tell us all about it," called out one of them.

"Eat eggs—that's the best thing," yelled another.

That girl, Evelyn, told the boss, and he laughed, sort of meaningly.

I lost my temper and started to answer back; but as that only made them worse, I just had to shut up and take it.

Early that afternoon that Evelyn took it on herself to boss me around a bit.

"Alice, you go over and feed the mangle for a while—Maggie's tired," she said.

I had been over there about ten minutes before she hollered—

"That's all right, now, Alice—you come over here and fold for a while. Maggie, you go back and feed."

Her tone was too bossy. I flared up harder than I had ever done before. "I ain't going to fold—do it yourself," I snapped back at her.

"Come on now, you fold," she said threateningly.

"I ain't going to fold—it ain't my job," I yelled. "I'm here to shake out clothes, and I'm going to shake out clothes or nothing.

"Well, I'll just go and ask the boss," said Evelyn. "We'll see about this."

I started to take off my apron.

"You don't need to see about it," I said. "Just because you go out with the boss at night, you don't need to think you can run this whole laundry."

She had never had that said to her before. All the girls had always been respectful to her. I could see the color flame up into her face, and she got so mad she couldn't speak. I thought sure there was going to be a fight.

"What are you going to do, Alice," asked one of the girls, as I reached for my hat.

"I'm going to quit; that's what I'm going to do," I said. "I ain't going to be bossed by any such chippy as her." I jammed on my hat and made for the office.

"You can't get your pay till Saturday," the boss said to me. "We don't pay off till then, and you know it. Going to quit, are you? All right; there's plenty more."

It was only two days till Saturday. I knew I could get Henry Marsh to support me till then.

He didn't say anything when I told him I had quit, except, "Well, there's lots of other ways of making money."

And I was beginning to think that for myself.

I called around at the laundry on Saturday for my pay.

Just as I was entering the door of the laundry I happened to see an elderly man standing by the curbstone. He stepped forward and spoke to me.

"Hello, Pearl," he said.

And that was where I plunged full length into the muddy river.

Now that I had come to the real thing, I was awful scared. I was walking fast—kind of nervous.

"Ain't you made a mistake?" I flashed over my shoulder.

"My!" said the old man. "I guess I have."

I went inside the laundry, drew the $3.50 that I had coming to me at the time I quit, and came out again. The old man was still there.

"Pardon me," said he, stepping up close and not talking loud, "but don't you room near here?"

"Yes. What of it?" I was sassy as you please, on top. Really I was saying over and over to myself, "What am I up against now? What am I up against now?"

"I—I thought you probably had a room near here, that's all," said the old man.

I happened to look down just then. The old man had a roll of paper in his hand; and I could see that paper shaking as his hand trembled.

I started on a step or two. He followed.

"I'm coming along," he said. "Is that all right?"

"Oh," I snapped, "you couldn't stand it at my price." I was getting onto myself. I grinned.

I would need money. Why shouldn't I just take this chance that came along, and make my first money all by myself? Henry would like it.

But I couldn't quite bring myself to give up to this old man. It went hard against the grain. I didn't like the little red lines in his face.

And really, though I answered him so quick, anybody can see I said just the wrong things. We women who sell ourselves are supposed to be all submission, all meekness to men—we cringe and flatter and make them think they are lords of creation—just so we can get the money out of them.

I was a lot too fresh; it shows how green I was.

"Well, but couldn't we come to terms?" the old man asked.

I kept hurrying along that sidewalk.

"Of course," I snapped out. "If you got ten dollars to part with, come right along." There! I had made the break. At the same time I knew he wouldn't take me up. So I felt brave and I felt safe, both at the same time.

He fell back, giving a little laugh.

"Oh, I couldn't stand for anything like that, you know," he said.

"Then, so long!" I answered, and went on alone.

I walked on a block, slower, thinking it all over. Then there came a voice again over my shoulder, and I shuddered.

"I—I—I—just wanted to say it's all right about that ten dollars," said the old man. "I say, kid, you're worth it, all right."

All of a sudden I wanted to run away. But I didn't. I had caught the ring of that ten dollars.

That sounded like a lot of money to a girl who had always been poor. The reckless side of me, that new mood, started to come to the top. Well—since everything pointed that way, I'd be game. I drew a big breath.

"All right, then; but mind, you put up that ten dollars as soon as you come into that room!"

"All right." He nodded, trying to smile. That roll of paper in his hand was shaking and trembling more than ever. I decided he wasn't so very old at this thing himself; and I felt easier about it, as I led the way up the stairs and opened the door to my room. If he was new at it, so much less chance of his being diseased. I had heard about that, and how horrible it was.

"Come in," I said. He walked in, took a look around, laid the ten dollars on the bureau, and then turned and looked at me. I was looking down.

All of a sudden his hand quit trembling.

After that old man had left me, I sat on the bed and turned over that ten-dollar gold-piece in my hand.

This was the thought that came to me.

"And I worked all week in that laundry, for just six dollars!"

The demand had won out at last.

Only the other day I heard of a woman—a good woman, and a brainy woman—who had put on rough clothes, gone out from her home, and taken a job in a laundry, without giving her real name.

She wanted, she said, to see what the life of the working-girl was like. She had plenty of money—she didn't need to go to work at all; but she wanted to see for herself, she said, the way those poor girls were treated, and how they felt while they were trying to live on such small pay.

That was a fine thing for her to do. She could surely do lots of good work for better conditions, after that. But as I got to thinking about it, another idea came to me—that woman really, after all, didn't get any true insight into the feelings of the girls she worked with.

How could she? She wasn't really up against it. It was just play for her.

Suppose that same woman, with her two weeks of play-laundry-work, lost her money and had to work in that laundry or starve. She would feel mighty different. She would be getting the real thing, then.

"You keep on at some job, Alice," Henry Marsh advised me. "Don't let people get the idea you are regularly in this business. You've got to keep up the appearance of being young at this business if you want to make money."

I took his advice and went out to look for a job.

But, don't you see, it wasn't the same as it had been before. I didn't really want to find that job at all.

All the time, in the back of my head, I had this idea, "I don't really have to work at all, if I don't want to. I can quit any time I want. I'm independent. I've got this other way to live."

And people who feel that, generally find their job getting too hard for them.

I hadn't ever minded hard work. I had lots of life to me, and I would sooner be busy than not. I never was lazy; didn't like people who were.

But once I had made money this other way, it was all different. I lost even that liking for work.

I tried other laundries; and I tried restaurants; then I tackled candy stores; then I got a private telephone exchange. I would start out on each new job with the best intentions. Pretty soon some little thing would come up—one of those little disagreeable things that are always happening everywhere; I would have to do something I didn't like, or somebody would be cross, or the boss would speak to me sharp, or I would quarrel with one of the other girls.

And instead of just taking those things as they came, telling myself it was all in a lifetime—I would quit the job.

You see, I was always certain of the "demand." There was no such demand for waitresses or laundry workers. You had to beg for a job like that, and keep right up to time if you wanted to hold it. But this other demand—this demand made by the men—was always there. It was waiting to be supplied.

I didn't need to earn money, I thought. There was money always waiting on the streets. Just a glance out of the corner of my eye as I walked down the sidewalk would bring the man—if I cared to do that way. If not, there was Henry Marsh with his cigar shop, always willing to "send his friends along."

So, if you think I liked the way I "made money on the side," you are badly mistaken. Even then, long before I had known the worst side of the life, it sickened me. Some times I wished I was dead—me, with all my cheerfulness.

But my head was now fairly out of sight under the waters of that filthy, muddy river. Its slime was all over me, body and soul. Why didn't I "get out of it," you ask? I did try. You can't climb out of those things just by saying, "I will quit."

The filth of that muddy river made me too weak in body and soul to make any real hard effort. I just drifted along, unhappy, disgusted, reckless—sunken.

I was "supplying a demand."

❧❖☙

After the old man left me, and I had rested a while, I called up Henry Marsh, at his cigar store.

"Hello, kid; how have you been spending the time?" he said.

"I've made ten dollars—all by myself, too," I told him. He laughed his peculiar laugh over the telephone.

"Good! Fine! Now you can get a few of those clothes you need. Well, maybe I can help you now. How about it?"

He referred to his offer to "send up his friends from the shop."

"Don't do anything right away, please," I said. "I want to talk to you first."

"All right," he consented. "I'll be home in an hour."

During that hour I thought over a good many things. One was this: Was I a "prostitute" now? I had sold myself for money; that ten dollars was proof. Well, just what is a "prostitute"?

I didn't like the name. I said it over to myself several times. I didn't like it at all.

Evidently a prostitute was one who sold herself for money. Well, I wondered, was there anybody in the world, according to that, who didn't sell herself or himself for money? Didn't everybody supply some demand, in some more or less disagreeable way? And wasn't everything always for money?

Everybody who does something that goes against his best self, just for money, is a prostitute, but sexual prostitution is lots worse than any other. It hurts other people—it breaks up homes and it spreads disease. Besides, it is just a living death for the prostitute herself. No other kind of prostitution has that horror about it.

But the "demand" is there, and it's got to be supplied. Only, don't blame the women that supply it. Everybody supplies some demand—the demand that happened to hit them hardest when they were weakest.

As I sat there waiting for Henry Marsh to come home, I didn't know that I was in for one of the hardest lessons of my life.

He came strolling in with a smile and a word of congratulation to me.

"By the way, girlie,"—his voice dropped kind of low, as if he was ashamed to ask—"I'm a little short of money. Could you lend me, say, eight dollars till Saturday?"

If I hadn't been the greenest of the green, I would never have stood for that. Since then, seeing so many of my poor sisters kept deeper in this life by some beast who takes their money, I have shuddered to think what I did.

"How's it happen that you're so poor?" I asked. I was cautious about money by nature.

"Oh—a poor cigar-dealer can't take a girl out to dinner so often without spending some money, can he?"

Well, when he put it that way I felt ashamed.

I handed over the gold-piece and he gave me two dollars change.

"I'll give it back Saturday," he said.

I waited till Saturday. In the days between, Henry did as he had said. He steered some of his friends up from the cigar-store to my room. Not too many at first—he was careful to break me in gradually.

I kept myself up to it those first days with considerable drink. That helped. And I just stayed around that room or on the street. I didn't make any effort to get a job.

But all this time I never suspected what Henry Marsh was holding over me.

"Here's your money, Alice," he said laughingly to me on Saturday.

"It's the same gold-piece back again. I never spent it. You needn't mind the two dollars change."

I looked up, puzzled worse than ever.

"Why—why—what did you want the money for, then?"

Right away Henry Marsh got serious. He sat down, straddling a chair, facing me and leaning over the back. I can see him yet.

"You've got a talking-to coming to you, Alice," he said. "Do you want to know what I borrowed that money off you for? Well—just to see if you'd give it to me.

"Now, you listen to me—if you're going to get into this business, you've got to learn one thing—never give a man a cent. Your business is to get money from men, not to give it to them.

"Don't even loan a man a cent. Not under any circumstance. Just as sure as you do, you're gone. I've seen the thing too often not to know."

"Now, here's another thing, Alice," he went on. "What were you going to spend this money for—all this new money you're making."

"Clothes," I jerked out.

"Of course. Flashy ones, I'll bet. A big hat, with a light-blue feather; silk stockings that make the men stare; high heels to your shoes. A lot of lace and stuff that shows when you climb onto the street-car. A peek-a-boo shirtwaist that lets you show through like it wasn't on you at all. Going to paint your face?" He shot that question at me suddenly.

"I—I don't know," I stammered.

"Well, now, look here, Alice." His voice got more serious than ever. "Take my advice, girlie; don't do any of those things.

"If you're in this business for a good time, get out of it right away. Go and get a job cooking or laundering on nothing a week—you'll have a better time. There ain't any good time to be had here.

"No, no. What you're in it for is just the money, that's all. That's your only excuse—money. Now, let me tell you. If you go to dressing flashy, and painting your face, and looking brazen, you're just taking away from your market-value.

"A fellow will look after you as you go down the street, dressed up in those fine clothes, and he will say, 'There goes a peach.' But when it comes to the money, that same fellow won't come down with half as much as he will if he thinks you are kind of new.

"You ain't in it for romance, girlie. You are in it for money. It's just a business. And it's a rotten business."

Henry Marsh went on to give me a regular set of rules.

"Now, kid, you want to quit this drinking," he said. "After about a year of that, no man alive will look at you. You've got to keep your looks; and kid, you're not a bad looker now. You keep on drinking and see what you look like.

"Don't go without work. It pays to hang onto some sort of a job—just for a few hours a day, waiting on tables or something. It makes the man think you're fresh at this other business, and then your price comes higher.

"Put your money into the bank. Don't spend it. These good spenders never get anywhere. Save it up; then in five years or so you will have enough to buy yourself a little place somewhere and get out of the life. A woman can do that, too, if she's wise; but not one in five thousand is wise, kid. Are you one in five thousand?

"And you watch out and don't fall in love. That's just the same as if you tied yourself up hand and foot and gave yourself over to the man. It's all right for girls to fall in love who ain't in this life. But if you're starting out to buck this thing, you've got to buck it alone.

"And say, kid, never believe a word a man tells you. Never believe even me—after this. I'm telling you the truth now, but I may never do it again.

"A man, to you, has got to mean just one thing—dollars.

If he hasn't got money, you haven't got any time. Coax him, cheat him, lie to him, flatter him, make a damned fool out of him the best you know how—and get his money.

"After all, kid, it's the men that got you into this; and it's up to you to make them pay for it."

Some of it seemed impossible. How could I tell I might never fall in love? I wasn't in love with Henry Marsh, that was true; but I was seeing lots of men; mightn't one of them make me his slave? I could see the use of dressing quiet, and I'd quit drinking right off. If I couldn't get used to the work without drinking, I had no business in it.

Oh, but it was a hard, hateful, dirty game! But could I get out of it now? Could I go back to Grandmother Smith's? Could I try to support myself again? Wasn't I spoiled already by the "easy money" I had made—that "easy money" that was really the hardest money in the world?

One result of Henry Marsh's talk was that I made one resolve—to get out of the life for good and all.

But don't I wish every man that goes into a house of prostitution could have heard Henry's little sermon! These smug fools that come in, flashing their money around, thinking they own the world—honest, you wouldn't believe it, but most of them think they really have bought the whole woman, because they have bought her body for a while.

They don't know, the blind idiots, that the woman is saying to herself—

"Now, you fool, I'll put up with you for the sake of your coin; and I'll lie to you and jolly you so you'll come again—and bring more money. But so far as you're concerned—why, do you know what I'd do if it wasn't for your money? Don't you see how I despise you and hate you in my heart, for the way you have used me? Don't you think I would spit on you in scorn, if it wasn't just for your money?"

It may not be those words, but it's something like that feeling that is in every woman's mind when she bows down as a prostitute before one of these "lords of creation."

❧❈❧

Nearly a year passed, from the night I went to live with Henry Marsh, before I found myself in a house of prostitution.

That room next to Harry's—I came to call him Harry after a time, just as his men friends did—was vacant after a little while, and I moved into it. Here was my chance, now, I thought. Up to then I had only been seeing an occasional "friend" of Harry's. Now I had an apartment by myself; and I went into the regular business as a free lance.

Why did I make this change? Well—there were the shop windows.

It's all so simple. Just give a girl a little idea that she can make extra money in some way, and then you can safely leave it to the store windows to send her the rest of the distance.

You decent woman who is reading this, haven't you ever stopped in front of one of those lovely windows, and feasted your eyes on the silks, laces, lingerie, costly gowns and jewelry—things that just made your soul seem empty because you didn't have them? Is there any woman anywhere who doesn't love fine clothes? Well—how about the girl who has been poor all her life, and has never had any? How do you suppose she feels?

Well, I'll tell you how it makes her feel. There is a thick, strong plate glass window between the man, standing there, and those diamonds he is looking at; and at that, he only loves the diamonds because he can sell them. That plate glass window protects him from stealing them. But there isn't any protection to hide expensive dresses away from the eyes of the poor girl, who loves them for their own wonderful beauty; oh, few men realize how much she loves them, or how they reach out and take hold of her, mind and soul.

That plate glass keeps the men from being burglars. But it doesn't keep the girls from going and selling themselves.

Think of that the next time you look into a shop window.

I used to stand and stare at those lovely things, in my idle day times, with tears in my eyes—

Then my mind would fly forward to the coming night with its chances of money; and I would think of the men in horror, because I loathed that part of it, and hated myself for standing it. But I didn't see how I could go back to the drudgery and disgrace.

It's the sad thing about such dreams, that they can't come true. There isn't money enough for the girl, even if she sells her soul. The men and the madams get it all.

I don't think the love of finery can be a wrong thing. It comes from a woman's sense of beauty—she can't see much beauty in men, and she has to find it in clothes. But it isn't fair to turn that love of beauty to a woman's ruin. It isn't right. There ought to be some way out of it.

One idea I got crazy over was the thought of travel. I started to put away money when this notion came. I wanted to go to San Francisco—I'd heard a lot about it; and I wanted to work east to one place and another. And that was another thing that kept me living as I was.

The notion was put into my head by my new chum, a girl named Ella. I had known Ella in the old laundry days; she had been one of the girls I liked best, because she was "straight" in spite of being poor. But one morning I was surprised to meet her in that same lodging house where I was; and after a question or two I found that she was living almost the same sort of life that I was.

There was this difference: she was in love with the man she was with—crazy about him, mad about him, willing to do anything for him; while I was just sort of indifferent to Harry Marsh—at that time. Poor Ella! I felt so sorry for her! She oughtn't ever to have gone to live with that man; she was made for better things.

Ella was interested when she heard I was making a regular business of "seeing men."

"You know, if the right man comes along," she said, repeating some bit of gossip she had heard, "lots of times they'll take you traveling. They say just lots of the girls like you go traveling; and lots of them get married, too, and get good homes."

She believed that faithfully. And since then I've decided that that notion, in one form or another, is held by almost every prostitute in the world. Think of it—thousands of them—all waiting for the man to come along who will marry them, or else take them traveling; and they wait and wait, and years go by; and first they get nervous and worn, and then they get diseased, and by that time they can't quit drinking, and maybe they have got the opium habit; and there are other troubles, too, worse ones, that make their voices course and their faces hard and unwomanly. And all this time, tucked away in the secret part of their minds, is this same hope.

"Maybe if I just wait long enough, that man will come along who'll give me a home, or else take me traveling."

I was fearfully lonely those days. I was alone all day. After I met Ella, she and I became close friends; but we didn't see much of each other.

The only friends I had were the men who visited me. Some of them, the ones who came again and again, got to be what I thought real friends. They were all married men—that old man from whom I got my first money, and a railroad conductor who was a friend of Harry's, and several other regular visitors.

I was surprised at first to find many of my customers married men. But soon I came to look on this as one of the commonplace facts of the business. And those married men were free, too, in talking about their homes and their wives.

I could have told many a Westville wife and mother things that would have surprised her. I could have wrecked a good many Westville homes, caused a good many Westville divorces, except for that unwritten law that keeps a prostitute's mouth shut about what she knows. And I could have told some of those women, too, a few plain truths—truths that would have been for their good; truths that might have made their husbands stay at home, or might have safeguarded their own health in days to come. The prostitute, whether she is in a regular house or just on the border, lives at the very heart of a certain secret side of life; wretched as she is, she is guardian of many strange stories and people's fates.

Harry Marsh, all during this lonely time, was my one real friend. I used to make Harry sit and listen to my troubles till I guess his ears were tired with the sound of my voice.

I had started out not caring whether Harry lived or died. He had given me advice when I needed it, I thought; and I hadn't yet learned that it wasn't good advice.

But by the time I had been living with him three or four months things started to get different. I fought against the idea; but down in my heart I knew that I was beginning to care.

It wasn't a romantic love, especially—not a love a person would be very proud of. But it isn't human nature, at any rate not in mine, just to go along alone, and never care for anybody.

I knew I was in love with Harry, I wasn't glad about it. For, to tell you the truth, I didn't like the way Harry was acting.

"What's the matter, Harry? Got some bad news?" I asked one day, when I found him reading a letter. The expression on his face was the funniest I had ever seen.

"No; no bad news at all," he answered, hurriedly, and stuck the letter into his pocket kind of quick. I thought it was odd, but didn't say anything more; yet I wondered a lot about that letter.

And it wasn't more than a day or two later that something happened.

I was walking down the stairs of that lodging house early in the afternoon, dressed up to go out on the street, when I passed a woman coming up. The light was at her back, and I didn't see her face; all I could make out was that she was tall and handsomely dressed in black.

Just as we got to the same step, she going up and I going down, she turned and looked at me. And I pretty nearly fell down those stairs. She looked just like the woman in Harry's picture!

I got down to the street with my head buzzing. It was some time before I remembered that letter. Then the whole thing seemed plain. That other woman, the one Harry Marsh had loved, had come back.

I took a long walk to think things over. If there was another woman in the running at all, I would leave him. There were some things I just wouldn't stand.

It was almost night when I got back to the rooming house. I looked up from the street, and saw that Harry's window was dark. As I passed his door, I had all I could do to keep from turning the knob, walking in on Harry and that woman—if they were there—and saying, "Hello, dearest," to him. But I passed on into my own room.

I shut my door quietly and listened. After a minute or so I caught the sound of a voice—a woman's voice; then Harry's voice in reply. He was in there—with that woman!

"That settles you, you brute," I muttered to myself. "That's the last you'll ever see of yours truly, Alice Smith."

The next afternoon—it was Labor Day, I remember—I went out on the streets with my new plan whirling through my head. I was to leave right off—but where was I to go? What should I do?

There were two ways. I might get back to the old drudgery of honest living; this last throw down made me awful sick, and I guess I was sort of disgusted with this life anyhow. Or I could give up everything, take a "job" in a house of prostitution that one of my friends, a railroad man, had told me of, and just sink forever. I was desperate enough to do that.

I stood staring at a blue gown in a shop window, going over everything in my mind, when all of a sudden I turned my head around as if it was regularly jerked by a string. There, coming across the sidewalk toward me, was the one person I was hungriest for in the whole world—my dear, dear sister Emma.

"Oh, Emma!" I cried, running up to her. "Oh, I'm so glad to see you!"

I had to stop and wonder what she was doing on the streets that time of day; then I remembered it was a holiday.

Emma drew back a little bit; and something seemed to hurt her and me at the same moment. She gave a quick glance at me; and I could see what she was thinking. My clothes were better than I used to have.

"Where are you working, Alice?" she asked in a queer, stiff tone. All of a sudden I couldn't have looked at her to save my life; but I was so glad to see her it seemed as if my heart would break. Yet I kept control of myself.

"Emma, honest, I'm not working anywhere just now," I told her. "I'm living with Harry Marsh. And you know the rest, don't you?"

She gave me a cold little look—a look that had a lot of shrinking in it.

"Then grandma was right," she said. The voice didn't sound like Emma's. "Grandma told me I wasn't to go to see you, even if I ever found out where you were living. I'm sorry; I wish it could be different. But it can't. I'd better say good-by."

She gave her shoulder a little shake that sort of brushed off my hand, and walked quickly down the sidewalk.

I stood gazing after her, my heart beating fast, and tears running down my face. At that moment I wished I had died. I loved my sister more than I loved anybody in the world; had loved her from the first moment I laid eyes on her. Now she had cast me off.

Then my clothes—I hated them. They were better than Emma's; but I felt that in their very goodness they cried out to everybody what I was. And my hair was piled up high in a pompadour as big as a church tower. I felt like a coarse, dirty woman of the streets alongside of her—I, who had thought myself still decent, in spite of the way I was making my money.

I walked back to the rooming house. Harry was in his room—alone, but I didn't care. It wouldn't have made any difference.

"Good-by, Harry," I said. "I'm going away. I'm going to leave you for good. I'm going to turn straight."

I expected Harry at least would say he was sorry—he might look a bit surprised. But he didn't even seem interested. I had yet to learn that men don't care for women like me, except for just a short space of time.

"Are you?" he asked. He gave an odd sort of laugh. "Going to be straight, are you, Alice? Well—here's luck."

So once more I packed my straw basket.

✦✛✦

I went right off to an employment bureau. I have had dealings with these places before; and I knew enough to give them a good account of my usefulness in the world. On the basis of my calling myself an "experienced waitress" they sent me to a little place called the Traffic Men's hotel, out on the edge of Westville.

The first thing I did after moving into my new room was to get my sister on the telephone.

"Emma," I said, "I couldn't stand meeting you like that the other day. I wanted to tell you I've gone away from Harry Marsh."

"Gone away from him?" Emma's voice seemed uncertain, as if she didn't quite know whether she ought to be talking to me or not.

"Yes, Emma, I'm going to be straight again. Honest I am. I've got a job at the Traffic Men's hotel. I don't know whether you could come to see me now, but anyhow, that's where I'm going to be. Good-by."

I hung up before she could say anything. I was so afraid she would say she couldn't come to see me. And I wanted her to think it over. Then I turned to face my new life.

I was determined I wouldn't go back to Harry Marsh; I wanted to put that three months as far behind me as possible—so far that it would never come up again.

I plunged into my new duties with energy. That first day as a waitress and chambermaid combined—it was a small hotel—left me tired, sore, worn out—happy. Not in three months had I gone to bed with such a feeling of doing the right thing. I was a regular heroine.

The morning of that second day, I had a queer feeling that I might expect Emma. I dreamed about that meeting as if I had been away from my dear sister for years, instead of just weeks.

The third night I had a new thing to worry over. I went to bed tired as could be: aching all over; then all of a sudden I was wide awake. I could no more sleep than I could fly. I lay there, with all kinds of awful thoughts flying like mad through my head, one after another; and I felt so nervous and shaken to pieces that at times I wanted to scream.

Here was the way it looked to me: I had heard of men who had been heavy drinkers and had tried to quit. Well, I could figure out that I was in just that same situation. Here I had had this unnatural life all this time; and now that I had stopped it all at once, it left me nervous and weak. It was just one of the powerful ways the muddy river had of holding me—a fearful way. Would I get over it?

This was harder to face than anything else. Those nervous fits lasted for days. Many times, in those next days, I felt desperate enough to get up at night, dress in my flashiest clothes, go out onto the street and plunge back into the old life. It took all I could give, to keep from it. This clean life seemed to have so little in it—nothing but hard work, and being bossed and nervous nights and days, and that awful tiredness from the drudgery; and poor pay, and no chance to buy pretty things or ever have any fun; while the old life, though I knew it would be suicide to go back, called and held me in a grip stronger than I had ever dreamed of.

I was getting new meanings from that empty phrase, "Quitting the life."

Well, I held on tight to my job; and it started after a time to get easier. I was less nervous, and after a week or so I began to feel as if I might win out in time.

But I was worried over my sister Emma. Why didn't she come to see me? Wasn't she going to forgive me? Wasn't she ever going to take me back?

I had been at the Traffic Men's hotel over a week. One afternoon I was snatching a few minutes' rest, up in my little room, when there came a sound as if somebody had brushed against the door, rather than knocking on it.

Into the room rushed Emma—much as I had run into Harry Marsh's room three months before.

"Alice!" she cried out.

"Oh, Emma! I'm so glad you've come!"

I hardly noticed, in my joy at seeing her, that her face was stained as if she had been crying. I put my arms around her and held her tight, and felt so happy and so tender—I hadn't felt that way for so long—that I'm not sure but I cried myself.

"But what's the matter, Emma?" I asked her presently, as she didn't stop sobbing, but just held her head down and shook all over.

Then she got control of herself and told me, all in a breath.

"I—I wanted to come to see you long ago, and grandma wouldn't let me, but she said today that if I came to see you at all, I could just s-s-stay, and be b-bad like she said you were. And I came anyhow."

"Why, Emma!"

I could hardly believe my ears. Emma turned out, too, just as I had been, and just because she wanted to see me!

But would just that have caused all this trouble? Wouldn't it have to be something more?

"Emma," I cried out, "who's the man?"

Then my sister just put her head down lower still and sobbed harder than ever as she told me. For there was a man, it seemed, and she was in love with him; and when he tried to call at the house grandma had made trouble, because now grandma was suspicious of all men. She couldn't see any good in a harmless love affair. And she had been telling Emma that she, too, was "bad," just as she had told me.

Emma didn't say so in so many words; but from little things she let drop as she became quieter, I knew she was feeling that same hard rebellious way I felt the night I had gone to live with Harry Marsh. Emma was on the edge of going to her lover and telling him she wanted to stay; and she was reckless, and goodness knows where she mightn't have finished up.

"I'll just go," she cried out. "I won't stay. He'll take care of me. He loves me."

I knew here was danger. I had traveled this same path myself.

Maybe now I could make a little good come out of my experience.

"Emma," I said seriously, "you listen to me."

Then I talked to her as if I was years older than she was, instead of being really younger. I told her all about my life— things about it that made her shudder and shrink away from me; and I didn't spare myself, but laid it on thick. I showed her what men were like, and how they acted toward the girls that got into their power; and I told her about the "one man," and my struggle to get away from the life, but how I was afraid I couldn't make it go.

And I told her that if she once left home, she was in for the same thing. I didn't leave any room for doubt.

By the time I was through, Emma was staring straight ahead, her breath coming short and quick.

"Now," said I, "you go back to grandma's and tell her I sent you, and tell her plainly you ain't bad, and ain't going to be bad, because Alice has tried it and wishes she had died first. And maybe she'll see the truth, and fix it all up."

So Emma went, after first having a long visit with me; and she did fix it up with grandma, and later on she and her young man were married. So I have always felt happy about that.

I was left alone again with my task of making good.

The proprietor of that hotel had a son about my own age. When I first laid eyes on that boy I suspected trouble. I don't know whether he might have seen me on the street, or whether it was just some look about me as if I had "seen life." The old life, I know, had left its stamp on me, in the way my eyes looked, and the way I glanced at men, and in a dozen and one little things I wasn't conscious of. And this boy saw them. One day in the hallway he met me. I was sweeping.

"Hello, sweetheart," he whispered as he went past. He came back that way a moment later, then he whispered, "Hello, dearie."

I didn't make any answer. But I thought, "Here's trouble."

It was several days later—I was near the close of my second week there, and was feeling a little bit better each day—beginning to think I might make it go, after all, though I was getting awfully lonesome. I had finished with the dining room work, and had just put out the lights, and was groping my way toward the door in the dark.

I heard footsteps, and stopped, startled. It was that boy.

He came up close, reached out and put one arm around me. With the other he gripped my wrist tight.

"Say, dearie," he said, "let's go upstairs together. I'm onto you, kid."

I jerked my wrist free, stepped back and slapped him in the face so hard it scared me. Then I made for the door and slammed it, just as he got wits enough to swear.

I went up to my room, lay down on the bed and felt real sick at heart. What was the use of trying to make good, if somehow it stuck out all over you that once you had been bad? What was the good of a world where all a person's breaks, all a woman's mistakes, dragged on you and weighed you down and took away your strength and put their brand on you forever?

I had taken that one wrong step. Wasn't I ever to be free again?

Early the next Saturday morning the dish washer in the kitchen said to me as I passed:

"I hear you're going to get the run today. I'm awful sorry."

A little later I met the proprietor.

"You can mop up the dining room floor this morning instead of this afternoon," he said to me. I looked at him square.

"The new girl can do that, I guess," I said. "I'm wise to your game."

The man flushed red.

"And I'm wise to yours, you——," he said brutally. "You've been giving this house a bad name, my son tells me—having some of the guests come into your room at night. You are lucky I don't hand you over to the police. You can get your money at the desk."

What was the use? I packed my things once more in that straw basket, got my money at the desk, and went out into the street, discouraged.

Should I just give up now and go back again to Harry? I came to the corner of the street where he lived.

Then I turned sharp around and made for the employment office. Maybe I could live it down yet.

The employment office sent me to a town in the mountains on what would have been a splendid job, if I could have held it. It was for an "experienced waitress," which I was not; and the place was a popular summer hotel.

I came to the place on a rush Sunday, and that very first dinner I went about a mile high. I wasn't fitted for a waitress' job; it's a hard strain and you have to keep your head no matter how hard you are rushed; a thing I never could do.

"I thought you said you were an experienced waitress," snapped the proprietress to me after that meal.

"I did say I was," I replied sullenly. I was worse discouraged than ever.

"Well," she said, softening, "you can get your meals here

until you've found another place. There's a laundry down in town that might have a vacancy."

I went down to that laundry. The proprietor didn't have a place for me, really, but he seemed to like something in the way I asked him for work, and he took me on.

"I've got a new good job for you, young lady," he said to me three days later. He was a very kindly man with blue eyes—one of the few men I ever met who was good to me just for the sake of being good.

"There's a little new restaurant opening down the street," he explained in a low voice. "It's being started by one of the old girls from the 'line' here, you see. She's trying to get out of that life, poor girl; and she's saved up $600, and now she's putting it all into this little restaurant. I do hope the poor woman makes a go of it; but she doesn't know the first thing about the business, I'm afraid."

The "line" or "red light district" in that town, as in most mountain towns, was altogether too big for the size of the place. There were four or five houses, all in a row, facing on an alley; and that alley ran along right behind the little new restaurant this woman was opening.

I went over and made myself known to my new employer; and she told me right away I could have the job. There was something about that poor woman that laid right hold of me. You could see she had suffered fearfully; afterwards I learned that she had been one of that great majority of girls who aren't really strong enough to stand the strain of the life; she had dragged through the old ghastly round of disease and hospitals and operations and sickness and hunger and want—the same road that is traveled by eight fallen women out of every ten. But all her suffering hadn't made her heart hard; her speech was often vulgar, she swore like a man, her voice was coarsened, and her skin was rough from the paint she had now quit using; but in her wrinkled eyes there was a kind look, and she was always helping take care of some poor girl from the "line" who might be in need of help. She had the soul of charity; it had been given her by her suffering, and she never blamed anybody for anything.

Her little restaurant started off with a rush. But even I, with my little experience, could see she would have to call a halt. The cook sent up the orders too large; and the menu offered too much for the money. She had no head for business; didn't know the right things to watch for.

I liked my job just great. She paid me mountainous wages— $9 a week; and I got tips, besides. And she let me arrange that little restaurant just the way I wanted to; and that always did appeal to me.

I would shuffle those tables around and decorate that little place until it looked as pretty as could be, with pine cones and evergreens hanging here and there, and flowers on all the tables. I loved that way of doing; and for the first time I started to feel as if I might really be some use, and get over the shame of those three months.

But just then I began to get letters from Harry Marsh.

I don't know how he found out my address. When that first letter came, it seemed to wake up something inside of me—a longing—not for the old life, but to see him. It made me remember all over again what I had never wholly forgotten— the way I had come to care for him, before I left him; and all that he meant to me.

He was lonesome, he said. And he wanted me to come back. He wrote regular love letters now, and said he was sorry for things that had happened, and promised to see no more of other women. I could guess from this that that other woman, the brilliant one whose picture he kept, had left him again; and I was glad, though I knew she was always liable to come back.

This restaurant, as I said, was right on the "line." The women from the houses facing that back alley used to come in there and get their meals. I knew what they were—their appearance didn't leave it in doubt any—and though I waited on them the best I knew how, I didn't get acquainted with them at all until a peculiar thing happened.

One night I went for a drive with a young fellow who drove a bakery wagon. He was a nice enough boy; but as soon as he got me out of town he started that same old line of talk that is always started sooner or later by every man.

I guess he didn't think I had had any past experience. It was the surprise of his life when I suddenly got back my old reckless streak, and told him, right out:

"You don't attract me any. Why, I used to keep an apartment, down in Westville."

He was surprised, but he realized then that I wasn't any such easy game as I seemed. Well, naturally I supposed he would keep it to himself. But a few nights later, as I was taking an order at dinner from a couple of those women, one of them grinned and said:

"You're all right, kid. You're just my style of a girl. No 'charity' about you."

Her companion laughed.

Well, my secret was out. But would it hurt me? Her voice had been kindly.

After that all those women who came to the restaurant made a good deal over me. It's a peculiar fact that professional prostitutes always hate girls who are immoral, as we say, "for charity." We look on them with something of the same disgust as the union man looks on the scab. They aren't honest; they aren't willing to come out and face the results of what they are doing; and then there's the money side of it, too, and it's true that such girls probably keep money away from some poor girl who is in debt to her landlady. But now that these women had found I wasn't a charity girl they made a lot over me.

I was willing to meet them on friendly ground, too, for the sake of their trade to the restaurant. I was all wrapped up, heart and soul, in the success of that little place. So I always met these customers' jokes with a smile and word or two of my own.

I was getting my old happiness back, those days. I used to do a good deal of singing about my work. One day I left the back door of the restaurant open, and went about my potato peeling singing like a Tetrazzini.

Pretty soon I heard a voice from a doorway across the alley:

"Come on over here, you little nightingale, and sing for us!"

"Sure, come on," another voice urged. "None of us old birds can sing like that."

"Come on over and have a drink," said a third.

"Oh, I can't go over now," I answered. "I'm busy."

But just the same, I was filled with curiosity to see what that house was like inside. I had heard so much about such places; had even thought I might go into one, some day; but I had never been inside of one. It just sort of captured my mind.

They kept on pressing me to come over, and finally I went. But I was so bashful when I got there that I just kept my eyes down, and that is why I can't tell you what that house looked like inside.

There were a lot of women there, dressed any old way except completely, and they made a big racket when I came in, and crowded around me; and one of them gave me a glass of beer. I didn't like beer, but I gulped it down; and then I made my escape as soon as I could because they wanted me to sing. But I liked them.

There was a bartender who used to come into the restaurant. I got to be friends with him. One afternoon, when the place was empty, I asked him a few questions about those women and their lives.

"Do they make much money?" I asked.

He looked real serious, and almost sighed.

"Poor girls," he said, shaking his head. "Poor girls! There ain't scarcely a one of 'em that ain't in debt—as to money, why, they go through hell for all they get. God knows what becomes of 'em afterward. It kills them in time. Say, you wasn't thinking of going there, was you?" He looked up sharp.

"No, I wasn't," I laughed. "But I like some of those women. They don't seem so bad to me. Some of them are as kind as can be."

"Oh, they're no different from other women," he said, sadly. "They are just as kind and friendly as anybody. But they don't get much chance. It's all a fight for them; and they never win."

That gave me a lot to think about. I was sorrier than ever for this woman I was working for; for by that time I could see that her restaurant was just on the ragged edge of failure.

One day I had received an especially sad letter from Harry. He must have been in an awful mood to write that way. He wanted me to come back, and said if I didn't he might kill himself—he couldn't tell. He also said my sister Emma was sick; and I felt real bad.

That same afternoon the proprietress of that little restaurant beckoned to me. She was sitting over her books, trying to add.

"Alice," she said, "will you add that column up?"

I did as she asked, wondering what was the matter.

"Now will you add this one up?"

I did. It came out pretty near the same.

"Read me the two answers," she said. Something in her tone made me look at her. She had two little bright red spots on her rough cheeks.

"This one's eighteen hundred and thirty-eight, fifty," I said. "And this one's nineteen hundred and two, twenty-five."

She stretched out her hands over that desk, hid her old leathery face down on one arm, and twisted a pen around in her fingers so hard it snapped in two. Then she doubled that arm around her head and burst out into sobs.

"Oh, —— —— ——," she moaned, "I've got to go back to the line. And I'm an old woman—an old woman."

I tiptoed away. There was nothing I could do.

I wouldn't take any pay for that last week. But that woman wouldn't let me give her back any of my past wages. "It wasn't your fault," she said. "I ain't taking charity."

So that was why the train a day or two later took me back to Westville. I had phoned to Harry Marsh I was coming, and he met me at the depot. I went with him to his room again, so lonesome and in need of comfort that I all but forgot I was a failure—a worse failure, even, than that poor broken-down woman.

***

It is with pain that I write this chapter in my life. You could never get me to tell exactly how it was that I came to enter a house of prostitution, if it weren't that I have made up my mind to tell my whole life story, painful or not; and also that the same thing happens so often in the lives of other prostitutes.

But please don't say, in reading about my misfortune, "Oh, she's different from other women. She wouldn't feel about children the same as ordinary women would feel." Don't be cruel enough to say that. The one difference in my emotions, when at last I found I was in a condition approaching maternity, was just that all my love, and my hope, and gladness, and wonder, were spotted and mixed up with another feeling—a terrible disappointment and shame.

I was barely nineteen when I knew for certain of my condition. It had been almost a year since I first went to live with

Henry Marsh; and it was six or seven months since I had given up my effort at "turning straight" again, and had gone back to being a "free lance" in Westville.

Maybe you who read this have made a losing fight, some time or other, to cut out cigarettes or whiskey. All the time you were holding out against them, didn't you keep on remembering how good you had felt, sometimes, before you quit? And when you finally gave up trying and went back to it, didn't you feel a sort of satisfaction—almost happy, though you were ashamed at the same time? Well, that's how I felt. I don't think anybody in the world really loves the idea of giving up what you call a vice; and even if you have been told the vice will kill you in time, you always think, "Well, maybe it won't."

Then, out of a clear sky, came this new trouble. I was in a condition of coming motherhood.

At first I just wouldn't believe it. It was too awful. I had, as I thought, taken every care of myself; and I couldn't understand why this thing should have come to me. Hadn't I troubles enough already?

I was afraid, of course, to tell Harry. He would think I was awful green, to let such a thing happen; and he would laugh at me and maybe scold and abuse me a bit. He was getting to do that, once in a while now, as he got sure that I was in love with him and wouldn't answer back like I used to.

So I let the weeks slip by.

One day, after I had been sitting in my room, idly, by the window for an hour, I caught myself up, all of a sudden, and felt real angry.

What had I been doing? Well—I had found myself right in the middle of a day dream. I—a prostitute. Such a day dream as honorable mothers-to-be have, I guess; a dream about my baby, and what he would look like, and the color of his eyes and hair—I wanted a boy—and how I would have to take care of him until he was bigger and not so helpless; and how he would be all dependent on me, and look to me for his very life; and how I would love him all the years he was growing up.

I brought myself up with a round turn. Who was I, to let myself be thinking of such things? Wasn't I a prostitute? Wasn't I an outcast? How could I ever let myself go ahead and have my baby, no matter how much I might want him, so long as there was that shadow? Why—only think; I didn't even know which of my "friends" was my baby's father.

When that thought came to me, I know I felt the deepest agony the prostitute ever feels—that awful pit between her and "good" women, the cruelty of the curse laid on her by everybody. It was all the worse because I knew that, except for outward things, I was just like all other women; that day dream, with its hope and longing, had brought me closer to them than I had ever been in my life.

Why not go right ahead and bear my child? What right did they have to stop me?

It was an impossible thought; but I let it stay on a moment because it was so sweet. And then I couldn't get rid of it.

But no; the world hadn't any room for babies without fathers. If that child was ever born alive, I would surely some day have him reproach me for being the most selfish creature alive—a woman who went ahead and brought a child into the world, knowing perfectly well that the child's life could never be anything but a burden to him and to everybody else.

I remembered all I had ever heard of men and boys born out of marriage. The shame had conquered every one of them. Some had turned criminals and were in the prisons and jails all over the country. Some had been lunatics. Some had finally committed suicide. And all because of an idea!

What was marriage, anyhow? I thought it over, and I felt angry because I couldn't put my finger on the answer. Was it a holy sacrament? Well, I had seen too much of husbands who came down to visit me, to believe it was very holy. Was it so as to make sure about health? I had seen lots of crippled children, stunted children, blind children, who were born of legal marriages; and nobody ever criticised. Then what was this marriage, that was so strong it could make me suffer like this? Wasn't it just an idea?

I couldn't find any better answer. It was an idea—sometimes a good idea, sometimes a bad one; sometimes right, sometimes wrong; sometimes true, sometimes a horrible lie. Well—anyhow, it was there; everybody had it; and it was too powerful for me. It could crush me, easy enough, and all my little longings.

I guess the strongest things in the world are some ideas.

Then I gave up. There were only two ways out. Either I would persuade Harry Marsh to marry me, and give my baby a name; or else I would have to find some way to be a murderer. To set myself against that great idea that children must be born only by married women, would just mean worse than death for my baby—

Never, never in my life, could I have a child.

Well, this thought didn't make me cry, or anything like that. It just sort of soaked into me and became a dead part of my heart and soul. It is there yet. Never in this world can I have a child.

I tried to tell Harry about my trouble a good many times before I succeeded. Somehow I felt in advance what his answer would be. But I didn't foresee all that he would say.

Finally I chose a bad moment. But I don't think it made any difference. He was beginning to drift away from me, anyhow.

One night he stepped into my room, while I was lying down. I was feeling pretty bad that day.

"Oh, Alice, I've got some tickets for a show tonight," Harry called out. "What do you think of that?"

Under ordinary circumstances I might have thought a good deal. He hadn't been paying me too many little attentions lately. I was sick and blue as could be.

"That's good," I answered. "Better look up some of your friends. I ain't going."

"Why not?" He wasn't especially pleased.

"Oh—I'm tired," I answered.

"Tired? You're always tired these days. I never saw anything to beat it. Tired day in and day out." He seemed kind of sore about it, as if he had been thinking it over before, and was waiting for his chance to say something. He came over and sat on the edge of the bed.

"Honest, Alice, what is the matter with you? You never are in for any good times, any more."

I had been telling myself, here was my chance. So I got myself together while he spoke; and now I sat upright, looked at him square, and said:

"I ain't thinking of you, because I've got lots else to think about. I'm going to have a baby."

He took it well. All he said at last was, "H'm."

Then I got my surprise. Harry got up off the edge of the bed and looked down at me, as calm as you please.

"Well," he said, "I haven't got the money to see you through. You know that. A woman like you, in your condition, generally has the sense to take care of herself. You can make your own money in your own way. Better be looking out for a job in some house."

He walked toward the door.

Good-by to all my dreams, I thought as he slammed the door behind him. Here I had been telling myself that he might make me his wife. How absurd. How foolish! Harry Marsh do anything that wasn't just for his own good!

That was my call to get busy. No more of this day dreaming.

I would need money; I would have to make it myself; and the sooner the better.

I wasn't brought into the world to be a mother, but just a prostitute, it seemed. Very well, then—a prostitute I'll be; a real one, not just on the border. I couldn't be a mother, anyhow; then I might as well go the whole way. No use holding back; what was the good?

My friend, the railroad man, called that night. I led the talk around to the subject I wanted, then asked:

"Do you happen to know any house where they want another girl? I'm looking for a job."

"Well, say, I do, kid," he answered. "Over at the town of Zephyr, at the end of our division, there's a bunch of little houses—places with two or three girls apiece—and I heard last night that Nellie, the landlady of one of them, is going away for a while. She wanted a girl to help out while she was gone."

"Could you put in a good word for me?" I asked. He used to spend one night in Westville and the next out at Zephyr, at the other end of his run.

"Sure, kid," he said. "I'll do it."

Very well. I had found my way to make money at last. Now I could save my baby from being born without a name—or at all.

❖

That last day of my life with Harry Marsh was full of happenings. I was to leave early the next morning on a train that would take me to my new "job"—my first place in a house of prostitution.

I might as well say good-by to Ella, my chum, I told myself. Ella would be sorry I was to do this. She was living with her young man, part owner of a saloon; but she hadn't been "seeing friends," the way I had. She would feel bad at losing me.

I stepped into Ella's room, the way I did now and then, with just a knock. She was lying face downward on the bed, her head buried in a pillow.

"Hello, Ella," I called out. "I've come to say good-by. I'm going away."

Ella twisted around and sat up. There were tear marks on her face.

"Why, what's the matter, child?" I asked her. I hadn't got so very close to Ella; but we were good friends, at that. I guess she didn't feel she knew me yet well enough to tell me her troubles, because she only answered—

"Nothing."

"Well, there's matter enough with me," I said, full of my own affairs. "I'm going away tomorrow morning. And it's good-by for me."

"Why, where are you going?" she asked.

"Out to Zephyr, that's where," I told her. Then, getting mad at the thought, I added, "I've got a job out there. I'm going in a 'house.'"

"Oh—Alice!" She drew a big breath. The idea seemed to shock her. "What on earth are you going to do that for?"

I was in a brutal mood. I spoke right out.

"Well, I'm going to have a baby. And I've got to make money to get rid of it. That's what for."

I had expected her to be startled; but I didn't expect to see her turn around all of a sudden, throw herself onto the bed and burst out crying harder than ever. Her hands sort of clawed at the pillow.

I was over by her in a minute.

She seemed so little and helpless—she didn't have as much strength as I had; and now I knew that her trouble was the same as mine. And I knew how she was feeling.

Then I got a new idea. Maybe her trouble wasn't quite so bad as mine, after all.

"Ella," I said, bending over her, "there's just been only the one man, hasn't there?"

She nodded.

"Why, then, you're all right," I cried out. "You're lucky. Oh, Ella, how I wish I was you!"

Ella sat up at that, and stopped crying, and we had a long talk.

"But there's one place you can go to," I told her. "Your Jim won't have to take care of you until afterward. There's the Crittenden Home."

"I know. I've thought of that. But, Alice, I haven't got the money to get the things I need. I need ten dollars. I can't make it—your way. And Jim won't give it to me. He's sore."

Then another idea came to me. Harry Marsh had led me into this; or I felt as if he had. I got sort of mad. It was his duty to see me out of it.

I went right around to Harry's cigar-store.

"Harry," said I, "you ain't through with me yet. I've got to have twenty-five dollars, right this very afternoon. And you're going to give it to me."

Never in my life had I spoken to him like that. It sounded now as if I hated him. He was real surprised.

"Why—I haven't got it, girlie," he said, soothingly.

"I don't care if you've got it or not. You've got to get it. That's all there is to it."

He got sort of mad.

"But Alice"—

"There ain't any 'but' about it. I need that money, and it's up to you. I'll give you till two o'clock; I'll be around here then, prompt. And, Harry, if you don't get it—there's some law about helping a girl to go wrong—delinquent, they call it, don't they? Well, Harry, I'm coming around at two. Good-by."

I was on hand at two o'clock. I stood there in front of Harry's cigar-store, and he came outside without a single word and passed me twenty-five dollars in gold. And without a word I took it and went away.

I got that twenty changed into five-dollar pieces. Then I wrote a little note, saying, "Dear Ella: Now you can go to that Crittenden Home. Have your baby; and I hope it's a boy, and a darling. Please let me see him some day. Alice."

I wrapped three five-dollar pieces in the note, and shoved it under the door of Ella's room, quiet. I guess she was asleep at the time. Then I packed my old straw basket—I had brought it out from home not so long ago, and now look where it was going!—and went to a cheap rooming-house, where I stayed that night. The next morning I took the train for the town of Zephyr.

I hadn't supposed any of the girls from that house would come down to meet me. As a matter of fact, I didn't give any thought to what I would do after I got to the little town; I naturally supposed I would find my way without any trouble to the "Redlight District."

As I stepped off the train, I saw a painted woman in a black brocade coat step on; and I supposed this was the landlady who was going away. A girl with a big blonde pompadour, carrying a suit case, got off just ahead of me; and a couple of women, who were waiting there, stepped up to her with a whispered word or two, and walked on, one on each side of her. I went away from the depot without anybody taking any notice of me.

I hadn't any idea as to what sort of looking place a house of prostitution in a town like this would be. I walked around quite a while, looking for the suspicious-looking place; but I didn't find it. I dropped into a restaurant to get lunch, and came out again and kept on with my wandering.

I was getting tired. Should I ask one of the men? There were lots of men on the streets; and at the end of town I had seen a couple of big factories of some kind, and there were big railroad yards, too; so I guessed these men must be night-shift workers. But I was afraid to ask.

At last I saw a policeman—a regular country cop, with a cheap brown suit on, and a great huge star pinned outside of his coat. He was the only cop in town; and he looked it.

I stepped close up to him.

"I beg pardon," I asked, softly, "but can you tell me where I can find the 'Redlight District?'" My! That sounded like a terrible and important phrase, that "Redlight District!" I kind of rolled it out, as if it was something real big.

He looked at me close, but didn't seem to find anything at all funny in the question.

"Sure. You go down that way two blocks, then over to the right. You'll see a row of little houses with red doors. Just a little distance."

Evidently the Law, in Zephyr, knew all about prostitution.

I went as he had pointed. There were the little houses with red doors, just as he had said, and some plain-looking cottages across the street. On the doorstep of one of those cottages was sitting a woman—one of the two I had seen at the depot.

"Say, is your name Alice Smith?" she called out to me. "Well, say, me and my partner tried to meet you at the depot, and you was so young and innocent-looking we passed you right by. We was looking for a full-fledged old bird. Come right in."

She was breezy and hospitable, and I took to her.

I followed her inside the house.

"Guess the joke's on us, all right," she laughed. Then the other girl I had seen at the depot came up. "Katie and me was down to the train to meet you; but we was on the lookout for a blonde. That railroad fellow said you was a blonde. Well, when this other girl got off the train, we see she had a big yellow pompadour, so we up and introduced ourselves. She seemed sort of surprised"—she stopped and laughed—"and I guess she had a right to be. She's a waitress in a restaurant here, and says she, 'I make my money honest!'"

I decided this must be "Big Annie," who was taking the place of the absent landlady. She showed me where to put my things—the place was just a small cottage, with an ordinary kitchen, and a couple of bedrooms plainly furnished, and a parlor with a couple of tables and a picture or two and a rickety old piano in the corner; and there was a little front porch with a red electric light globe hanging over the door. There wasn't anything about the place that looked bad or "Bohemian" at all, so far as I could see; just dirty and kind of worn-out.

"Big Annie" talked right along, in one unbroken streak, while I was getting my things into place. Then I did one thing that I guess looked sort of funny to her. I took out of my straw basket some stuff I had bought to make a dressing-gown, and had cut out already. There wasn't any sewing-machine, but I was used to doing my sewing without; so I just grabbed my little workbag, that had needles and thread and scissors and everything, picked out a chair in that parlor, and got after my sewing, as domestic as could be.

"You're an industrious one, ain't you, kid?" exclaimed Annie. I think she liked it. But it made her think I was green, I guess, because after a minute she drew up another chair, closer to me, and said—

"I guess I'd better tell you how it is here. There's several things you might need to know. Tell me kid—ever been in a 'house' before?"

"Not a regular house," I told her. "I had a room in Westville, by myself."

"Well, that's all right. I might's well explain this is a two-dollar town. No matter what you do for a man here, you can't get over two dollars as a usual thing—it's just the way of the town."

"Is there much money here?" I asked.

"Well, can't say that there is. Too many women in the business. There's four other houses right on this block, all little ones—two of 'em's got two girls apiece, and one's got three, like this one, and then there's a negro house that's got five girls. They don't more'n make their board."

"What are those little places across the street, with the red doors?" I asked.

"Oh, those are the 'cribs,'" she answered. I wasn't much the wiser, because I hadn't ever heard of a "crib" or a "parlor house," and didn't know the difference. I learned afterward that the cribs were used by unattached girls living by themselves, and taking as little as a dollar. But some of the most energetic girls lived that way, because they wouldn't have anybody to watch them, and now and then might take a chance at picking a man's pockets, if they could get him drunk.

And just as I was wondering about them, here came a woman loafing along kind of slow down the middle of the street—no hat, her hair half down and all angled up, dressed in an old dirty garment that had slipped down from one shoulder, leaving one arm and her breast bare. She waved her bare arm to Big Annie, yelled something I didn't understand, and disappeared behind one of the red doors.

"That's Mad Susie," said Annie. "It's fools like her that spoils our trade. Just rotten with 'syph,' and gives the whole business a bad name. You was asking about money. On pay-nights it's pretty good. Maybe a girl will take in twenty-four or twenty-six dollars, one of those nights. The rest of the time it ain't any good—maybe six dollars some nights, maybe nothing. They's two pay-nights a month—the railroad pays off on the thirty-first, and the foundries on the fifteenth. Those are the heavy nights. You got here just in time; it's the fourteenth today."

"How about board?"

"The regular charge here is ten dollars a week," said Big Annie. "I'm taking the madam's place, so you can pay that to me."

She went on to give me more intimate advice not printable here—on the right use of disinfectants, carefulness about disease, things that were expected of a girl, and other such stock-in-trade of the prostitute's life. Some of it I knew already, other parts I hadn't dreamed of with all my experience.

As she was talking, in came a couple of other girls. I was introduced to them by name; they were from the other houses. And one thing I was sorry for was that I had given my right name, like a little fool, when I came into the house. I hadn't known that these women all had some name to hide behind, and somehow it hurt me to hear my name, that had once been as clean as anybody's, passed around on their lips. I felt degraded by it.

Girls from the other houses began to come in soon, including three colored women from the negro house. I didn't like that, but it was all the same to Big Annie—it's pretty democratic in those country places. It wasn't long before the place was in an uproar, everybody talking at once, and drinking.

Big Annie drank and joked with each new visitor; and I wondered how she stood it, until I found that she had a bottle of colored water that looked just like whiskey. But once in a while she would drink out of the bottle that had the real whiskey.

One thing that I noticed in the talk of the visitors puzzled me. They kept saying, "My pa, he's coming tonight," or "When did your father go away?" or "My dad won't be around till Monday."

At first I wondered if these girls could have their families right here in town, and yet be working at this business. But

I decided there must be some other explanation, when one of them turned to me, as I sat there sewing, and said, with a laugh—

"Alice ain't got a 'pa' yet. Never mind, kid; you'll get one soon enough."

Then I understood.

It got time for dinner; and the girls left for their houses one by one. Big Annie and Kate, the other girl in the house, went out to the kitchen to get supper; they wouldn't let me help because they said it was my first night here, and they would entertain me.

Pretty soon the smell of cooking and the rattle of plates went all up and down that little street, just as if those houses were so many homes. Then the dishes were cleared away; the doors were shut and the blinds were pulled down; it started to get darker; and one by one, along that little street, gleamed out the red porch lights.

I sat in that parlor waiting—and trembling. This was worse than my room in that lodging-house. There, I had been at least by myself, and I only knew a few men, who were my steady callers. But here I was a stranger; and this room was open to anybody, any man or beast who might care to come in.

It was like sitting in a shop window, marked "For Sale," to be handed over to the first customer with the price.

The stair outside creaked; there was a heavy footstep on the porch; then the door opened. In that instant I know I stopped breathing.

"Hello, Annie," said the man who came in. He glanced around the room. "Hello, Kate. How's tricks?" Then to Annie again, "I see you've got your new girl."

Somehow, I felt relieved right away. I remembered this was a quiet night, and it wasn't likely, I told myself, that there would be any horror, or any money either, about this night.

I liked the looks of this new man. He was middle-aged, and well enough dressed, and he seemed thoroughly at home in the place. He acted as if he owned it. I wondered whether he did really own it.

Annie got up and brought some beer. She poured out four glasses. They sat around there for a while, drinking a little and talking about the landlady's going away for a trip; and by this time I had choked down a couple of glasses of the stuff, out of sheer nerve.

"The kid don't like her beer," said Annie, after a while, with a grin to the visitor; I was still trying to make out who he was.

He turned and looked at me for the first time hard. I looked back as easy as you please. I liked him.

"All right, then—let's try her on whiskey," he said finally.

Annie brought out her two bottles again. Now, as she poured out the drinks, I noticed that the visitor paid her a ten-dollar gold piece, and she gave him his change all in dollars. He sat there, smiling at me while I got ready to drink my whiskey, and he was shuffling that pile of dollar pieces in his hand, like you shuffle poker chips.

I'd never tasted whiskey before. But I gulped it down, and almost choked. They laughed.

"Better than beer, isn't it, kid?" laughed the man. And after that he paid most of his attention to me in the talk while Big Annie sat in the background, looking pleased with herself. I wondered why.

"Let's have some more of that," said he presently. The glasses were filled again, and he threw out another dollar, still shuffling the rest of the pile in his hand, and waiting.

And that was the last thing I remember that night; the bottles of whiskey standing there, the glasses, Annie's face, and that man sitting and waiting, playing with that pile of dollars, and grinning at me. Then everything sort of went out.

It was late the next morning when I woke up.

"Oh, Annie," I called out, as I dragged outside. "What do you think? I must have been pretty far gone or something. I let that man get away without getting any money from him."

I expected Annie would be mad. But she just smiled, as if she was satisfied.

"It's all right, kid," she answered. "He'll be all the better friend to you for it. And he's a man that will make a good friend, and help you out, too, if you ever need help."

She went away as if she didn't want to be asked any more questions. But later in the day I caught Katie, that other girl in the house, and asked her.

"Who was that fellow that was with me last night?"

"Him?" she said. "Oh, that's Jack Peters. He owns the Elite saloon—the biggest saloon here," she answered, but I had the feeling that she was keeping something back. She sort of smiled when she said it.

I didn't see anything of Jack Peters the second day that I was there. This was pay-day at the foundry; and by the time that night's work was over, I wouldn't have known him if I had seen him.

The rush started early in the evening and lasted until way in the small hours. That little bare parlor was pretty crowded most of the time, and Big Annie was kept busy waddling after drinks. There were several fellows in the crowd who could rattle the piano, and they kept that creaky old instrument going until it nearly forgot its age. On the surface, it seemed like a very gay night.

I know that it wasn't nine o'clock before I had to start drinking, so as to forget how weak and sore I was, and how I was paining. I can't describe that pain; you have to experience it to know it. I hadn't ever faced such a night before—and, remember my condition. But it would have been awful anyway.

I didn't waste my time over beer, but made for the whiskey first thing; and I needed every drop I took.

One thing that got on my nerves was that question, repeated I guess a dozen times during the evening: "Where's your new girl, Annie?" The men all had heard there was a new girl, and naturally I was the big attraction. I heard the next day that there had been a fight about me, on toward morning; but by that time I was too far gone really to know what was happening.

Along toward afternoon of the next day I woke up, feeling half-way dead and ready to go the other half. When I got awake enough to remember everything, I just turned my head over on the pillow and cried. I reached out and counted the money I had taken in. Twenty-eight dollars—I knew that was good, for that town. I've found out since that fourteen men a night is nothing at all remarkable, at any rate in the cheaper houses. Well, it seemed I was to be a "good money maker."

And it was those very words that Irish Annie met me with, when I turned in my ten dollars for the week's board. "You're a 'good money maker,' kid."

Eighteen dollars clear. I looked forward and tried to figure out how much I would need for that coming affair with the doctor. At least a hundred. Maybe two. Well, say I made my expenses on the nights between pay day times; and say each pay day got me twenty-five dollars clear. Four pay days—two months. And every week of those two months would make the final agony greater for me when it came.

"Annie," I said. "You said I was a 'good money maker.' Well, I'll need to be, I guess. I'm in wrong, Annie—I'm going to be a mother, unless I can find some doctor who's willing to help me out."

"Gee, you poor kid," was Annie's reply. "Well, there won't be no trouble about finding a doctor. Almost any doctor'll fix you up—for money. They talk about the honor of their profession a lot, but you jingle. That's the best answer. And if they need another, tell 'em you're from the 'line.'"

"But I won't be able to work at all during that time," I said. "I don't know how I'll live or anything. I haven't got a cent of money but what I'll make here."

"We can take care of you, kid, I guess," said Annie kindly. "I'll tell you what I'll do; Nellie won't mind, I guess. Instead of paying me ten dollars a week after this, you just give me a third of what you make. When you don't make anything, we won't get anything; and when you are making good, then we'll get better than just the ten dollars. Let's put it on that basis. And you can stay here right through."

I agreed to that gladly. I shouldn't wonder if in the end the house came out ahead; but anyhow, I didn't have to worry so much. Few landladies would have been so generous; many of them would have just turned me out.

There was one more thing that Annie said:

"Well, kid, you'll need a good friend now, more than ever. It's a lucky thing you didn't take any money from Jack Peters the other night. Hang onto him, kid; he'll make a good friend."

But the next afternoon the phone bell rang.

Annie answered. "Hello," she said. "Oh, that you Jack? How's tricks? Why, sure we can; I guess so. Wait."

Turning to me she said:

"It's Jack Peters. He says he's been out hunting and got some wild duck. He wants us to come up to dinner at his joint. Better come."

"You bet I'll come," I answered. Katie, sitting there, gave another funny grin, and later I caught a wink passing between her and Annie.

The Elite saloon, I found, was next to a restaurant, and there was a back room behind the bar that was connected with the restaurant kitchen. Annie led me right in through the saloon, with a laugh and a dirty joke at the bar. "I'm coming around to take a look at that new girl pretty soon," said one of the fellows, half drunk; and Annie laughed. "Come ahead; she'll accommodate you, all right." We went into the back room.

Jack Peters was on hand. He served a good dinner, with that same air of owning everything and feeling at home, as he had shown down in the house. He was an open-handed sort of man; free with his money and full of funny stories and jokes, and I liked him.

"My young Jack came down to see me today," he told us. "You must see my kid, Alice," he said to me. "Six years old now, and bright as a dollar. Say, that's one great little kid. Wish I could see more of him"—he gave a little sigh—"but then, I'd have to see his mama, too. And she wouldn't like that. Neither would I," he added, laughing, and I felt as if I knew his whole story.

But I didn't—only his end of it.

I began to understand, by the end of that dinner, why Jack Peters made such good friends of us women. It was just that he naturally hated forms and conventions. He hadn't been happy in his home life; and so he had got that idea so many men get, that everything respectable is just a sham, and that respectable people are all liars. So he went to the other extreme, and made friends of us women. That's a pretty common road for men to travel, when they are unlucky at home; it's one of the roots of prostitution, this unhappy marriage proposition.

Jack opened quite a bit of wine. I was still full of whiskey from the past two nights, and the wine tasted awful good to me. Besides, I was fast learning what is pretty near the first lesson to learn in this game—that if a girl doesn't want to suffer and break her heart, she will just have to stay drunk, at first.

We all got home pretty late, to find Katie doing the best she could to hold the visitors till we came. Then there was the work to do; and at the finish, when everybody else was gone, Jack Peters came and stayed out the night with me.

I heard Big Annie laughing as she went away to bed.

❖❖❖

During those next few days I had plenty of chance to wonder why Jack Peters' visits to me caused such a lot of excitement.

The girls from the other houses came over to visit us quite often. I couldn't help seeing that they took a great deal of notice in me. They seemed to be interested in me for some reason.

Annie would always greet them with, "Here's the kid. She's been five nights straight with Jack Peters." Was that a sort of distinction, I wondered. They didn't talk like that with any other man; other men, if they were mentioned at all, were just talked about like so many dogs. But not Jack Peters; he was spoken of not with respect exactly—no man was spoken of with respect—but with a kind of interest.

I explained it all to myself by saying that Jack was the most prominent saloon man in town, and that most of the houses bought their whiskey and beer from him; and that he was naturally a prominent character among the women. Most likely he worked up quite a bit of trade for some of the houses, in his saloon—for I was beginning to see how close together the saloon and the houses of prostitution really were. I could see for myself, for instance, that seven out of every ten men who came into our house had been drinking at some saloon; and I knew how just a little suggestion from the bartender, or a picture, or some other chance hint made to a man when he was a bit drunk, would just send him our way as easy as could be.

One day I was walking down the main street of the town. There's a difference even in the way a harlot walks through a town; all the men whistle at you and make remarks, and you're supposed to take it as if you were looking for it, when really, most of the time all you're after is to get away from that house, and the smell of whiskey and disinfectants, for a while.

I was with a girl from one of the other houses. We turned off down a side street. Just at the corner while I was right in the middle of a laugh, and had my face stretched wide in a grin, I almost ran into a little plainly dressed woman, about thirty-five, but looking older—her face was the sort that you could see never smiling again.

I had just a glimpse of that sad face, and in the same glimpse I could see that the woman knew who I was. She met my eyes square, and held them square, as she stepped aside to let us pass. My laugh died short, but that foolish grin stayed on my face. And just as my look broke away, I could have sworn that her eyes filled with tears.

For some reason, I couldn't tell what, my heart started beating fast.

"Who was that woman?" I asked my friend.

"Don't you know her?" She gave me a funny side glance.

"No. She looks pretty solemn. Maybe I've seen her somewhere."

"Well—that's Mrs. Peters. She's Jack Peters' wife. He don't live with her, you know."

So that was why the woman had looked so strangely. Some of her "kind friends," no doubt, had pointed me out to her as a "friendly" little service. But her eyes had filled with tears at the sight of me. Poor little woman!

All the happiness—such as it was—dropped out of me, all of a sudden. I felt like a murderer. I couldn't get the picture of that little, faded woman out of my head. The face showed that she had suffered. Well—I had suffered, too; was suffering then, in fact; but my face didn't show it. Oh, if she could only know the truth!

But I put that idea out of my head. She couldn't ever know the truth about me. There wouldn't be any use trying to let her know that I knew what pain was, as well as she did, and that I wasn't just a thoughtless, light woman, playing with her husband for fun. But how could Mrs. Peters ever understand my life? I could understand hers, all right, but if I could cross that gulf between us, why, she couldn't. That was all there was to it. People can never understand the class below them.

So I went on, sorry for that little woman, but unable to do anything.

Anyhow, I told myself, if Jack Peters hadn't stayed faithful to her, it was probably her own fault. That is the perpetual excuse of the woman who comes between a man and his wife— that the wife is somehow at fault.

But it wasn't till later that I saw this little woman's whole sad story, and knew that it wasn't anybody's fault—just the way things are.

One afternoon Jack called me up.

"Come on up to the saloon," he said. "My little Jack's up here, and I want you to see him."

Naturally I was all for that. To have a chance to play with a little child—oh, I can't tell you what it meant to me.

It was a dear little youngster, too. His blue eyes looked up at me as if he didn't care whether I was a prostitute or the Queen of England. Here I was at last with a tiny bit of a human being, who didn't know anything about men, nor about the "underworld," nor of passion, nor sorrow, nor judging other people's faults. I didn't know when I might have another chance. I played with that kid until he had to be taken home; and he didn't want to go.

After that, Jack used to send a porter up to the house for his son often, bringing him down to the saloon, and let me play with him. He saw how happy it made me; and by that time he was caring too much about me to think what that other poor woman, the baby's mother, must think.

And one day, with a laugh, Jack repeated a remark the little fellow had made—and I felt glad I was a prostitute, and not a mother, so that I might never be stabbed to the heart by a remark like that.

"If you scold me again, mamma, I won't live with you anymore; I'll just go and live with that sleepy girl, the one who plays with me."

He had called me "sleepy" because my eyes were weak, and gave me that look.

And Jack had thought it was funny. But then he was a man, and I forgave him.

There were other things Big Jack trained Little Jack to, that I could see were going to hurt the mother worse yet in the years to come. At the time I thought them cute and bright. He used to stand up to the bar, and the bartender would ask him, "What'll you have?" and the little fellow would speak up, "Pa'll take a lager, and I'll have a grape juice." And the men around the bar used to teach him how to smoke, and he would throw his head back and chew the end of a cigar as if he was the cheapest sport in town.

All this time I was sinking deeper and deeper into the spirit of the life I was living. Night after night it was the same—that little, plain parlor; that creaky piano; men coming in, with their talk, ordering drinks and trying to jolly up; fat Annie, who didn't work unless it was a rush night or she happened to want to; and that constant flow of dirty language from both men and women—curses, vile songs, the smell of whiskey and of disinfectants; and, later in the evening, the "work."

I was getting to take the "work" in an easier way; but I was miserably ill most of the time, and naturally I wasn't getting any better as the weeks passed by. I always had that awful fear hanging over my head—of the horror that was coming, with the doctor.

No wonder I kept myself filled, night after night, with drink and tobacco smoke until I didn't think or see or really live, at all, except in a sort of dim fog.

I knew I might be losing my good looks; I didn't care. I knew my health couldn't stand the way I was going; but what difference did it make?

My one comfort was Jack Peters. I told Jack my troubles, and he understood, and always told me it would come out all right. He was my great comfort—the only one I had.

So the days wore on; and two months had passed, and I was just getting ready to face my big trouble. Also, I was getting used to Jack Peters' nightly visits, and so was everybody else. Even Annie, though I could see she was tickled to death over something about it, got used to them. And I wondered more and more why she was so interested.

Then all of a sudden the whole truth came out.

It was late one morning. Jack hadn't left me yet. The whistle of the train, that reached Zephyr about noon-time, woke me up, and it wasn't very long afterward that I heard the front door of the house slam.

"Say, here comes Nellie!" exclaimed a voice.

Then the house door slammed again. Then came big Annie's voice, calling out—

"Alice! Oh, Alice! Get Jack awake and out of there, quick! Tell him Nellie's coming!" I heard her add, as if to herself, "Lord! I didn't expect that woman for two weeks!"

I heard her dart outside and slam the door.

Jack was awake. He didn't lose any time about getting up. It wasn't more than a minute or two before he stepped out into the parlor. I followed.

Alice

Out on the corner standing talking to Big Annie and one of the women from another house was Nellie, the landlady, dressed as I had seen her that day when she got onto the train. Annie was talking and joking with all her might, and I had to laugh to see how she was trying to hold Nellie back.

"Well, kid, shall I get out the back way?" Jack asked me, sort of laughing. "I guess I'll just stay around and say 'hello' to Nellie when she comes up."

I didn't see why he shouldn't.

"How well do you know her?" I asked, carelessly.

"Oh, we're old pals," answered Jack. "I've known Nellie— let's see—ever since she was in high school. Ten years, I guess."

Nellie reached the steps. Jack, smiling and kind, stepped forward to meet her. He looked too pleased.

"Why, hello there, Jack!" she called out. He shook hands with her and grinned. I watched the thing through the window, and could have killed both of them.

"You dog! You dog!" I kept saying over to myself, until I heard a chuckle just behind me. I turned around and saw Katie standing there, watching, too.

"It's all right, kid," said Katie.

"Look here, Katie," I said, facing her square. "Jack was Nellie's lover, wasn't he, before I came?"

Katie didn't want to answer. But I made her. "Sure he was, kid," said she. "But it wasn't your fault you done as you did. You didn't know."

"But why didn't Annie tell me?"

"Ask her," grinned Katie. "She done it on purpose. She hates Nellie."

And then Nellie came in, laughing and talking, hanging onto Jack—my Jack—with both arms. And out of the window I could see the other girls standing on the doorsteps of their houses, all down that block, and on the steps of the cribs

160

opposite, and all of them doubled up with laughing. They had been waiting for that day for two months. I felt shamed before the whole world.

"Here's Alice, Nellie," chattered Big Annie. "She's been working in the house ever since the day you left. She's a good money maker, too, the kid is."

"Well, I've got to be going," said Jack. "I'll come back tonight." He got out of the room; and when he got down to the street, seeing me staring out through the window, he winked at me. Then he walked on; and Mad Susie, who lived in a crib across the way, laughed after him in a kind of shrill shriek, and kept on shrieking until she went inside her little hovel and banged her red door.

Nellie went to put her things away, and I walked back into my own room to think it all over.

Nellie's lover! I had supposed he was my lover, not Nellie's. Well, we'd see about that. I was ready to go to that doctor for my operation, and every day and night I was pretty near ready to die; but here was a chance for a fight. I wasn't going to give up Jack Peters.

But what bothered me most was the thought that I had broken one of the hard-and-fast rules of a harlot's life. I had taken away another woman's lover.

During those two months I had been learning the unwritten laws that govern the underworld. Everything, at first, seemed upside down—just the reverse of the laws that rule the regular world, up above. But I came to see that those laws were very important; and maybe it was the ordinary laws that were upside down.

One of those laws was that no woman was ever supposed to give away to a respectable person the name of any man that had visited her.

Another law, just as important, was that no prostitute was

ever supposed to "cut out" any other prostitute, with her lover. It was this rule that I had broken.

I was surprised when I first heard of this law. In the world I was used to, it seemed to me it was just the other way around. If a girl ever got a chance at another girl's sweetheart, most of the time, she would think it quite a feather in her cap to "cut the other girl out." But in the underworld, all the women were outcasts together. They had a lot of real human sympathy for each other. The last thing they would ever do would be to take away another woman's chance of getting out of the life. And this was exactly what a regular lover might mean.

Of course, in larger cities where there are houses of all sorts, there are a good many shades and castes, just as in respectable life. But here in this little place it was all democratic. And, of course, too, there are some women who will break that unwritten law on purpose, and do everything they can to win away another woman's sweetheart; but they aren't the majority, and they aren't looked upon with any friendship or favor by the mass of the women. They suffer for what they do. On the other hand, some madams won't even entertain in their house the lover of a woman in another house except just to let him buy drinks.

And here I had taken away the lover of my own landlady— or had been trying to. I felt real bad.

But then I thought—

"Why, after all, it was Big Annie that did it. I didn't know Jack was Nellie's. I was just green to the life."

Just then, outside my door, I hear Annie and Nellie talking. Annie was showing Nellie how much the house had earned in Nellie's absence, and going over the business affairs. The walls were thin, and I could hear every word they said; and I supposed they knew it. They came to the end of their business talk. Then Nellie, in a changed voice, said—

"Say, Annie, I wanted to ask you. Has Jack been around here much in the last two months? How's he been amusing himself?"

I could just hear the satisfaction in Big Annie's voice, as she said, trying to sound sympathetic—

"Aw, say, Annie, it's awful. I thought you ought to know it. Jack's been laying up with the kid."

Nellie kept her voice very quiet.

"How long?"

"Since the very first night that you went away. The kid didn't know who he was. I tried to stop him"—her tone was fine—"but, gee, what could I do?"

Nellie stopped to think a moment. Her voice was shaking, in spite of everything, when she asked:

"Didn't the other girls put the kid wise?"

"Now, honest, Nellie," said Irish Annie, seeming real indignant about it, "that just shows the sort of a bunch they are around here. There wasn't a one of them girls in this whole town that would tell the kid the truth. They all thought it was a fine joke on you."

I thought she overdid it a bit. And I guess Nellie thought so, too. Because she didn't ask the natural question, "Then why didn't you tell the kid yourself?" but just said, "All right; give me that money."

I heard her push her chair back. A moment later the front door slammed.

I came out of my room and faced Annie.

"I heard all about it," I said. "Where's Nellie gone?"

"Uptown, I s'pose," Annie answered. She was jubilant. "She's going to get drunk, I bet. Kid, you're a smart one. 'Tain't every day a girl like you comes into the business. Nellie ain't so much. She's bossed me for a long time—a long time," she added, seeming to go back over a lot of memories in her mind.

Afterwards we heard that Nellie had gone drifting from

one saloon to another, drinking more and more and cursing and talking about Jack and me and Big Annie. I stayed in the house, and kept out of the way when Nellie came back, late for supper ugly with the drink. I was worrying about the coming night, and what would happen. She kept going after the whiskey-bottle.

It wasn't late before Jack walked in; he was expecting trouble, I could see, and I liked him for coming right out and facing it.

It was all right for an hour. Jack and Annie got to talking over the girls in another house, and Jack said, "Well, I can't see anything in that Belle. I just can't see anything in her at all."

"That's funny. And you ain't particular," broke in Nellie, suddenly. Her voice was as nasty as could be. She hadn't spoken for a long time. We all looked around.

"What's it to you whether I'm particular or not?" asked Jack.

"Well, you ain't," screamed Nellie with a curse. Her temper flared up hot and so did her voice.

Jack kept his voice down, but he was mad clear through.

"I wasn't so particular ten years ago, that's true enough," he said.

"Ten years ago? You know what you done ten years ago?" yelled Nellie. "I wouldn't be here today if it hadn't been for you ten years ago, you ———. And now you go chasing off with the first kid that comes along, just like you did when you got married to that other little fool. Oh, you call yourself a man, you ———." She broke out into curses that made Jack turn red and bite his lip.

"Come in here, kid," he called. "I've got something to say to you."

I didn't move; I was afraid to. Nellie never took her eyes off Jack.

"No, you don't, damn you," she yelled, and grabbing the

whiskey-bottle by the neck, threw it at him. He ducked quick, and the bottle went flying past his head and into my room, where it hit the wall and broke. Then Nellie made for Jack, half-crazy; and I was glad she didn't have a knife.

Jack just grabbed her wrists and held her off. He was too strong for her; and pretty soon he had her sitting down on a chair crying; then, after a good while, Nellie was all broken down and sobbing.

"Get her to bed some way, Annie," said Jack, "and then you and the kid come up to my place. I want to make a proposition to you."

With that he walked out; and we got Nellie to bed.

I asked Annie, as we were walking up through town to Jack's saloon—

"Had Jack and Nellie been together long, then?"

"Long? My, I should say so. Years and years. Why, kid, I've heard Nellie say they went to high school together. And that was where Jack won her, and she ended up in this life. He broke away for a time, and got married, and still came back to her; and that's why Jack and his wife don't live together now. The wife was Nellie's chum, too, in years gone by."

I was ready to face my big ordeal. I had saved up a hundred dollars and was bracing my courage to undergo a "criminal" operation.

The other girls on the "line" in Zephyr knew about my condition and what I would have to face. They were very sympathetic. "It's all right, kid; we've all been through it," they told me. But they none of them went so far as to say it wasn't horrible.

I don't think there was a single woman on the line there

who hadn't been with child at some time in the past—generally when she was new to the life. My experience, I found, was very common—to live as a "free-lance" for a year or so, then to come up against this new trouble and to have it wreck everything. The girl who starts in for herself, as I did, knows a few things, but she rarely knows enough to keep herself out of trouble. And all through my life in the "underworld," in many different houses in different parts of the country, I haven't met one woman in ten who escaped.

Practically every one of my friends ended up her story with, "And so that was where I wrecked my health, kid, and I've never been good for anything since." Most of them had never fully recovered. Some had been in good high-class houses before; but they had had this sort of an operation, and their health had been broken. Now they were condemned to drag on through the cheaper houses, and see the worst class of men until they died, torn with disease.

No wonder that I had said to myself, a hundred times—

"Oh, I'll just go ahead and have my baby. I want him"—oh, how I wanted him!—"and I can't face this ghastly thing. It isn't natural, and it isn't right. It might kill me; it's almost certain to hurt me; and, anyhow, I've got a right to be a mother. Every woman has a right to be a mother, even if she—"

But when I reached that part of it, I would just lose heart and give up. What I would have said was, "even if she isn't married." And that wasn't true. Women who aren't married had better die rather than bring a child into the world; because the world will take its revenge on that child. And it's a fearful revenge.

I wasn't going to give birth to a son and have him wear stripes some day, or kill himself. I couldn't go contrary to that great, cruel idea—the idea of marriage. The world had that idea; and who was I, to try to go against the world?

Jack Peters told me there was one doctor right in Zephyr who would fix me up. He was the village druggist, an old fellow. There was another doctor there, who had the best practice, who wouldn't touch such a case as mine for any money.

But this druggist-doctor didn't appeal to me exactly. He knew I was a prostitute; and he wouldn't care much whether I lived or died. I reasoned that if I could go down to Westville and get a doctor there, one who didn't know what I was, I would be better treated. It might save my life for me.

So Jack bought my railroad ticket and told me that if I wanted a little money, he would send it to me; but that he didn't have much. I went down to Westville alone, as desperate as I ever was in my life.

Westville is one of the largest cities on the Pacific Coast.

I only went to what I thought were safe doctors—those who had the most expensive offices in the business part of town with electric signs to guide their patrons. I told them plainly what I wanted. I knew it was illegal. So did they.

"Two hundred dollars," said the first, a respectable-looking man, instantly. I hadn't told him I was from the "line." I gave my name as Mrs. Boyd.

I couldn't stand that price. I left and went to another.

"I don't make a practice of handling such cases," said this one—a brisk, middle-aged man with a pointed beard. "But I'll see you through for—say—one hundred and fifty dollars. It's a risk."

That was more than I had, too—I couldn't earn that in two more months. And I couldn't afford to wait so long. It would kill me.

So I tried yet again. "Two hundred with drugs, and two hundred and fifty the other way," said this man.

I went still further. "Mrs.—Boyd, you say?" questioned a young fellow. "Er—in what profession is your husband?"

"He's a broker," I said.

"Well—I could possibly see you through for one hundred as a first payment, and additional payments as demanded," he said, carefully. That proposition to "bleed" my husband's pocketbook was a nice one. If I had had a husband, and taken that up, we would have been paying that young doctor yet.

To make this short, I went to other doctors, but not one of them named a figure under one hundred dollars. The more stylish ones came higher.

If I'd explained that I was a woman of the underworld, the price would have come down—and so would the quality of the service. Underworld women don't have any friends who will prosecute in case of death.

The only man that refused was an old French surgeon—a tall, thin old man with a white mustache. "Get out of here—get out of here!" he cried, with his hands raised. "I wouldn't touch your case for a million." He was the only one I visited that wasn't willing to stretch a point.

In the end I went back to Zephyr. I put my case into the hands of that village druggist and doctor. I had to take the risk; I was poor.

At first he said he would "see me through" for twenty-five dollars. I paid him that. He performed the work. Later on he collected thirty-five more from Big Annie, who was taking care of me. At least, Big Annie said he did; but from things I learned about her, I knew there was another possibility.

So at last the horror was over with. I didn't come very far from dying. Of course, that doctor didn't think I was worth much to the world, and didn't give me proper care after the worst part was through; and it was just luck that brought me out finally without blood-poisoning. There wasn't a hospital in town, so I stayed right in the house, and paid Annie a dollar and a half a day to look after me while I was sick.

Five days after the operation, weak and dizzy and sad and sick, I dragged myself up out of bed. I had a queer, unreasonable streak of pride on; I wouldn't ask Jack Peters for a cent, no matter how broke I was.

"How much money have I got left, Annie?" I asked her.

"It's all gone, kid," she said. "But you needn't worry. I'll take care of you for a while yet, and you pay me later."

"That isn't my way," I answered. "I'll go back to work tonight."

It was part desperation, part madness, part of my old natural obstinacy I did go back to work that night; and I made six dollars. Then I collapsed and was sick in bed for two days; then I went back to work again for a night and was sick again for a week; then I started to get stronger, and as soon as I got stronger I would go back to work and pretty near kill myself. I didn't care if I did die; I had nothing left to live for.

I came out of that trial changed in many ways. I seemed to have more sympathy for other people. I could see their troubles plainer, and their faults plainer, too, so the faults excused themselves. And that was where I started to quit judging others; today I haven't it in me to feel real hard toward anyone for anything they do. So the results of it all were good in one way. But it seemed as if, after that time, I wanted children more than ever; and that emptiness in my life has always kept getting worse, right to today.

"Alice, you're lucky that doctor left you in as good shape as he did," Big Annie said one day. And then she told me a story that was quite famous in that town; I heard it afterward from others.

"This old Dr. Phillips, the one who treated you, got the scare of his life one day about ten years ago. Up to that affair, he was the main physician of this town. It was some town in them days, too; that was before it 'died' and there was a lot of dance halls and gambling joints, and a big 'line.'

"There was one woman lived in this very house. Kitty, they called her. She was as bad as the worst—got into a fight every time she got drunk, which was right along. She stayed that way till one day along comes a fellow named Jim North, a professional gambler.

"He was a hard one, too. Well, he started out being Kitty's 'man.' A regular one he was, too—took every cent Kitty made, and gambled it away, and used to beat her up to make her give him more. But she was crazy about him, and it's true that he never paid a bit of attention to any other woman.

"I don't know why it was; but both of 'em seemed to change after a little while. Kitty cut out the booze little by little; and Jim—he'd never drank much—got so he wouldn't throw his money around so free. The girls got to understand that they was both saving money—the money Jim won by gambling, and the money Kitty made in the house—and that they was planning to get married when they had enough, and get out of the sporting life.

"Every one of the girls took to helping them along whenever a chance turned up. And things was going along just fine, when one day Kitty fell sick. She'd been careless. It was the same trouble you just got over, kid.

"Well, it seems Kitty didn't tell Jim North anything about her fix. Ashamed to, I guess. But she just waited till she was sure, then she went to this same Dr. Phillips you went to—at that time he just about owned the town.

"He performed the operation on her. And I suppose he thought, 'Oh, she's just a prostitute,' because he never took care of her right. It wasn't three days before she was dead.

"They took the news to Jim, while he was sitting in a card-game down in a saloon. He was a gambler, and wasn't given to showing his feelings. He went right on playing, and they said afterward he cleaned up every cent of money around that table before he quit. Then he took his winnings, got up from the table, and walked out of the place without saying a word.

"Jim kept control of himself so good, the girls all come to think he didn't care. He got up a fine funeral for Kitty, and spent a lot of money, and managed everything himself just like as if she had been his wife. Then, when she was underground, he just said, careless, to some of his friends—

"'Well, boys, I guess it's some other town for me.'

"Some of the boys walked with him to go to the train. Jim stopped off into a shop and bought a gun and cartridges, loaded the gun and stuck it into his pocket, saying, 'I'm going over to a new town and I may need this.'

"Up on the next block, as they were crossing the street, Jim dodged over so he was on the inside of the sidewalk. And just as they passed that building where the doctor's office is, he broke away from his friends and ran up those stairs.

"He was too quick for them. They heard him burst open the door, upstairs, and then came a shot. Then Jim ran downstairs, just as quick as he had come up, and saying quiet, 'I've got that —— —— ——; now for the train,' he just walked along with the boys. And he got out of town all right, inside of five minutes.

"But he hadn't killed the doctor. Just wounded him, and the man got well. Jim had killed his reputation, though, and that doctor's a poor man today, 'cause the story got out all over town. Nobody ever heard of Jim again, though it was reported he committed suicide.

"And yet they say that outcasts don't care."

❖❖❖

The night Nellie, my landlady, and Jack Peters had had their big quarrel over me, Jack asked Big Annie and myself to come up to his saloon. "I've got a proposition to make to you," he said.

"See here, you girls won't be able to live with Nellie any more, after this. She'll try to get even on you, Alice, and she won't like Annie any too well, either. Now, I think you girls had better get into a house of your own. Did you know the Twins went away today?"

The Twins were two girls who were in the business together at Zephyr. They looked so much alike you could hardly tell them apart unless they were together. We knew they intended leaving.

"Why don't you take the Twins' house, you two? Annie, I'll set you up in what drink and other stuff you need to begin on. You can pay me back later. You run the house, and the kid here'll work with you, same as she did when Nellie was away. If you want a third girl, get one from Westville."

I could see Big Annie swelling up with pride at the thought of being a real madam, not just a substitute one. Her ship had come in at last.

"Sure, we'll do it," she said.

The next day was pay day. It was afternoon when Nellie came out of her room, looking tired and worn out.

"Say, Nellie," Annie told her, "if you think I'm going to stay around here after the way you treated me last night, you're off. I'm going to move today. And the kid's going with me."

"That so? All right, then, you can go." Nellie didn't sound a bit mad; only tired and lifeless. She knew she had lost Jack Peters for good and all. And she was pretty old in the game, and losing her health fast.

She turned to me.

"Did you say you were going, too, Alice? Can't you stay at least tonight? It's pay day on the railroad today."

"No; there's something wrong around here," I said. "I didn't know anything about what was doing, but I guess you and me couldn't get along after that."

So Annie and I packed up our things then and there, and moved over to that other house before supper. Jack had sent down some beer and whiskey, and towels and stuff, and there was furniture of a sort in the house already. We saw as much of a crowd that night as we would have seen in Nellie's house; and Big Annie started to feel real prosperous right there.

A couple of days later a girl from another house, paying us a visit, told us, "Nellie's gone away—did you know that?"

It was true; the poor woman had packed up her things and quietly left town, without letting anybody know. So far as I know she was never seen in Zephyr again, and her life and Jack Peters', which had been so strangely bound together for so many years, were separated at last for good and all.

I never heard of Nellie again. That is the way with women one meets in this life; they come and go, and they drift here and there, never staying long at one place or in one house, excepting sometimes in the larger cities; restless, wandering, never contented, always thinking they can do better somewhere else.

Big Annie's airs, now that she had a house of her own, got worse and worse. She had been bossy enough while she was just taking Nellie's place; but that was nothing to what she was now.

I was broken in health for the time being, and while I would be well one day, and able to work one night, I would be sick for the next three or four, and have to lay off. It seemed as if my heart was gone, and my courage; I couldn't bring myself back into the old way of doing. I didn't even care enough to drink. I was just weak.

This didn't add to Annie's good temper any. She took care of me at first as well as anybody could have. Then she got tired of it. She got so she would scold at me pretty often; and besides, I wasn't making any money, but was just dragging along, as so many women drag, always a little behind, and always in debt to the house.

Jack Peters pulled me through.

"Annie's getting worse all the time," I told him one night. "I can't work, and I ain't making any money, and she keeps nagging at me. I can't help it if I do just drag along. That operation was enough to kill anybody."

"You say she scolds you, kid?" I hadn't told him anything about it before; I'm the kind that keeps my mouth shut about things like that.

Now that I had begun, it all came out. "She nags at me all the time. I've been sick longer and worse than I'd thought for, that's all. I can't blame her, though. Of course, I'm not making any money at all."

Jack didn't say anything then. But the next day he called me up, and I went to his saloon—just as Annie and I had done before.

"Kid, I'm going to take you away from Annie," he said. "Nellie's old house is vacant. Of course, you're a real young girl, and all that, but I think you've got brains enough to run a little house. Let's get a couple of Westville girls up, anyhow, and make the try. I'll stand back of you."

A house of my own! My Jack was kind. I felt better right away.

Annie and I had a quarrel when I told her about that. She wasn't like Nellie—she couldn't hold her temper so well. But at first she tried another trick.

"I've been meaning to warn you, kid," she said. "There must be something the matter with you. I've had several complaints from men. You'd do best to go back to Westville."

I got mad. "You show me a single man who says that," I told her. "Till then, this place is good enough for me." Then she got mad and threatened to hold my clothes for debt; but Jack had given me the $15 to pay her, and she couldn't keep me from going.

This time Jack fixed things up fine. He sent down some new furniture to the little house; and he had his nickel-in-the-slot piano from the saloon taken down there, and he sent down a special selection of drinks, with different kinds of whiskey—I was the only madam in that little town who could ask that question, "Rye or Scotch?" of her guests.

I was very young looking, in spite of my sickness; in fact, I wasn't yet twenty-one. The girls I had working for me were both a good deal older than I was. It used to tickle my pride, when a man asked for a drink, to get up to serve him myself, and see him stare. It felt great to be a "madam." And I always loved to run things.

As to making the money from the girls, knowing all the time how they made it, that bothered me a little—just a little. But I told myself, just as I suppose any business man tells himself, that that was the way the thing was managed. You had to have others working for you; and you had to take a good bit of their money, if ever you wanted to get anywhere. I couldn't see that it was any worse to take money made by other girls in a brothel than it is for a man to take money made by workingmen in a factory. And can't yet.

In my new position as madam, I got to know something of how the law looked upon the houses of prostitution.

Every month, that policeman—the only one in town—came around and collected $5 from each girl, and $10 from the landlady. If any Westville girls were in town on the first day of the month they had to pay up their $5, too. The cop used to give a regular receipt for the fee; but I don't know where the money went to.

Then there was a liquor license to pay of $25 a year. I went into the house the latter part of April, and only had to pay part of that fee, but on July 1 they collected the whole amount.

In that town there wasn't any "protection" to be paid for, except that $5. The house rent only amounted to $30 a month for me; the girls who lived alone in the little cribs paid a rent of four bits a day. I laugh now when I write these figures; but then, I have since seen San Francisco and other cities, and the huge rents extorted there from the houses; and I have heard of the crib girls, in days when cribs were common here, paying for the privilege of living in them. And naturally, the higher the rent, the more the girls must make—any way they can.

There was a doctor in Zephyr who was supposed to make an examination of us girls, and who used to appear regularly and make his collection of $5 for a fee; but never a sign of an examination did he make.

I had a real examination just once while I was there. Big Annie, down the street, had never got over the shock to her pride. Her house was at the corner of the block, and she used to stand on her porch and yell at every man she saw entering my place: "Don't go there—you know what you'll get!" So I just paid a doctor—the best one in town, not that druggist— to look me over and give me a certificate; and after that Big Annie quieted down.

Jack Peters made his regular headquarters at my house. He used to keep an eye on all the business affairs, though he never asked me for a cent of money. I would have given him money if he had asked, though, because he was so kind and I came to care for him and depend on him so.

There was only one thing that bothered me; and that got worse and worse. I kept meeting that poor little wife of Jack's. And after hearing her story—how Jack had loved Nellie first, and ruined her, and then married this woman probably in a fit of remorse, and later gone back to Nellie again—I felt sorry for her. I would have done anything I could for her—short of giving up Jack.

One evening, after I had been running that house for several months, I was sitting in that little parlor. There came a knock on the door. I opened it. Standing under that red electric light on the porch was the bowed figure of this little woman—Jack's wife.

It was up to me to speak. But it didn't come easy. I was real surprised.

"Good evening. Er—won't you come in?" I said.

She stood there a minute, trembling, and I could see it was a lot harder for her to speak than it had been for me. I thought what an effort it must have been for her to come to that place.

"I came to see if Jack was down here," she said finally. "I wanted to see Jack, or—to ask you about him." She spoke very slow.

"He ain't here yet," I answered, sort of quick and hurried. That girl inside her room started to sing, just then, and the little woman shuddered.

"When he comes," said Mrs. Peters, "will you—would you—ask him for some money for me? He is supposed to pay the grocery bill and other bills; but he hasn't paid anything—lately."

I felt awfully ashamed. Jack, of late, had been spending quite a bit on me.

"I'll do what I can," I answered. "Sure."

"Please do," she said, and I could see she was kind of dignified, for all of her being so little and weak. "We can't get anything to eat, little Jack and me, the way things are now."

All of a sudden she put her shawl up over her face, turned away and fairly ran down those steps and up the street.

I told Jack about it that night, and he fixed things up and promised not to let them go that way again.

◆❖◆

A few weeks later I was glad to leave Zephyr for good and all. The big foundry, that made half the life of the place, was closed. It killed the town. For my part, I wasn't sorry, because meeting with that woman sort of got on my mind till I worried about it nights. I was pretty sick, too; and Jack advised me to go back to Westville and rest until I got strong. He said he would support me and come to see me often there.

I was back in Westville. As the train rolled in, I couldn't help thinking what a different girl I was from the girl that had left there to go into a house at Zephyr.

For one thing, I was a year older. In that year I had been in three different houses of prostitution; had stood an operation; had associated only with one kind of woman, had hardened into a thorough "sporting woman." Yet in some ways I knew I was softer-hearted than I was before; my trouble, losing my baby and all, had made me more gentle.

There were two things I was looking forward to. One was seeing Harry Marsh, the man who had ruined me; I was sort of curious to see him now, because when I was in trouble, a year ago, he had turned me loose and sent me into the sporting life. Another was seeing my chum, Ella, the poor girl who was to be a mother, and who had gone to the Crittenden Home with the money I had given her.

I didn't dare think of what was deeper still in my heart—the longing to see my sister Emma. I hadn't let myself think about Emma. But when the train was rolling toward Westville and I knew I was to stay there, for a while at any rate, the thought of Emma came to me and stuck there. It hurt worse than anything.

But first of all, my business was to get well. I was so weak I could hardly walk; the jarring of the train pretty nearly killed me. Yet this was months after my operation.

If the train was hard for me to stand, then the hack that took me to my old boarding house was worse. I could hardly walk up those stairs—the same ones I had rushed up, that night when Grandma Smith had turned me out and I had gone to live with Henry Marsh.

Jennie, the landlady, my old friend, greeted me with:

"Why, here's little Alice back again. Say, I don't think I've got a key right now that'll open Mr. Marsh's room."

"You needn't try," I answered. "Give me a room by myself—an inside one. A cheap one, too, Jennie; I'm sick, and I'm poor."

She was surprised, I guess, but she took me to the room. And once there, I collapsed, and had to have a doctor sent up. Jennie was kept busy the rest of the day piling hot applications on me.

"She ought to be moved to an outside room," said the doctor.

So when it came time for Harry Marsh to get home, Jennie went out of the room. She must have held Harry up on the landing, for a few minutes later she came in, without a word, and started to move me.

"What are you doing?" I asked, pretty weak. Then I knew. "No, don't do that," I said. "I'm going to stay here."

She put me down again; and a little later there was a knock on the door, and in came Harry.

"Say, little girl, I'm awfully glad to see you back again," he said heartily, and all of a sudden I found out that I didn't love him, and didn't hate him now—I had done both—but that he was just ordinary. He had no hold on me now.

"So you're out of your other troubles now, are you, Alice? Well, I'm glad it's all through with. I've thought of you a lot. I—I hope you don't blame me any for it, girl."

"No; I don't blame you exactly," I said slowly. "Only you know, and I know, that there was one time when you could have prevented me going the way I went—and you did not."

"Well, at any rate, maybe we can get together again now you're back in Westville," Harry said, trying not to notice. "I'm still living in the same old room, you know."

"Harry," I said, "you and I are through. We're through for good and all. The sooner you realize that the better."

I only saw Harry Marsh once more in my whole life. I got well and wanted to move to another rooming house to get away from him. But I chose a time to leave when I knew he would be just coming home at noon-time, because—well, because I wanted him to see me going.

Harry came along one side of the hall, and I took the other side.

"Good-by, Mr. Marsh," I said, bowing as if he was just an acquaintance.

"Good-by," he returned, lifting his hat; then he stepped over in front of me quickly, and blocked the way.

"Excuse me," I began. He put out both hands and took me by the shoulders, bringing me around till I faced him square.

"Look at me," he commanded. "You look at me."

Well—I obeyed. He stood there a long time, until I started to laugh at him; then he sort of jerked away and stamped off down the hallway. I never saw him again.

The first thing I wanted to do, now that I was better and able to get about, was to look up my old chum, Ella. I hadn't heard from her in two months, and I was worried. I went around to the Crittenden Home.

"She ain't here. She ain't been here for some time," said the attendant. I thought she was pretty bad tempered about it, and I wondered why. But at the same time I was more worried than ever.

Her friend, the saloon man, who was the father of her baby, ought to know.

After two or three calls at his saloon I finally caught him over the phone.

"Where's Ella?" I asked.

"Who are you?" I was sure the voice sounded sort of alarmed.

"I'm Alice Smith."

"Oh!" He seemed relieved. "Well, I can't talk over the phone. Be in front of here at 12 o'clock. Good-by."

The saloon man—his name was Jim—came to the door of the saloon, saw me, and beckoned.

He led me right on toward the back, through a sort of shed, out into a back yard all littered up with old bottles and papers, dodged between a couple of buildings, and finally turned into a dark, close little passageway. I could see that it was an old musty house that had been moved back long ago to make room for new buildings.

And here, in a room so dark I could hardly see her, was Ella.

She was lying on a sort of couch. When she heard us coming she started up in alarm. "It's only Alice," I said; then she fairly ran up to me and hugged me and cried—you would have thought the poor girl never expected to see a human being again.

I started to get mad. There was something about all this I didn't like.

Jim stepped over to the couch.

"Look here, Alice," he said. "Ain't he a fine baby?"

I took it in my arms—and pretty nearly broke down. "It's a fine baby, all right," I answered, kind of rough, "but what kind of a place do you call this to keep him in? Is this the best you can do for Ella?"

Jim looked sort of embarrassed. He turned to Ella. My eyes were getting used to the light, and I could see that both Ella and that poor little baby were just as white as a sheet, and that Ella had great rings under her eyes.

"Alice, sit down on that box and I'll tell you about it," said Ella. "I'm hiding here. I'm afraid all the time. You see, I ran away from the Crittenden Home."

"Why, what was the matter?"

"After the baby was born they were going to keep me there. I was afraid they would take the baby away—people used to come and adopt children, sometimes, and pay the home. Well, I was pretty weak, and the work they gave me to do was in the nursery; and one night they forgot to take away the keys."

She gave a weak little laugh.

"There was three of us, Alice—three girls, and three babies, and three suitcases. There was just thirty cents in the bunch. 'Here's the car—we'd better ride,' said one of the girls, and we got aboard, bound to get away from there, if it took our last cent.

"So I found Jim, and he got afraid the authorities would be after him, and he hid me in here. I've been here a month."

She hadn't any clothes to speak of, and the baby was wrapped in an old petticoat; and there hadn't been decent food, or anything. I could have killed Jim. But I felt fine that afternoon when I cashed a ten-dollar check Jack Peters had just sent me, and spent just about all of it buying baby clothes and things.

I was pretty sure the Home would not be so very anxious to get back its inmates. So we moved Ella to a decent little room. Jim sort of hung back; I couldn't make out his position at all.

Since I was better now, I went to "work" again. I didn't go into a regular house, but I made myself known to several saloon men, who used to call me up when they had customers who were willing to spend money.

Then I took to doing as lots of those Westville girls used to do—traveling around the country to make money on pay days and holidays in the small towns, and in between, picking up what I could get in Westville. It was a wretched life, and I was so lonesome I couldn't stand it long. After a while I found a little six-girl house not far out of Westville; and there I stayed.

There was great excitement just about the time I came to this house. That little town had a mayor who was a stock rancher and a pretty rich man. He had come on a few visits to the house, had got to know one of the girls, and had regularly fallen in love with her.

All the girls in the house were looking forward to the wedding. It was one of those things that only happen very seldom; but when they do happen, they wake up all the hope that is in the heart of every prostitute.

I had a chance to get acquainted with the lucky girl. She was a lovely character, too—as sympathetic as anybody I ever saw.

I told her about Ella.

"Oh, I'm so glad I'm going to be married!" she exclaimed right away. "See here, Alice—I'll have a big place, a ranch and everything; and I want that poor little girl to come and stay with me for a month. She'll be welcome for that long; and by the end of that time she ought to feel a lot stronger, and maybe something will turn up."

That wasn't the spirit of cold charity. That was human understanding and love. And Ella took it that way; and stayed there a month while she and that dear baby got over their paleness; and while she was there we tried to get that Jim to give the child a name, but he left the country, and later another man, a good man, found Ella and married her, baby and all. So today—and I always love to think of it—she is a happy woman.

VOL. 123. 62nd YEAR. TWENTY PAGES.

EXTRA

ussins Attac

The Bulletin

SAN FRANCISCO, THURSDAY, JANUARY 25, 1917.

200 UNDERWORLD WOMEN PL
WITH THE REV. SMITH A

WHAT SHALL WE DO? THEY

Women of the redlight entering the Rev. Paul Smith's church, at Leavenworth and O'Farrell streets, th

ister, Unable
Reply, Saddened
w Voice of Outcasts

ul Smith, head of the present vice
ay stood in his own church before
audience ever assembled in San
perhaps, in the world—an audi-
two hundred women of the
bedraggled finery and bear-
faces the marks of ill health.
despite the traces of rouge—
a voice of sorrow:
that I have ever been sadder
m right now.
ome some questions that
ered. I cannot answer
me is to be done?"

local underworld that this dramatic
visit was to be made. A crowd of
made onlookers had assembled, in
addition to motion-picture, and
cameras, men and newspaper reporters.

The women passed to the church
r along a lane in the crowd
ich filled the overflowed deck
spicly and overflowed down
de streets
ESITED INTO CHURCH
seeing how many of the women

WHO WILL ANSWER?

Over two hundred women of the
underworld today asked the
Rev. Paul Smith, leader in the present anti-vice crusade.
the eternal question "What Is To Be Done?"
The question was asked in the Methodist Episcopal Church
at Leavenworth and O'Farrell streets, where the women had
assembled.

It was perhaps the most dramatic confrontation of the
underworld with the upper world in all the history of the age-
old problem of the social evil.
The Rev. Mr. Smith's answer was in effect, "I do not
know."
He said the whole startling experience was the saddest in
his life.

Tonight a mass meeting is to be held in Dreamland Rink.
Will an attempt be made there to answer the query of the
Magdalens?

there were, the Rev. Smith,
the door to stop his nud asked
form to stop the main mody
extruded, excepting the bystanders soci-
porters. Then the overflowed news-
than onepor than one hour later they
were forced to run the gauntlet of the

As the women passed through the
start some busy their heads, some
out their faces from sight there lovered
murely under the collars of cheap
overcoats

THE MINISTER SPEAKS.

Within the church, when all
were seated and the doors closed,
the Rev. Smith rose and addressed
them.
"I do not know what this morning," he said, "while
ing I received a telephone call
mons, but said and me and said
of a house

SPEAKS FOR WOMEN.

A woman neatly clad in a suit of
shepherd's plaid, a fitellgent appearance and evidently controlling
her nervousness by a strong effort
will, arose and took the seat which
the pastor offered.
The Rev. Smith, he made a brief
speech, in which he said;
"I do not want to be
derstood as waging
against vice."

If I would meet a group of women
of the underworld and confer with
then.
I consented.
"The woman who called me up
will now go to the platform I should be
pleased to have her occupy the
place."

Magdalenes Throng
Church in Dramatic
Cry for Help in Woe

It is not trying to persecute
any of the women who are the
victims of the conditions
instigated on the poor.
We will help too things that I have
town district, and that is as far

"I am very glad to have this
opportunity to confer with you
and to hear a word from the
other side of the problem. No
one than I am more sympa-
thetic to the desires I am. Any woman
who desires to some
older, she wants to find
help to the best of my abilities. I
cannot the attacking I agree
with only the exploiters who
who exland and men who make
the traffic

"Our investigations have nothing to do with the Examiner and
call. They have that printed things
in my paper that I did not say.
My experiences have been set
forth only under their own sig-
lot is them one been whole
not put in there."

The woman who in
platform that
this

There was a volley of loud ap-
plause from the two hundred women in the auditorium.
"Most of the women here pres-
came from the districts 'Age continued. "The sphere are among
the well-to-do. Those girls are
better off in houses of prostitution than they would of in
drinkable houses at least they
get what little protection the
(Continued on Next Page, Col. L)

LATEST NEWS

GRAND CROSS GIVEN—MACKENS

BERLIN, Jan. 25 (via London)—
upon Field Marshal von Mackensen the Grand
Cross, it was officially announced today.
At the same time he named the Field Mar-
thanks, of the Fatherland for
(Note—The only one of the Field Mar
Cross in Fe

LATES

SELECTED LETTERS
TO THE EDITOR

WOMAN-MADE CIVILIZATION BORN OF LOVE TO DESTROY INEQUALITY AND INJUSTICE

In their letters to The Bulletin many outcasts say men are kinder to fallen women than women. This is only a seeming truth. Men give women the first kick and the last. Prostitutes mistake men's mock good fellowship for friendship. Men have only contempt for the fallen. On all sides I see hostility to their victims revealed by their attitude toward the story of Alice Smith. They scoff at reforming a prostitute. Scores of men fill pulpits, but only a few have had a public word of sympathy for the moans that come up so pitifully from this man-made underworld. Editors sneer at the tragic outcries of sinking women. The more, in their own private lives, these editors have done to create Alice Smiths the more bitter are their sneers. I have followed all the letters in The Bulletin offering aid to the outcasts, and I noticed that of the helping hands outstretched 90 percent came from women. For the first time women of the upper world really understand how much they have in common with women of the underworld.

I am proud of my sex when I see irreproachable, high-minded women like Mrs. Tucker, Miss McLeon and Mrs. George bravely pioneer their way to help the lost women escape from their hideous lives. I, too, would help, but my husband will not allow it. He will not let me even know a woman who has been talked about. He himself told me that before we married he was with two women in one night, and yet he always thinks women guilty and wants me to avoid a woman who looks queer or has been divorced. He is terribly down on suffragists. He thinks women inferior to men and should stay at home and be good wives and mothers. His idea of my being a good wife is to do as he tells me, always agree with him and to think he is the cleverest man in California.

Yet he is a good man and is thought to be an excellent husband. He is very prominent in all movements for public improvements. He thinks women will set back progress because they are so narrow-minded.

I obey my husband. I have obeyed him for years. I began obeying him because I wanted to show my love. Now I obey because he supports me. I don't know how to earn a living in any other way. So I have a great sympathy for women of the underworld who must depend not on the whims and passions of one man in a day, but of ten. Think of ten husbands in one day! Ten odors of tobacco, ten odors of whiskey, ten gross, sensual, egotistical, tyrannical brutes in one day! But I sometimes think that if we wives ever told our story it would be as horrible as that of Alice Smith. The worst of our story is that it can never be told. Marriage is finished and settled. To get a new husband would do me no good. I have what is known as a "model husband." Another husband would probably be worse. I understand my husband's faults. It would be more than I could stand to find out another man.

Men are not kind to women of the underworld. They are not kind to their wives. To be sure my husband gives me my meals, and, in a growling manner he would not use to any man of his acquaintance, signs checks for my dresses, but he is not kind. Sometimes I feel that I am only a cheap, safe mistress who cannot escape.

I believe that my husband and men are quite unconscious of their brutality both to women of the upper and of the lower world. They are as nature intended—violent, dynamic, destructive creatures with incidental uses, but never intended to do anything fine. In creating hybrid grapes, after the act of fertilization, the wind wafts away the male. Among lower animals the male knows not his offspring. The tomcat kills his male children that he may be the only tomcat in the neighborhood. Frequently, the deer murders his young. Man, the highest animal, is so unimaginative that creation is obscenity. All through vegetable and animal life the female is the custodian of life. This has made her a highly specialized, sensitive being—the custodian of love. She knows love. Men know only a stormy frenzy that they call love.

Man does not like this awakening of women. He fears she will destroy civilization. And she will. Man-made civilization with its inequalities, injustices and hatreds must go. In its place will come a woman-made civilization born of love.

A Married Woman

No Love at Home,
But Wife Lives for Babies

In looking through your letters from the public in last Monday's Bulletin I was very much interested in the one which was signed "A Married Woman." She hasn't a very cheerful outlook of life, and there are scores of married women placed in her position who need to change their viewpoint and not their environment. I, too, am a married woman and my case is similar to hers, only where she gets dresses I don't get them, and I have two children to keep looking decent out of my scant allowance.

I have many in-laws to feed and keep up appearances. I have a large house and do all my own work even to pressing trousers. My children are small, so I am kept indoors and without news of the outside world except from papers and magazines.

I have a step-son who is old and willing enough to beat me when he sees fit, and an aged man who dictates what I must or must not do, because I married his son.

My hubby places his relatives first, and his wife—well, she isn't included in his list at all. He will sit down to a hearty meal and eat in three minutes a dessert it took an hour to make. He never talks shop; I am not supposed to know what he makes or what he spends his money on. There is no family life here: no joy, no music, no harmony, no visitors, because I seldom invite them the second time, as I do not wish outsiders to know what they would surely learn by coming here.

Everything in the house is in the same place his first wife had them, even to the lard pail, when I would give anything to have a little touch of individuality to my movements. To many natures this would mean nothing, but how I have suffered from it no one will ever know.

My health has always been the best, my temper none too good, yet Christ said: "Take up thy cross and follow me," and I know this is my cross and I must bear it.

On the other hand, having a good education, the use of a nearby public library, the ability to see my way clearly before me, I will not stagnate nor fill my mind with bitter thoughts or my face with lines of worry. I am young yet, the world is before me, and I am not sticking to a man because of the material things I get from him.

I have many things to be thankful for which others pass by or fail to see. Slights and insults fell by me like water off a duck's back because my little ones mean so much to me. I can't and wouldn't leave my "ideal husband" because he is the father of my children, both of whom are well endowed with strength, health, and courage (which my hubby knows as temper) and, thank God, will yet be useful man and woman.

Hope this letter will be of some use to someone who sees it and knows there is more than one kind of

A Married Woman

Another Woman in "Red Shadow" Fears the Whole Truth About the Night Life Will Not Bear Telling

Outcasts are not supposed to have a voice, but I cannot help writing. I am not a denizen of the "segregated" district, but a free lance, like many others. I am the widowed mother of two small children whom I am supporting and educating by "living the life," after I had tried to support them in what is called legitimate ways. Men are absolutely repulsive to me in nearly all cases, but I can sacrifice my body and my instincts for the sake of my offspring. Of course, they shall never know.

I could write a book myself. Slight of body, but pretty—so I have been told, and what woman doesn't know for herself—I imagined I was in love when I was sixteen. He was a drummer and paid periodic visits to our town. With all his superficiality and thoughtlessness—it should be called irresponsibility—he was kind and lovable. I can still say this, despite the grievous wrong, the eternal shame, he brought to me.

Like many other girls I had dreams. I imagined a handsome, fairly well-to-do fellow would visit our country town and fall in love with me, and I with him.

The man came, but what a delusion. I say that because I have since learned that many other girls in this life have fallen in the same way. Yet I don't know who is to blame.

I think, perhaps, the display of fine clothes and hats by women is largely responsible for the downfall of many girls of what you call the underworld. Not that I was particularly weak that way—at that time—but so many girls have told me their lives.

There are so may angles to this problem that you must not hope to solve it. All you can possibly do is to make a few people think, perhaps.

Even married women enter the life for short periods, unknown to their husbands, as a rule. Not always. Some calamity puts the husband on the verge of insanity, and the wife, for love of him—perhaps for the sake of their children—makes the horrible sacrifice. It seems incredible, but—.

There are three women in this house—a "first-class parlor house"—who are supporting their children. Four others send money home to their parents each week. One girl is caring for a crippled sister. Five give "all they make" to the most despicable creatures on earth—male parasites. The three others are known as "wise guys"—they have bank accounts ranging from $10,000 up. The landlady is worth $100,000 at least.

For what is the use of even trying to tell you what I know. I can only hope that Alice Smith is older than I and, therefore, knows more. I am 21.

Your proposed narrative is important, but I am afraid it cannot depict the truth. Men are men, and seventy-five per cent of the patrons of this house are married men, many of them fathers. THIS IS A FACT. There is a code of ethics in this life which binds us never to expose a man. If such were not the case, well, so many "respectable" men would be seeking cover that there would be a general closing up of business, with no profession exempt.

Respectable women are so ready to condemn the demi-monde and condone the acts of men.

Should God turn his searchlight on civilization we should all immediately become brothers and sisters, and we might really get together and try to redeem our so-called humanity.

I am weak at expressing my knowledge, and yet I want to do it. I am conscious of a striving not to offend, yet I feel deeply, oh, so deeply. I would give my life—if the lives of my children were assured happily—to tell you the whole truth.

As it is, I must content myself with this letter. May God, or whatever Supreme Intelligence is over us, guide the pen of dear Alice Smith.

ALMA GREENE

BEGS VIRTUOUS NEVER TO CAST STONE AT WEAK

I would like to voice my sentiments regarding "A Voice from the Underworld." The public seems to think we are a different species from the rest of humanity, but we are not. Almost every woman here has someone depending on her—relatives, I mean. I have a good old mother, God bless her, and as long as I can give her the necessities of life I can hold my head up, look you square in the eye and say "I should worry about public opinion."

Suppose she should find out, you suggest? Well, we are all taking chances, even our moral men and women. They say to themselves every day "I'm glad nobody knows what I am doing or what I have done." Is society going to take care of my mother and me when morality closes in on us?

No man was the cause of my downfall, just plain dollars and cents, which everyone is struggling for and which millions get just as immorally as we, only they are not caught at it. I don't wish to offend, just to state plain facts.

Who is it that responds to the call for aid, whether in sickness or deep sorrow, but the women you call outcasts? Go to the hardest-looking one and tell her an imaginary story of some one in deep distress. See how quickly the features soften and the heart responds. Is that a sign everything is dead within?

Who carried the buckets of water through the streets the night of the fire, giving to all who were parched with thirst, with the remark: "Drink this; it's better for you than beer tonight?" One from the underworld. I could relate many other incidents of the big-hearted, heroic things they did that night.

But, I send out this warning to any contemplating the step. Don't. The ice is thin and only strong swimmers survive. And to those who haven't sinned—Please don't cast too many stones, as they only make our lives just a little heavier.

Neilson

MEN FLEE BEFORE POLICE

The Hegira of the Magdalenes

Three of the women driven by the police from the vice resorts. In the rear is a negro entertainer who, likewise, felt the effect of the moral crusade. Below is one of the policemen enforcing blockade.

GERMANY PLAYING FOR TIME

By CARL W. ACKERMAN
(United Press Staff Correspondent
With Ambassador Gerard. Copyright, 1917, by United Press.)

PARIS, Feb. 15.—Warning against the menace and German submarine activity in American waters and against German peace propaganda.

GOES TO JAIL FOR THE LIBEL OF WASHINGTON

(By United Press.)
TACOMA, Feb. 15.—For having written an article libeling the memory of George Washington, R. H. Harter today began serving his sentence.

SEVEN ACCEPT, NINE DECLINE, VICE PROBE

Two acceptances and one declination of places on the vice commission were received today by Mayor Ralph.

FOUR CAFE MEN ARE CITED ON GIRL'S CHARGES

Carl Martin and Peter W. Wimandy, proprietors of The Breakers, a resort at Mason and Ellis streets; Alex Davidson, proprietor of the Cafe Louvre, Hill and Powell streets.

LEFT HUSBAND AND CHILD TO MAKE OWN

PROGRESS MADE PUTTING DOWN CUBAN REVOLT

(By Associated Press.)
WASHINGTON, Feb. 15.—State Department reports from Cuba today indicate the government is making progress in putting down the Liberal revolt.

Awaits Wanderer 9 Years; Asks Divorce

OAKLAND, Feb. 15.—Abandoned all hope for her husband's return after nine years of waiting, Mrs. Allison McDonald filed suit for divorce today.

The Servant's Story.

20-Year

A Voice from the Underworld

PART IV

It was two years from the day I had entered a house of prostitution. I had started on the most utterly reckless period of my life.

I have seen girls, time and again, come into houses of prostitution timid and afraid, just as I was; not used to swearing nor drinking nor any of the rest of it. At first the life will make them more timid than ever. But after a while they get hardened; then they get stronger; and at length those same girls are as reckless as anybody. The life molds them. But it works the other way, too; for many a woman who has been taken from this life, by some stroke of good fortune, has seen her old recklessness just disappear under the influence of kindness and love. There isn't such a thing as a human being that can't be degraded, and there isn't any human being that can't be raised.

It took me just two years in the life, before my recklessness reached its height. I had got rid of Jack Peters, and now I took on first one and then another man, throwing each down as soon as I was tired of him.

I was great on clothes in those days. I had a wardrobe that looked like the property room of a comic opera company. I used to love to dress up in my very flashiest, and go down to Westville in broad daylight, parading the streets and showing off my finery as a sort of insult to the decent women who dressed plainly and lived placid lives.

I made quite a bit of money. But I didn't put away a cent of it.

I spent quite a lot on drink. Not for myself especially, because I was not a very heavy drinker, even at that time, but when the crowd got together it seemed as if it was always my treat. I liked it that way. And the other girls seemed to look up to me as a sort of leader.

What about the softer side of me—the side that had come out so strongly when I faced maternity? Well—that didn't have any chance to show itself. I never would let it. I could even quarrel with a woman, or throw a lover down, without getting specially angry or worked up over it. My heart, if I had one, kept out of sight. My feelings were never roused. It was easier that way.

One night I put on my most stylish gown, with everything else to match, and went into Westville. I had a date to meet a man at a certain saloon that had private boxes—a place where all the "higher-up" prostitutes went. To look at me, you wouldn't have thought that I was just a girl in a $2 house. But somehow the chance to get into a better house hadn't yet come along, and anyhow, I guess I liked to be a big frog in a little pool.

All the boxes were full when I got to that cafe. It was 11 o'clock that night, and my friend was late.

I walked up and down the aisle between these boxes once or twice, and then the proprietor saw me. I was a stranger to him, but he knew what I was in a moment; my clothes didn't leave it in doubt any, and then, there was the fact of my being in that place.

"Say, go into that fourth box," said the proprietor. "There's a madam from some house up in Canada there; she's down looking for girls. She's a good fellow."

I went in and introduced myself to the madam. It was myself, not she, that ordered the drinks. We soon got to talking.

"Why don't you come up to Canada with me?" she said. "It's good pickings up there; I run a $3 house and girl like you"—she looked me up and down—"can make $130 a week."

I thought to myself that if she put the figure that high probably I ought to make $50; which was more than I was making where I was. There was something about the woman I didn't quite like—she wasn't dressed so well as I was, and she hadn't offered to part with any of her money for another round of drinks, but what was the difference? If I didn't like her house, I could change.

"I'll go along with you," I said. I made a date to meet her the next afternoon. Then my friend came in.

She wasn't to leave for a couple of days, and meantime I helped her get together a few more girls. I found out how she went about it—she had gone to every big saloon in town, and offered each bartender a flat rate of $20 a girl. That was why the proprietor had steered me in to her, and he got his $20 for that bit of work.

The next day the madam—her name was Lily True—and I went into one saloon, and there was a girl waiting for us. At first glance Lily gave a sniff and turned away. The girl certainly didn't look very good. She was just a child—about 16, and her clothes were awful. Her shirtwaist was dirty and had a big tear in it, and her black skirt was all spotted, and her shoes were broken out, and her hair was just tumbled together any old way. She had an unhealthy complexion, and the way she looked just then any man living would have run away.

"What's your name?" I asked.

"Verna," she said.

"Been cooking and sweeping at $2 a week, haven't you?"

"Yes," she answered. "But no more of that for me."

"Come along with us," I said.

Lily and I took her up to our room. Then I regularly dressed that girl up. I hadn't but about $20 left in my purse, but I bought her some false hair with little curls around her forehead, and then I got her a face massage, and some silk stockings, and slippers and by buying some things and giving her others from my outfit I soon had her looking so she would be noticed anywhere. It was lots of fun to see that child improve.

That bartender got his $20, too. So did three others, and in a few days five of us were ready to start.

I couldn't help noticing what a penny-pincher Lily was. She never parted with a cent that she didn't rub first on both sides. All the time we were getting those girls she never treated, never paid for a meal unless she just had to, and I suspected she would try to make me pay the room rent. I decided I would keep my eyes on Lily.

At the depot that last day, I noticed that Lily put two of us girls in each lower berth. That made me suspicious. She was paying the expenses as they came along, but I knew she would hand us each a bill later, and we would enter her house in debt to her.

We stopped over at a town midway to our destination. Lily went out to look for more girls; and then we five got to talking. They were all younger than I, from 16 to 19, and new at the life, and they looked up to me as a sort of a leader.

"I don't think Miss Lily's doing the right thing to make us stop over and pay our own room rent," said one girl. "She's pretty cheap," said another. "Oh, well," I said, "she'll add it all on to our $12 a week board—"

"Twelve a week board!" they all screamed. "Why, she told us we were to pay her one-third of what we made!"

That made me suspicious. If she had put them on a one-third basis, I reasoned, she must know that there was more money to be made by the house that way. Maybe it was a good place, just as she had said.

Just then Lily walked into the room.

"See here, Lily," I said, as impudent as could be, though she was my landlady, "what about this? You've made a one-third arrangement with them, and I'm to pay board."

She stammered out some sort of explanation.

"You see, Alice, I wanted to do right by the girls. They're all new at the game, and, of course they can't make as much money as you can, with your experience. I thought they'd go on a third for a while till they learned more."

"Now, see here, Lily," I said, "you know as well as I do that the ones that make the most money are the new girls, and not the old, experienced ones. This kid Verna is going to be a lot better money maker than I am."

She knew that as true, and gave it up. "All right, then, I'll put the whole bunch on $15 a week board," she snapped, and though it was higher than she had promised me, I accepted it.

We got to our destination, a Canadian city, in the early afternoon. The houses were a couple of miles out of the city, which was a good sized one. I found out from one of the older girls that we were expected to wear silk or satin parlor gowns; I hadn't any of such nice material and I went into town and bought some for myself. Lily, the madam, went into town, too, and bought some—for all five of us new girls, and when she handed me my bill that evening, here was the item, "Material for parlor-gowns," with about three prices marked opposite it.

Then there was a little test of strength between Lily and myself. I took that bill and blue-penciled it. She had charged us each for one full berth-fare, though we had doubled up; and she had added a quarter apiece to our room rent for that night we had stopped over, so that she wouldn't be out anything for her own room; and she had overcharged the hack-fare, and several other little things of the sort. We quarreled over every item of that bill; and at the end I was several dollars less in debt to that house than Lily had wanted me to be.

But the other girls were afraid to say anything to her; and they accepted their bills just as she handed them in. Little Verna especially was in debt to the house. That is the constant effort of almost every landlady—to put a girl in debt. It gives them a hold on the girl.

It was a sad fact about Lily that she was born entirely without tact. And tact is the one thing necessary for a landlady to have; without it she just can't get along.

Lily couldn't seem to make a "go" of it with the girls. For one thing, she made the mistake of setting a very poor table. There was never enough to eat; she was always giving us such things as kidney stew; and there were never any green vegetables or the little things that go to make eating worthwhile. She sat at the head of the table and served things out, and there was never any chance for a girl to pass her plate the second time.

Lily had been placed in her position as madam by her lover, a business man. But one night I heard them quarreling, and I knew then that her pathway wasn't altogether one of roses. He was threatening to take the house away from her if she didn't make more money. Then I realized why she kept down so on the food.

One day little Verna came into my room. She was crying.

"Oh, Alice," she said, "Lily just gave me my bill to the house. I'm five hundred dollars in debt."

"Why, kid, how did your bill get that much? You had to buy clothes and everything, of course, but aren't you making good money?"

"I'm making money, all right, and paying her every cent of it, but, Alice, I don't think Lily's giving me credit for what I do pay her. I just can't see that five hundred at all."

Another girl, Geraldine, was in the room at the time. Geraldine was what we always called a "stool-pigeon." She went right down and told Lily what Verna had said. Presently there came a call for Verna to see the madam.

I went along, too. There was a nice quarrel between the four of us, including Geraldine; and at the end Lily reached out, grabbed Verna's papers from her hand—all her receipts and bills and everything—and tore them up before I could prevent.

The poor child didn't have anything at all to show for her work. She was in the madam's hands. She owed just whatever the madam said.

Well, there was no way out of it. But I decided to move. I told Lily so.

"No, you won't," she yelled. "I ain't taking the risk of bringing girls over the boundary, just to have them skip to that other house."

But I walked right out of the place when the madam wasn't looking, went to a house a few doors away, knocked, and told the lady who answered that I was one of the girls from Lily's, and I wanted to work for her. I told her how Lily had been doing. I didn't know whether I would get refused or not; but she took me in.

Only a little while after that, Lily's lover and business manager took the house away from her. Both houses, hers and the one I was now in, went under the same management. And Lily went away, and I never heard of her again.

If ever a prostitute's life in a house could be bearable, my life at this time should have been. It was a three-dollar house, and the only men who came out there at all, came to spend money. There was very little of the hoodlum element hanging around—the sort of curious, vulgar, morbid crowd that makes such a terrible place of the San Francisco segregated district.

But I was restless; if I stayed too long in one place, I might get to thinking about myself again, and going over all my past life, with its disappointments. It wasn't long before I got the longing to move on to new places, to see new things and new faces, and to keep myself occupied and busy—anything to keep from thinking.

There was one girl in our house named Annabel, who had a story to tell that I must repeat, as near as I can to the way she told it to me one afternoon in my room. Annabel was a quiet little girl with hay-colored hair. I knew she had been a street-walker, but that was all, until she opened her heart to me and told me her story. It's a story that has happened often, I dare say; and it is exceedingly likely to happen again, here in San Francisco, before many months are past.

"It all occurred in the big city of C——," said Annabel. "There'd been a shake-up in the police, and a lot of the houses had been closed up all of a sudden. It threw a lot of us girls onto the street.

"I was shy on coin at the time. I didn't have enough to pay my railroad fare to another city of any size. There was only one thing to do. I just had to get out and 'hustle.'

"At first I found it paid fine. The men took to the streets, you see, just like we girls did. But at the end of about three months I started to suspect that the cops were all getting to know me. I could see I'd have to leave town pretty soon; but I put it off from day to day—you know how a person will do.

"So I got caught. The policeman on the beat where I worked hid in a dark doorway; and I guess he got the man to wait and speak to me right on that spot. When the fellow stopped me, I put up the usual objections—trying to get a line on him—then I decided he was all right, and said, 'Come along.' We went up to my room.

"It wasn't five minutes later till there came a loud knock on the door. 'Open the door,' said a man's voice. I was scared, but I hesitated, since I was deshabille; but the man with me walked right to the door and opened it. In came that big policeman on the beat.

"'Well, little girl, I guess it's the jug for you at last,' he said, and I started to get good and scared. 'Get on your duds. Never mind the feathers, you won't need them.'

"'Why, what's the matter?' I asked. I tried to seem surprised.

"'Oh, come on, now; don't try to pull any of that chirp noise,' said the cop. 'You know I've got you right.' And just as he said that, a queer thing occurred. The man who was with me had walked right out of the room, without the cop's even asking his name. Then I knew what was up. It was a 'shake-down.'

"I pretended to be frightened worse than I was.

"'Where are you going to take me?' I asked.

"'Why, to jail, of course. Didn't think I was going to invite you for a joy-ride, did you?'

"I sat down on the bed and started to dig down into my stocking.

"'Well, I'm not going to jail,' I said, as if I meant it. 'I've got bail money—see?' I held up a little roll of bills and cash—every cent I had.

"The cop came up close. I could see him sizing up that roll.

"'You've been pretty slick, kid,' he said. 'I've been onto you for some time. You'd orter had sense enough not to try to fool me. In police court tomorrow it'll be at least twenty-five dollars fine, and maybe a jolt in the stir; they're getting stricter all the time. But I don't want to see you go to jail—I'll tell you kid, I'll let you go this time. I'll relieve the judge of a little extra work in the morning—he has too much anyway. You can pay that fine to me—and don't forget I'm on the beat after this.'

"'But I haven't got $25,' I said. 'I've only got $16.'

"'Oh—that's all right, anyhow,' he replied. 'You can owe me the nine. Say, you got no kick coming; you know you've been getting by for three months.'

"He took my sixteen dollars and went. I knew what that meant for the future, all right enough. It meant I would have to come through with something every week.

"I saw him a few days later and gave him $3; and a little while afterward, since my business naturally went up, now I was protected, he raised me to $5.

"The cop had another proposition to make pretty soon. He had a friend down on the next street, he said, who kept a rooming-house; and he hinted that I ought to get my room from her. You know how a girl works it, when she's on the street—she lives in one part of town and works in another, and gets a room every night in some lodging-house that ain't particular. And when they get onto her in that house she is charged more than the ordinary room rent, and there's lots of little tips that have to be handed out here and there.

"Well, I took his hint—I had to—and his 'friend' charged me $1.50 for the privilege of using that room for a few minutes, maybe two or three times a night.

"Well, you know how things went after that. I tramped around in the slush one night when my cash was low, and caught a fierce cold; but my cash wouldn't have been low if it hadn't been for that policeman. He got worse and worse. Finally he would be waiting around in a convenient doorway almost every time I went upstairs to get his share of whatever I might make.

"Then a strange thing happened. One night the cop on the next beat called to me across the street. Somehow or other he had got to know me, though I never worked on his territory.

"'How much are you giving Jones?' he asked, meaning the cop who was 'protecting' me.

"'I don't know,' I replied. 'I can't keep track of it all. He's after me all the time.'

"'Guess,' he said. I guessed it at $15 a week.

"'Well, say,' he suggested, 'why don't you come over and work on my beat? I'll give you a squarer deal than Jones does. I'll make it $10 a week straight, and you can get a room at the G—— house for a dollar a night.'

"I was getting awful sick of Jones. I never thought of consequences.

"'All right; I'll get that room at the G—— house tomorrow night,' I replied.

"Well, I walked back across the street, turned the corner, and went a couple of blocks when I heard a man coming behind me. It was a drizzly night, and few persons were on the street; this looked like a chance, and it was the first in about three nights. I slowed up to let him overtake me.

"He slowed up, too. Just as we passed a street lamp I said, 'Good evening.' He stopped. He was a big man, with clothes that bulged out at the knees and elbows, and he had a big ugly scar across his face.

"We fixed it up all right and went right up to my room. I walked over to the dresser, telling him to make himself at home, then I turned around. I'll never forget what I saw.

"He was facing me, with his coat thrown back, and the thumb of his right hand was shoving out a portion of his suspender through the armhole of his vest. On the suspender was a badge, marked 'Special Officer.'

"I felt weak in my stomach when I turned away from that dresser and saw the detective's badge staring me in the face," she went on. "But I made up my mind I wouldn't let that cur know I was scared, if I could help it. His derby hat was on the back of his head, and that scar across his face looked uglier than ever.

"'Well, how do you like my jewelry?' he sneered.

"'It ought to be in the junk pile, same as you,' I flared back at him. 'No man who's really a man would ever pull a trick like this on a girl. Any man who goes out of his way to make a reputation by fooling a girl is just a dirty dog.' I was mad clear through; I stepped toward him, my hand raised. It was a foolish thing to do.

"He grinned at me and put his hand in his pocket. 'A revolver!' I thought; but it wasn't. Only a pair of shiny handcuffs. The sight of those things took the heart right out of me.

"'These are for you, little one,' he said. 'You need taming. About six months in the workhouse, and then a good swift kick out again.'

"I don't remember what I did exactly; but I sort of withered. I think I sank down on the floor and grovelled at his feet. When I think over that night, that's the one part I can't remember; and I'm glad, because I probably did something I ought to be ashamed of. If I did get down and grovel, nothing on earth could make me do it now. To bow down before the detective—that's what I can't see myself doing; yet maybe I did it. I can't remember.

"The next thing I knew, I was in a closed wagon, bumping over the cobbles. There was a dim light back of the driver, and I saw two policemen sitting at the rear of the wagon, one on each side. I had an impulse to scream; but I didn't. I thought of everything I knew that would keep up my courage; and it's funny, but I remembered some of my old Sunday school teachings. I've often wondered about that; I guess they belong just as much in a patrol wagon as anywhere.

"At the station a fat man with spectacles and an ornament on his sleeves asked me my name, age, address and a lot of other questions, in a voice that sort of seemed to come from his shoes. I started to answer meekly, but all of a sudden I realized what it meant, and afterward they told me it took three men to hold me.

"Then I was sitting on a board in some kind of a dark pit and staring at a barred door. I wanted to beat against that door but I didn't have the strength to get up. After a long time a man came in and unlocked it. 'Up to court,' he ordered, glancing at me coldly.

"I was shoved into another wagon; and when a door was slammed behind me and the horses started, I came out of my dream and realized I was in the 'Black Maria.' Several men, handcuffed together, were with me. All at once I felt better. Those men knew—they felt, they understood. It wasn't so lonely any more.

"'What's the matter, kid?' asked a young fellow sitting opposite of me.

"'Oh—just arrested, that's all,' I replied carelessly. 'What's yours?'

"He had blue eyes and light curly hair, with good features and teeth, and he couldn't have been over twenty-four. He answered just as careless as I had.

"'The rope for me, I guess,' he said. 'I croaked a guy last night. It was an accident; but I've got a record as long as your hair, and that means curtains.'

"'You're joshing,' I said. 'You couldn't kill a fly. You're in for petty larceny.'

"Do you know, I think that hurt his feelings. He didn't speak right away, but just looked at me. His look and his remarks about my hair reminded me that my hair was down, and that my hat was lost somewhere. I twisted up my hair as well as I could, though I had lost half of my hairpins.

"But that fellow had told me the truth all right. He was hanged six months later.

"As I went into the courtroom I happened to see a man whose face seemed familiar, but I couldn't just place him. I pleaded guilty when my case was called, but the judge wanted evidence, and 'Junk Heap' testified. The judge asked me if I had anything to say, but all I could say was, 'No, Your Honor.' I had heard other people call him that.

"'Have you any friends or character witnesses?'

"'No, Your Honor.' It was getting hard to stand the staring crowd. 'Please hurry, Your Honor.'

"'It's a clear case,' declared the young judge. 'Fifty days or a $25 fine.' He jerked out that last in the same sort of way as you'd say 'Transfer, please,' or 'Pass the butter.' Somebody grabbed me by the arm and led me to the clerk's desk—but my heart sank. I didn't have any money. How could I pay that fine?

"Just then I saw that familiar face again. Now I remembered. It was a man I knew—he had picked me up on the street once and visited me once after that. His face was bloated, but he didn't have a bloated soul, I guess.

"'Pardon me, but can I have a word with the lady?' he said, and then he led me to a corner inside the railing, with that awful crowd staring all the time.

"'You don't remember me, I guess,' he said, 'but what's the difference? Can you pay your fine?'

"'No. The copper kept me broke.'

"'Well, then, I'll pay it for you. You wait here.'

"He went away a few minutes, then came back and told me it was all right. I could have hugged him. But I didn't. Instead, I asked him if he would go up to the police station and find my hat. He was gone quite a while this time, but at least he came back and said my hat wasn't there. He seemed kind of sore, too, and I could guess how the cops had acted toward him, just for trying to do a service for a girl like me.

"I went home bareheaded on the car, and everybody stared. I found my hat that night down at the rooming-house where I had been arrested; the proprietor had taken it. He gave it to me, and I never went to that house again.

"Well, I had to go right back to work; there was nothing else to be done. I was broke altogether and hungry. I stepped a few blocks over and found that policeman who had talked to me the night I was arrested. 'I'll work on your beat for $10 straight,' I told him, 'but you'll have to give me time to pay you. I've been in trouble.' He said it was all right; and he showed me the rooming-house he had spoken of.

"It wasn't two weeks before trouble came again. Jones, the policeman I had deserted, naturally missed me and my money. He found out that I had gone over to this other fellow's beat to 'hustle,' and he laid for me. One night he stood across the street and beckoned. Like a little fool I went over; and he asked me for money. I told him I didn't have any, and that if I had I wouldn't give it to him.

"'You know what will happen to you if you go to court a second time,' he said. 'I'll put in a knock that'll bury you at least six months.'

"I pleaded and begged; but it wasn't any use. He wanted money. At last I fished down into my stocking again and pulled out two dollars—every cent I had in the world. Then he got after me good and hard, and before he let me go he made me promise to come back to his beat.

"That was the only time in my life I ever seriously thought of suicide. I went home so downhearted that I sat on my bed most of the evening picturing what it would be like to kill myself. Alice, I got up twice and walked to the door, meaning to go out and jump off a pier, and both times I came back, afraid to turn the doorknob. I was awake all night.

"Since I didn't have a cent I went without eating the next day; and when I walked out onto the street that next night, I was desperate. But I was lucky. I ran into some money first thing. Then I went and had something to eat and felt better.

"That same night my policeman called me over to him.

"'Jones and I had a fight over you last night,' he said. 'Say, kid, don't go over to his beat under any circumstances. He's awful sore. And look out anyhow. He's after you.'

"It wasn't but two nights later with all my care that I was arrested again—this time by another plain-clothes man.

"My game was up. I went through the same experience; only this time that young judge remembered me. Jones was on hand to put in his knock, and I was given six months in the work-house.

"The police wouldn't pay any attention when I asked leave to send somebody to my room to pack and store my trunk. I was sent to the workhouse, and that room rent piling up all the time; and it wasn't till I had been there three days that I arranged it. There were about twenty-five women in there, and I learned that one of them was to be discharged the next morning, and asked her. She put my trunk in storage and sent me the receipt.

"They dressed me in a gray dress, and I had to sew on a machine all day. The work helped to pass the time; but the food wasn't fit to eat, and the cells were full of bedbugs.

"It was just two days before my time was to be up, counting thirty days off for 'good time,' when I had a visitor. It was Jones, the policeman.

"'There's just one place in this town you can work and be safe,' he said to me, 'and that's on my beat. I'll go easy on you till you get on your feet.'

"Then I knew it was he that had tipped me off to the plain-clothes man who had arrested me. He had the upper hand on me, all right; if I said anything rash I'd lose my thirty days 'good time.' I made out I was grateful to him and he promised to leave $5 at the desk for me so I wouldn't go out broke.

"But I never went back to Jones' beat. The day I got out of the workhouse I met a girlfriend who told me of a man that was looking for girls to go to a small mining town where he had opened a dance-hall. I went with my friend to the man; and he got my trunk out of storage and put me on the train. Since then it's been the houses for me; and when this is through with, I don't know what will come next. But then, does anybody?"

My old friend Slim, the professional gambler, had hunted me out. I was restless, and ready for a change; and when he said, "Let's go on the road together, girlie," I was eager to take the suggestion.

Slim was too clever to be merely a professional gambler, pure and simple. He traveled as the representative of a large schoolbook and office fixture house. He was a very successful salesman, he said, and I always believed him.

But with a deck of cards, Slim put his salesmanship in the shade. There was nothing he couldn't do with a deck. Such little matters as dealing every third or fourth card were easy for him. He seemed to know every card, and where it lay, and you never could catch him.

He and I would come into some town, put up at the best hotel, and register as Mr. and Mrs. Freeman. Slim would stroll down to the lobby and presently coax three easy gentlemen into a game. As for my part of it, a word to the bartender would always be more than enough, providing the word was accompanied with a little cash.

Probably the most daring thing we did was to go the rounds of the summer resorts. Everybody warned us against it. We would take a cottage out on the edge of the little summer city of tents; and then, speaking to the bartender, I would begin business. No trouble about that; all the men would be eager for amusement. At some of these places I even went so far as to keep liquor on sale in my cottage. The risk was big; and at times Slim and I didn't let it be known that we were together, except just to the bartender.

But in any case, it wasn't safe to stay but two or three weeks at any one place; for some of those summer resorts were on United States government land and arrest would mean the realest sort of trouble.

When that summer was over Slim and I traveled on the regular route that he followed in his book selling. Here he introduced me to some of his friends; he was very well known among the traveling men, and I always felt perfectly at home, because they all knew as well as I did what I was. I only made money when I wanted to; and little by little I got to dread the idea of ever going back to a house.

I admired Slim for his neatness at the cards, just as I have always admired anybody who was efficient. But there were certain things about Slim that I didn't like. For one thing, he was horribly jealous of me, and at one time threatened to shoot me. When a chance came along to go with another man, I left him with little regret.

Then began a new affair, which I can't think of yet without feeling bad. Try as hard as you can to be an outcast of the most reckless sort, to shut your heart against every emotion—it's impossible to go on forever and not run up against something tragic.

Poor Charley, the man for whom I left Slim, came of wealthy people. His father was a merchant; and Charley himself had learned the art, and was a skillful salesman and judge of goods.

When I met him he was traveling for his father's house. After our acquaintance had gone further, I noticed that he didn't seem especially robust, though he kept up his health and spirits all right. But it wasn't till I had been actually traveling with him for a while that I found what the matter was.

"What's wrong with you, Charley? You're always coughing," I asked him one day.

"Well," he replied, looking at me queerly to see how I would take it, "the physicians call it tuberculosis. I call it the 'con.'"

Adventuress though I was, that staggered me. Tuberculosis! Except for some minor troubles, I had kept my health pretty well so far; but I didn't want to face anything like that.

Of course, I thought first of myself. I'd leave him right away. I'd go that very night.

Then I looked at Charley; and for the first time in two years or more I felt sorry for a man. His eyes had agony, and sorrow, and reproach, and desperation in them. He felt it all so strong that I had to feel it, too, whether I wanted to or not. It was a sort of crisis to me. It needed some shock like that to break through the hard shell around my heart.

"You needn't worry, Charley," I said, and I know my voice had a new tone in it. "I'll stick with you. I won't leave you on account of that."

I couldn't say that I wouldn't leave him on any account, because, although I was sorry for him, in the back of my head there was the plan of finding some other excuse to leave him as soon as I could. The very name of that disease filled me with dread.

It satisfied him, anyhow, my saying it like that. We kept on traveling together. But then there came a change. Charley lost his job.

It seems his father, who managed the firm, had heard that Charley was traveling with a woman. He was strict in his ideas—at least, that was what Charley and I thought—and as I learned afterward, had written to him, objecting to the way he was acting. But Charley had answered he would keep to me anyhow—he cared a lot, I guess—and this was the result.

"Never mind, Charley," I said. "I'll support both of us till you can find another job."

I wouldn't have made that proposition to a well man.

Then came the days when I really knew hardship, and sank almost to the very dregs of a prostitute's life. The only thing I had was clothes. What I experienced in those days I can't tell you. I didn't go to a house—Charley wouldn't hear of that; but I walked the streets and "hustled," and I took any money I could make, and I drifted from one town to another, according as the police started to demand tribute money. I felt the burden of supporting a man on my earnings.

Charley honestly tried to get one job after another. I was always looking over the papers, going through the advertising columns for some place for him; but he never could keep at work long.

Why didn't he hold them? Because his whole character seemed to be leaving him. I hated the thought then, and fought against it all I could; but I know now that I was to blame.

There's something about that sort of a love-affair—when a man has sacrificed everything for a woman, and is so in love with her that he can't leave her, and yet knows that she doesn't love him—that seems just to drag a man's better nature right out of him. Little by little Charley was losing his courage and his perseverance, his physical strength and the strength of his mind.

I told myself that I was helping him to keep up, and that if I should leave him he would die. Maybe I was right; maybe he would have committed suicide, as he often threatened; but at any rate, I know all the time that it was really myself, and not his illness, that was sapping his strength. He was in the grip of a passion that was eating his life away.

A whole year passed in this wretched poverty. We had drifted all up and down the Pacific Coast—from Canada to Los Angeles. There was always the worry about Charley's future plans; and one day, when he got a letter from his father that he brought right to me, I made a resolve.

"See here, Alice," Charley said, in a matter-of-fact tone, trying to keep the eagerness out of his weak voice, "my dad writes that if I'll give you up and come home, he will set me up in business."

"Go ahead and do it, then." I halfway meant it; but Charley thought I was joking.

"You bet I won't. Nothing like that. But say, Alice—don't you see what we can do? We'll work our way home, then I'll just pretend I gave you up—don't you see? Then the old man will do as he says he will; and after a little while I can bring you to see him, and I'll tell him you're the girl I'm just engaged to. We won't say a word about all this other business. And after he sees you he'll be tickled to have you for a daughter-in-law. Oh, kid"—his voice was almost breaking, he felt it so keenly— "can't we do something like that? It isn't impossible; you can do it. You can put it across."

"Well, we'll try it, Charley," I told him, as cheerfully as I could. "We'll work our way north, anyhow, and see."

It was my plan to take him back to his father and leave him there—to die. He wasn't going to last long, with that disease. It was getting worse all the time. He had stopped all efforts to take care of himself.

We started to work northward. I tried with all my might to make money, anywhere and everywhere I could—aboard trains, on passenger boats, in little towns. We were barely able to get enough to eat, let alone do much traveling.

I remember once when Charley came to our cheap little room in one town, all tired out with his failure to find work. "Go ahead and get supper alone, Alice," he told me. "You've got money, haven't you? I'm broke."

"Sure, I've got money," I said. I fished down into my stocking and pulled out two lottery tickets. I just let him see the end of them. "See there? I've got money." He thought they were bills, and I went out and walked the streets all evening, picking up a miserable dollar and a half, which was just the price of the room I had to get.

At last we seemed to go stranded for good and all. It was just a little over halfway back to his home; we had been trying to "drive" the conductors on the way, which means dodging them by getting off at stations and walking ahead to the front cars where the tickets are already gathered in; and it hadn't been a very good success. We had stayed in this little town for quite a while; it seemed as if we couldn't ever get out of it. I was discouraged at last.

There was another thing, too, which Charley didn't know anything about—among the men who had been helping me to make a living was one that seemed to be coming again and again. And I knew that if I said the word I could change over to him in a minute, and end all this hardship—for myself.

One morning I found a job in a newspaper that looked right for Charley. He went to the place and came back with a disappointed look on his thin face.

"What do you think?" he said scornfully. "That old food offered me a dollar a day for the first week, two dollars for the second, and so on until I got up to five dollars a day. I'd like to see myself working for a dollar a day. I never did that in my life, and I don't have to do it now. Yet it was a good place otherwise," he ended up, regretfully.

Then I got mad. I guess he didn't realize what sort of a life this had been for me, compared to what I was used to.

"See here, Charley, if that's the way you're going to act, we're through," I declared. "Maybe you're too good to work for a dollar a day; but, then, maybe I'm too good to wait on men for a dollar and a half apiece, and that's what I've been doing for your sake. Don't apologize or explain. You can go and live somewhere else. You and I are through."

He took it hard; but I meant it. I picked up a little money, came back to San Francisco with the other man, and soon was better fixed. Poor Charley followed me, found out where I was living, and got a room, as I afterward learned, in the same house—where he could "see Alice at night, when she pulls down the shades, and that other fellow is with her." That was the way he told it to a friend, who came and told me.

After a while Charley's room was left vacant; and later still, I heard that he was dead. He died three months after I had left him. They said it was tuberculosis that killed him.

I was running away from a man. For once in my life I had known the feeling of fear. That affair, though it meant much to me, has no bearing on this narrative of my underworld experiences. It is enough to say that when I walked toward the ticket window of the ferry building and met this man my heart sank.

There was only one place in the world where he wouldn't follow me. Back home.

"Where are you going?" he asked me.

"I'm going away." I didn't dare meet his eyes.

"But where to?"

Now, it is a fact that I didn't have any very clear idea where I was going to. He had suggested Sacramento, on a certain occasion some time before, and I had thought then that he was trying to get rid of me, and the thought had made me crazy. It came into my head now; should I go to Sacramento?

I started to answer. "I'm going to—" Then, just as I was starting to say Sacramento, another idea came into my head like a flash. He would follow me to Sacramento. There was only one place in the world where he wouldn't follow me.

I finished up—"back home."

"What? Way back there?" I had scored a point; I had surprised him, and it showed.

"Yes. Why not?" After all, I asked myself, why not? I'd been thinking of the old place for some time, off and on. Grandpa was dead now; but why shouldn't I go there anyhow and see the old folks—Uncle Ed—and my Billy, my boyhood sweetheart? Why shouldn't I? I cut the conversation short, went to the ticket window and paid almost my last cent for a ticket to Chicago. I knew of a house in Chicago where I could go if I liked.

So I went East on that train, full of the queerest sort of emotions. Five years since I had been that far east. Five years since I had come across the Rockies; and they were just the same, but I—after all, was I so different? Of course, new sides to my nature had been brought out and developed and hardened by the life I had been leading; but underneath it all, wasn't I just the same Alice?

Many things had happened lately to break the hard wall of defense that I had built around my heart. Grandpa's death; then the death of poor Charley, after I had left him; then this other affair, that was over with now. What a pitiful mixup!

So, without really putting it in so many words, I was deciding upon the place where my journey was to end. My ticket read Chicago, but my thoughts and heart were checked through to my old girlhood home.

When the train left the Rockies behind and started to run through that flat country I knew so well I lost heart. I saw what I would have to face.

How could I ever answer all those questions straight? How could I stand that close inspection? If I could creep quietly in among them it would be all right; but how could I? Those people would make the returned traveler the center of everything.

So I reached Chicago with the question still undecided. I gave a taxi driver the address to the house of prostitution, and he grinned.

I found the place neither better nor worse than a million other houses in big cities; there was a bigger crowd, more roughness, more idle men who didn't spend any money but just came to stare and to make foul remarks. But it was a better arranged house than one would find in the country. It was like going to prison to go back to the awful life of the house.

It wasn't three days before I went to the telephone and called up the railroad office.

"How much is the fare from Chicago to X——?" I asked. I hoped he would say twenty dollars; then I couldn't go.

"Eight dollars and fifty cents," came the answer. I felt as if I had both won and lost; for how could I answer all those questions?

At supper that night I told the other girls about my plan. I don't know why they were so lovely to me. Maybe it was because every one of them had a dream of going home tucked away in her own heart.

They appreciated the hard time I would have answering questions, too, and they thought up a lot of things that I was mighty thankful for later on, when some of those village gossips got prying at me.

One of the girls suggested that if I was a waitress I ought to have a lot of black aprons and plain white shirtwaists in my trunk, and so she and two other girls went out the next day, got a dozen each, threw away two aprons and four shirtwaists to make out as if they had been lost in the wash, and then took the rest around and laundered them so they wouldn't look all new.

So, dressed plainer than I had been for many a long month, and my heart beating with wild excitement, I took the train from Chicago to X——, and a crowd of girls came down to the depot to yell good-by after me.

In Chicago—sitting in my room in the house of prostitution, though he never dreamed it—I had written a note to my Uncle Ed, telling him that I was coming for a visit home, and would be there on a certain day. He drove in the seven miles to X—— to meet me in his buckboard.

Five years hadn't changed Uncle Ed so awful much, I thought, as I got off the train, and saw that face that had been so dear to me as a little girl. Five years! It seemed five centuries. And I wondered if what he saw in my face was not the time that had actually passed, but the time that seemed to me to have passed. In some ways I felt like an old woman.

But I chattered to him like a child as he drove the buckboard through the sweet-smelling country roads. I kept getting little shocks of surprise at seeing some old house or barn I had entirely forgotten, but remembered perfectly well now I saw it again.

And all this peacefulness and beauty that I remembered so well sort of took out of me the desire to be dishonest. I felt that I couldn't play my lying part so well. I wanted to blurt out the truth to them all, and be honest. But how would their faces look? How would I feel when they turned away from me? Would it be home, then? No; if I wanted any home-coming at all, I would have to get it by lying.

I stole a look at Uncle Edgar now and then. He talked very simply and very seriously. He seemed to think over each remark before he made it. I could see that he felt at a disadvantage, because I had seen the world and he hadn't; but he wasn't going to let himself be made awkward because of that. And the result was, he made himself disagreeable and heavy. By the end of the seven-mile drive I felt irritated with him, and knew I was to find the old place and the people fearfully stupid. And I was sick at heart because I felt that way. I wanted to love it all so much that I would stay forever—stay and be quiet.

Hazel, Uncle Ed's wife, yelled at me half a mile away and waved a white dish towel. Then I felt happier.

What a huge dinner they served! I ate till I was ashamed. And after dinner the neighbors began to pour in—and ask questions. Oh, I was thankful that the girls in the house had coached me the way they did. I told a straight story and kept my head; rather enjoyed it after the first effort; and though I was conscious of using a lot of slang, I didn't let slip anything worse. And that night, when I went to bed, I said to myself—

"So far, anyhow, not one of them suspects. I wonder how many nights I'll be able to say that. Three—maybe four. Then"—

Telling myself, "Anyhow, I'll die rather than go back to the sporting life again," I fell asleep.

They got up the next morning about the time I was accustomed to going to bed. But it wasn't too early for me. I had to laugh at the clock that told me it was a quarter past six, when I started out after breakfast to see the old house, the house where grandpa and grandma had raised me in the way I should go.

They had put up a new back fence, and the people that lived there hadn't been so poor that they had to rip off the pickets. I saw the shed where my Billy had left the notes under the chopping-block. And I saw the garden where I used to help grandpa do the spring planting. And right there I came upon something that was too much for me. I started to cry at last.

It was my doll's graveyard. It was way out at the back of the vegetable garden, in the corner by the fence. The soil, I knew, was full of dead dolls—dolls whose skulls had got cracked, or whose arms and legs had been wounded or torn off, or who had died, in the full height of their strength and beauty, of some mysterious illness. I had buried them there, and wept over each one, and had fixed up white stones at the head and foot of each little grave. I could see some of the white stones there still; the ground hadn't been disturbed. I stood there and laughed and cried together. What a foolish child's trick to bury dolls like that! Yet, after all, hadn't I buried more things than dolls—buried them forever?

I went home tired out. Then I had another shock. A visitor was waiting to see me. It was my Billy.

Billy—grown short and stocky, it seemed. His brown hair was all sunburned, and it didn't come down over his forehead the way it used to do when he was seventeen. He looked like what he was—a big, honest, awkward, country boy. But when I tried to talk to him, there was an awful time. Not a word he could find to say, and I babbled on and on, hating myself for doing it. He went very soon.

Billy called again a few days later. I was getting used to the place now, and had strengthened up some weak spots in my story, and was beginning to think that I might last through and have a good time after all. By the time Billy had come the fourth time, we started to talk more easily.

"I'm right where you left me, Alice," he said. "I ain't got a farm, and I ain't got rich; and I just work around in the summertime. I ain't gone ahead any. Who's there been to work for?"

Poor Billy! I couldn't get him out of my mind.

There was one old lady, the wife of a rich man, who held mortgages on most of the farms around there; and this old lady took it on herself to ferret out my secret.

"What's the matter, anyhow, Alice?" asked Hazel, Uncle Ed's wife, one day. "People are always asking questions. I can't see anything wrong with you; but these women are hard to satisfy. There's an awful funny atmosphere around here."

"I don't know, Hazel," I answered. "I don't see why there should be anything wrong. I've told them everything as straight as I could."

But she wasn't quite convinced. And one day when she saw that old lady, Mrs. Sharples, coming up the path to the house, I could fairly see Hazel's satisfaction. She was thinking to herself, "Now, if anyone can find out about Alice's life in these years, Mrs. Sharples can."

I got mad. I was sure of my story by this time; and I made up my mind I'd win this battle. I stamped into that sitting-room and sat down. It wasn't two minutes before the old lady began.

I sat there, with every look of friendliness, and gave her straight and quick answers for every question she asked. And she asked them, too, in a nice, friendly manner, as if she was really interested in me. It was a real battle, and I won.

After that, things were a little better, though the suspicion wouldn't stay down. I knew that if I got caught up in just one little contradiction, I was lost; and it hurt me all the time to think that even there among my own home people, there shouldn't be any sympathy held out to a girl that had been an unfortunate. The world had turned one side to these people and another side to me; but they would put all the blame on me just the same.

There was only one woman who was different. She was an aunt I stayed with a while.

"Alice, they're saying things about you," she said, "but I don't care. I'm not going to let it make any difference. I don't care if you did have hard times and took the easiest way out of them. Aren't you acting all right now? That's what counts—not what you may have done once."

I came pretty near to telling her the truth. But I didn't. She told me one little fact about her life, though, one day, which explained to me why she had such a big heart.

"You know, Alice, when I was a girl of sixteen I—got into trouble. There was a man—" She didn't say much more; but I knew. She had suffered. It's the people who have suffered that make the world fit to live in.

I stayed back there three months. At the end of that time I came to realize that I couldn't just live on and on with my relatives. And I couldn't marry Billy, even though the gossips said we were engaged. If you want to know why I couldn't, I'll tell you of one little thing that happened.

Billy went with me one day to pay a visit to an old chum of mine. This girl had got married quite young—before I left home, in fact.

We found her living in a house with four rooms. There weren't any flowers in the yard nor much of any fence. We stumbled upon the loose boards in the front steps.

She came to the door in an old dirty apron that had once been blue-checked, and asked us in. As she turned, a little youngster with a dirty face caught onto her skirts, and she scolded him. Inside there were three other little youngsters; and they were dears, but what a place for them to live in!

They all slept in one room—the six of them. Old furniture, old rickety chairs, an old cracked mirror, old carpets that fairly spurted out the dust as soon as you stepped on them. Those carpets had been swept till they were threadbare, but still the dust came in from outside.

The living room had had wallpaper once, but those little youngsters had seen some cracks in it and had torn it until it hung down in strips. We went into her kitchen and she had no conveniences, such as most housewives delight in. All she had was an old wood stove and some heavy iron pots and pans. She had to get her vegetables out of the back garden. And the girl herself, who wasn't yet twenty-five, was bent, yellow, old—lifeless. What wonder that she had a voice with a sharp note in it, and that her cheekbones were sharp, too? And what wonder that her place looked so dirty? With all that work, all those disadvantages, the constant fight to scrimp every cent, the yearly child, the dust, the wood-chopping, the old house and furniture—what woman wouldn't give up in time and let it all slide?

Her husband didn't own a farm. He was just a laborer—like Billy. Billy and I looked at each other. We both had the same thought—

"This was the way we might be if we were married."

I learned that I could make better wages doing housework around there than I had made five years before. They would give me $2.50 a week. But I was unfitted for housework after that other life. I was too weak to face that task. I wanted to try it; but do you wonder that I failed?

I felt that I'd made another failure, when I finally said good-by and left. One door of escape from the underworld life, a door that I had always felt stood at least ajar, had been opened; and where I had thought to see a way out, it just led into a prison.

I got aboard the train and went back to Chicago, worked awhile in that same house of prostitution, and then left again for the West.

❖

My failure to find the old home life bearable seemed to take something out of me. During all of those years, no matter how deep I sunk, I could always say to myself, "Anyhow, this is only just for the time. One of these days I'll go back home and live a decent life. They're always waiting for me back there; there's a home always ready."

Something seemed gone out of me when I got aboard the train at that dear little town of X——, and knew I was bound for that brothel in Chicago again. I was sick at heart. Why couldn't the home folks have seen things right? Why did I have to lie to them, and to keep on lying worse and worse?

Why should these people have been so eager to find out something wrong with my life? Why couldn't they have been all forgiving and broad-minded, like that one aunt who had suffered? I wanted to bury the past, to be good and stay good, but they had forbidden me to, just as plainly as though they had locked their doors on me. They had done it by their suspicion and—yes, and by their vulgarity. Every one of them would have been delighted to find out that I had been "bad."

Then I knew really what it meant—that word "outcast." And it made me feel very bitter—not angry nor passionate, but cold and bitter. And I felt that if I went back to the life and committed what those respectable people called sins, that it would really be their fault—that blame would rest on the respectable people who had cast me out.

"Aren't they making me 'sin' by their respectability?" I asked myself.

It was too unhappy in Chicago. I kept remembering how I had left that house three months before, saying it was just on a little visit home, but really hoping all the while that it would be forever. I was too near home still to be happy. After a while it got too much for me, and I left for San Francisco.

San Francisco seemed the natural place to go. I wanted to forget about everything. I thought of going back to Westville, which wasn't very far from San Francisco, but then I told myself:

"Harry Marsh is in Westville. He is in business, and he is 'respectable,' and though he could have prevented my life from going the way that it did, people don't look on him as an outcast. When he goes visiting, people don't try to pry out of him the history of all his past mistakes. I couldn't be happy in Westville."

So I came to San Francisco—to forget.

I lived alone for a while in an uptown apartment—doing a little "rustling" on the streets until I had a set of regular visitors. I was lonely and discontented—more discontented than I had ever been. One day, in a fit of moodiness, I sat down and wrote a letter to my Billy, back home. Just an ordinary letter, short and not saying anything at all, but the mere fact of writing was enough. I felt better afterward.

But there was nothing in my life except emptiness and the pain of my visit back home. At last that got too hard to bear, and the thought came to me:

"Alice, you've got to get out and have something happen, or you'll go crazy."

Where should I go? When I found the answer to that question I felt as though I had had an inspiration. I would go into a house in the "segregated district."

There was the place to forget, if ever such a place existed. I had heard of it many times, and had known several girls who had worked in it, and if there was a hell on earth that was it. You can see how reckless I was, just to go there deliberately. It was part the need for excitement, part the desperate longing for adventure, part—and mostly—that terrible feeling that I must forget about my home trip or go crazy.

I picked out a certain house on Commercial Street, and I went to see the landlady. She gave me a job without any hesitation. That's one discouraging thing about this life—the ease with which you can get work. Chances to work at anything clean are as scarce as diamonds, but there are a million opportunities at prostitution.

I'm just going to draw a few pictures of what I saw in the San Francisco segregated district.

Never will I forget my first night in the house. My great memory is of the crowd that kept reeling and surging through the parlor, where we girls sat waiting. It was a morbid mob—boys from the high school, kids in their teens, who were probably office boys, well dressed men, hoboes, old diseased wrecks; failures and fun-seekers, clubmen and criminals, the foul-minded young and the foul-minded old, all mixed together in one unhealthy, sickening mass.

Not one in twenty came to stay. Not one in fifteen came even to spend money on drinks. I felt that I had ceased to be just a prostitute, and had become an animal in a menagerie, to be stared at and called foul names.

Most of the men and boys would stand there in the doorway and stare slowly around at each of the girls in turn, with grins on their faces and that beastly look in their eyes that makes you hate all men. And the talk they would use! I was accustomed to hearing cursing and swearing, in a certain amount and degree, but before I had sat in that parlor an hour I heard things said that I had never heard before. When I had learned the filth that dropped from the lips of those men and boys—the boys hurt the worst, to hear mere kids talk that way—I began to understand a little more what prostitution really was. We were the men's big show; put there by men; kept there for the use of men, to be used as they chose and talked to as they chose, meant forever to be the satisfaction and the victims of their worst hours. Our business in life was to help men when they were at their lowest. Our trade was not our own; it wasn't even invented by us; it was created by the men when they had a mind to be lower than animals.

And they were lower than animals. I don't know whether animals have speech; but if they have, they don't use it as men do. And animals don't have prostitution. It took men to achieve that.

The house I was in wasn't one of the worst in the district. We had a locked front door, and the men and boys had to knock before they could come in. Many of the places in the district just have a swinging door, and the crowd that looks the girls over is, of course, just so much worse. I don't like to picture what it is for the girls in those places.

One other thing impressed me. The girls in that house seemed to be all set against one another.

"What's the matter with you?" the landlady said to me that evening. "Every time a man looks at you, you look the other way. How do you ever expect to make any money?" Well, I had been doing just as I always had done in Westville or in Canada or in Chicago. But then I began to notice how the girls had to do in San Francisco.

Whenever a man would step into the parlor every girl in the place would be up and after him immediately. They were supposed to compete for him; to solicit him, right there in their own parlor. I wasn't used to that. It was too bold for me. Maybe I was a prostitute, but I couldn't make myself stand up before a man, fawn upon him and win him away from the other girls.

That system led to a different feeling among the girls, too. Everywhere I had been before, the girls were pretty good chums. There was jealousy, of course, and fights now and then, and hatred between certain girls—just as there is, I guess, in a boarding school; but that was nothing like the meanness there was here. The girls seemed to hate each other and try in every way possible to slip it over on each other. There was that awful atmosphere of meanness and hate over the whole house.

I suppose it was worse, too, because the girls, for the most part, didn't live there in the house. They had their rooms, out-side, with their lovers, and just came to the house at night. They didn't get to know each other personally. I wondered to myself how I would ever have lived as long as I had done, if it hadn't been for the friends I had made among the women, and for the sympathy and frequent kindness shown in the different houses. But there was something about the San Francisco "dis-trict" that killed all of that.

I had come to that house to forget the burden of my place in the world. But it just multiplied it. Everything I had wanted to forget seemed all the more impressive in this fearful place. How the girls down there, the ones who stay year in and year out until they break down, manage to stand it, is more than I can see. I guess a person can learn to stand anything.

I wish I might tell you how it was that I finally quit the district. But there are things about this life, many things, but one thing especially, that I haven't been able to tell. It wouldn't bear the printing, nor the telling. I have tried to be frank and outspoken all the way through, and to tell conditions plainly, no matter how hard it was, but here is something that I cannot relate. I am in despair for the human race when I think of it.

So I left the district with my trouble, my dissatisfaction, my disgust, stronger in me than ever. As I went about the same old round of renting an apartment up-town and having the proprietor name an exorbitant price because he knew what I was, I said to myself:

"Alice Smith, there's just one thing for you to do on this earth. You've got to get out of this life for good and all. And you've got to be straight or die."

I had got to the point where I truly felt that I would have to get out of the underworld life or go mad or die.

Going home had opened my eyes. Those nights in the San Francisco segregated district had opened them still further. I had realized at last all that it meant to be a prostitute. Not only what it meant to me, personally, but also a little of what it meant to the world.

So as a first step, I did what the business men call taking inventory. I stepped off from myself, so to speak—sized myself up from a little distance, and tried to find out what stock I had on hand that I could use in my fight.

At first glance my heart just sank. I had never known such terror. Wasn't there anything, anything, that I could do in the world? It seemed not. I remembered that fight I had made in Westville, before I ever went into a house, to "turn straight." I had failed that time. Was I going to fail again?

But this time I felt differently about it. When I had made the try, five years before, I hadn't been so desperate. And when a man or a woman is drowning, or cornered by enemies, or starving, or truly desperate in some other way, there's no knowing what a powerful effort he or she can make.

I'd heard business men talk of debts and assets. Well, on the side of my debts—my health. Besides the general nervous strain, drink and abuse, there had been the first operation, and three other somewhat similar sessions with the doctor. I held out my hand and looked at it a minute. I couldn't hold it quiet; it shook. I thought how splendidly healthy I had been as a girl, and it nearly broke my heart to think of my wasted strength.

Then I'd lost all my friends. That was a fearful debt. There was not a soul to help me in my fight. Nobody to give me a hand when I needed it. I was at the bottom of a pit, and I had a rope—my courage; but there was no person to pull on the other end of the rope. I couldn't have any friends but men; and all men in the world would just try to keep me down. Charitable institutions would only get me positions where I'd be exploited and imposed upon because of my "record." I had no friends.

Then, I had no skill at anything. I couldn't wait tables now, even as well as I could once; I wasn't strong enough for that, nor for laundry work, nor anything else. I was a wreck.

Then, there was no opportunity, no splendid piece of good luck, holding out its promise to me. I had no rich uncle to die, and no well-to-do lover to marry me. And, by the way, this dream of a lover who would marry me had clung with me to the last. I had always thought that some day the man would come along. And my sudden realization that this was just a cruel, idle dream—that there was no such lover for me or for other women, and never would be. I wasn't going to be that sort of fool anymore. It was just trash and idiocy to hope for that; meanwhile, I was worse than wasting my life.

Well, there was my list of debts. No health, no friends, no chance. Bad enough to discourage anybody. But, as I said, I was desperate. When you are that way, you don't get discouraged. You can't.

What did I have on the credit side?

First of all, I saw right away, I had a little money. I wasn't such a "good money maker" any more, but I was making enough at this ghastly trade to pay my expenses and something over. But I had never known the value of a dollar; I'd always been a "good spender." If I had saved now, when I was in Canada, or when I was touring the summer resorts with Slim, the gambler—

Then I made a resolve.

"Alice, you take one year," I said to myself. "Make a vow, by everything holy and binding, that for a whole year you won't take a drink; won't go to a matinee; won't buy a single new dress or anything else that costs a cent; won't ride in a taxi or even on a car when it's possible to walk; no gloves, no hats, no silk stockings, not a new stitch in your wardrobe—for one whole year. Go in rags, if necessary. Vow that you won't lend a cent or give a cent away; that you'll just scrimp on food, and everything else. Meanwhile, work along as though you're doing now, in this apartment, and at the end of the year see where you stand."

I took that vow. I didn't have any Bible, but I held up my right hand and said something with the name of God in it. Maybe it wasn't a very good vow, but it did just as well.

My plan, you see, was really just to let prostitution kill itself, with me. The life was going to furnish me with the money to get out of it. It sounded a little like a person's trying to lift herself up by her shoe-strings, but I hadn't any other way.

I kept that vow. It took the whole year. In that time I didn't buy anything, didn't eat any more than I had to, didn't take a single drink, didn't buy a single taxi-ride. I kept on seeing men; but I didn't let myself get mixed up with any of them. No more lovers for me. I could see the foolishness of that.

That year did a lot for me. It made me strong in a way I would never have dreamed of being. I began to feel as if I was master of my life and of myself in a way that I hadn't been since Grandmother Smith took me West. I started to develop a little of what looked like business brains. I was as big a success as a penny-pincher, as I had been as a spender. And the simple life, even with prostitution attached, had its good effect on my health.

But if you think that year was easy, try it for yourself. I got through it, and I kept my vow; but there were many, many times when I nearly went mad. Just think—for years I had given all my desires, all my whims and moods and passions full play. Now I jerked them all up, suddenly; and that is a thing one can't do by merely saying so. Desperate as I was, it was so hard for me that I don't see how anything could be harder. I needed all my desperation; and if I hadn't been determined clear through, if I hadn't meant out-and-out every word I said when I took that vow, I would never have won—never!

It was nearly the end of my year. I had written the date down, and I thought of it often, the way a prisoner thinks of the date of his freedom. One afternoon I put on my hat—a sad-looking old hat, by this time—and made ready to take a walk in the park.

I opened the door of my room. And I was startled. On the threshold was lying a letter.

Who had found me out? It wasn't Billy's handwriting. But he was the only person that knew my address. This seemed a girlish hand.

I tore it open, and looked at the end of it the first thing. "Your loving sister, Emma."

I was trembling as I walked back into my room. I was afraid to begin to read it; and then, I couldn't see the page very plainly. It had been years since I had heard from Emma. I hadn't thought ever to hear from her again, unless I won my fight.

I have that letter yet. I'm not going to print all she said. It's enough to tell you that she and her husband, a laboring man, where planning to come to San Francisco and live. Emma had wanted to do that for a long time, she said, because of me. She had written back to the folks at my old home, whom she had never seen, to find out my address when word of my visit had come to the relatives in Westville. Nobody had known the address but Billy, and he had sent it out; and now Emma was writing to know if perhaps I wasn't tired of wandering around the face of the earth, and if maybe we couldn't find some little place and all live together. Emma could stand the truth about my life, she said, and wanted me to tell her everything; then she could help me to live it down.

A more beautiful letter was never written. It was like an answer to all the prayers that I had never dared to pray.

So that was why the last weeks of my vow were so easy to keep. I went around with a song in my heart, and a great thankfulness that my fight was won. And just after my year was up, I went down to the ferry building one bright morning with three handkerchiefs up my sleeve, because I knew I should need them when I saw my sister; and I did.

So that was the way the story ended. The bank held a little money—three hundred and eighty-three dollars, to be exact—enough to furnish a little flat for us two girls who had separated, suffered and come together again. The future faced us, though, because her husband was a poor man, and if I could have worried in those happy days I would have worried then; but I happened to remember a remark that a man—one of the thousands who had drifted through the old life without leaving a name to remember him by—had once made to me.

"I know what I'd do if I were you. I'd rent some flats, furnish them on an installment plan, and sublet them furnished. It pays after a while."

So that was the way I did. The little bank account ran dangerously low before those flats were furnished; and as to the installments, they aren't all paid up yet. But Emma and I today are living together, right here in San Francisco, with an income so tiny that it makes me angry now and then when I think of the way I threw money around at one time; but with all the poverty and scrimping to make ends meet, do you suppose I'd change back?

The hardest times, even yet, are when I venture out on the street and some ghost of the old days in the shape of a man, happens to pass and recognize me. Those are the moments when I want to die. Inwardly I am changed; why not outwardly as well? But since that cannot be, I suppose those encounters will have to stay, and keep me reminded of my sorrow for the past and my hopes for the future.

Emma and I dream of scraping together a little capital, some day, and leaving the city for some pretty little country town, where nobody will know us and where we can open a little store of some sort and worry along peacefully as the years pass. We are both young yet—I am under thirty; and I am sure that there is much happiness still left in life.

In closing, I want to say this to the girls who are still in the underworld—don't give up. Don't lose heart. But don't allow yourself to go along, year by year, in the hope that some man will marry you and take you out. That idea is a pitiful lie. There may be a few exceptional cases; but for ninety-nine out of every hundred there's only one person who will ever take you out of it, and that's yourself.

Most of you will have to make some sort of a fight to get out. Maybe you'll have a friend or relative to help; then it will be easier. But in any case, there's only one thing in this world that is harder and more appalling than the fight to leave prostitution; and that is to stay a prostitute. But the fight will try you out, and you will finish up well worthwhile in the world. And there's only one thing that can give you victory in that fight— you'll have to be in earnest. You'll have to mean it, desperately and completely. Meaning it will give you courage. And here's my prayer to give you sympathy. Remember that it's the people who have made mistakes and suffered for them, that make the world worth while.

And from the women who haven't had bad fortune, whose homes have sheltered them and whose friends were true-hearted, I want to ask this: Don't let your good fortune make you hard toward us. Try to realize that there are two sides to what people call "respectability"; one side that protects the people that are respectable, and the other side that makes "outcasts" of the people who aren't. Respectability is very likely to be a two-edged sword. But you women have sympathetic hearts, and that sympathy strikes deeper than just convention; and it is that sympathy that the "outcast" looks for more than life itself. Never condemn; to condemn may be to kill.

As to prostitution, I can see pretty clearly that it mainly exists because all men and some women have the idea of fun, of joking and pleasure, mixed up with their natural instincts of sex. As long as our boys and girls are allowed to think sex funny, prostitution funny, child-birth funny, or even to get too much pleasure into their ideas of reproduction, just so long you are going to have prostitution. That's the biggest root, I think; and the other big root is poverty. The fun idea makes men pursue girls, and poverty makes the girls too weak to resist. Both of these roots will have to be killed before the tree will die.

But in looking back over my past days, and the way prostitution began, grew, and finally killed itself in my life, I have a faith somehow that it will do just the same in the whole world; if you give it time enough. Such things as prostitution have a way of killing themselves.

Acknowledgments

We would like, first and foremost, to thank everybody at Heyday and the California Historical Society; they believed in this book from the onset and saw it through every detail of production. Special thanks go out to Gayle Wattawa, Lisa K. Marietta, Mariko Conner, Christopher Miya, Ashley Ingram, Steve Wasserman, and Malcolm Margolin, as well as Anthea Hartig, Shelly Kale, Charles Wollenberg, Jason Herrington, Patty Pforte, Adam Hirschfelder, and Hugh Rowland. We are honored to work alongside the likes of such talented, inquisitive, and dedicated individuals.

This project would not exist without the librarians, archivists, and historians that came before us. We would like to especially thank the staffs at the San Francisco History Center in the San Francisco Public Library, the California Historical Society, Woodhills Ranch at the Fremont Older Open Space, and the Bancroft Library.

This book would not have been possible without the support, input, and hard work of our collaborators, friends, critics, and comrades. Thank you to Peter Maravelis and Chris Carlsson for early guidance and inspiration; Henry York, Bochay Drum, and Ryan Hurd for their critical material assistance; Josh Sides for his contributions; Ruth Rosen for her academic expertise and for raising important questions during the editorial process; Della Heywood and John Whitehead for offering us their homes as writing retreats; Paul Yamazaki, Cassie Duggan, Tân Khanh Cao, Vanessa Martini, Jeff Battis, and the whole City Lights family for their expert advice and ceaseless encouragement; Andrew McKinley and the Adobe Books staff for finding us the right out-of-print books and filling us with enthusiasm; Kyle Livie and Robert Cherny for help shaping this work long before it was a book; the "de fem" art collective for the regular insight and keen feminist analysis; Ivy Jeanne McClelland and Jennifer Worley, whose influence helped keep this work contemporary; Patrick Kadyk for his unwavering support and friendship; Drew Murphy and the whole Apollo House for the late-night conversations; Sydney Cooke for cheering us on all the way; and to our mothers—Kathy Fieberling and Nancy Gross—for being our very first editors in more ways than one.

We would further like to thank the teachers, friends, and family that have instructed, inspired, and assisted us in so many ways: Steve Leikin, Sherry Katz, Glenn Fieldman, Joel Kassiola, and Hans Meihoffer of San Francisco State University; Jason Macario of the San Francisco Museum and Historical Society; and Aubrey Angus, Christina Lee, Karl Fieberling, Audrey and Bill Fieberling, Patricia and Frederick Gross, David and Dawn Gross, Earl Anderson and Lisa Johnson, Melissa and Aaron Nenner, Paul Anderson, Andrea Louise, and Hallie Christina Gross.

All images from the *San Francisco Bulletin:* June 23, 1913 (p. lxxxiv); June 20, 1913 (p. 34); October 24, 1914 (p. 42); July 22, 1913 (p. 96); June 28, 1913 (p. 104); January 25, 1917 (p. 184); and February 15, 1917 (p. 194).

Further Reading

Agustín, Laura María. *Sex at the Margins: Migration, Labour Markets and the Rescue Industry.* London: Zed Books, 2007.

Anonymous, with an introduction by Ben B. Lindsey. *Madeleine: An Autobiography.* New York: Harper and Brothers, 1919.

Antoniazzi, Barbara. *The Wayward Woman: Progressivism, Prostitution, and Performance in the United States, 1888–1917.* Madison, NJ: Fairleigh Dickinson University Press, 2014.

Asbury, Herbert. *The Barbary Coast: An Informal History of the San Francisco Underworld.* New York: Thunder's Mouth Press, 1933.

Bean, Walter. *Boss Ruef's San Francisco: The Story of the Union Labor Party, Big Business, and the Graft Prosecution.* Berkeley: University of California Press, 1952.

Black, Jack. *You Can't Win.* Port Townsend, WA: Feral House, 2013.

Boyd, Nan Alamilla. *Wide-Open Town: A History of Queer San Francisco to 1965.* Berkeley: University of California Press, 2003.

Bruce, John R. *Gaudy Century, 1848–1948: San Francisco's One Hundred Years of Robust Journalism.* New York: Random House, 1948.

Chambers, John Whiteclay, II. *The Tyranny of Change: America in the Progressive Era, 1890–1920.* New Brunswick, NJ: Rutgers University Press, 2006.

Chateauvert, Melinda. *Sex Workers Unite: A History of the Movement from Stonewall to SlutWalk*. Boston: Beacon Press, 2014.

Cherny, Robert W., Mary Ann Irwin, and Ann Marie Wilson, eds. *California Women and Politics: From the Gold Rush to the Great Depression*. Lincoln: University of Nebraska Press, 2011.

Connelly, Mark Thomas. *The Response to Prostitution in the Progressive Era*. Chapel Hill: University of North Carolina Press, 2011.

Davenport, Robert. "Fremont Older in San Francisco Journalism: A Partial Biography, 1856–1918." Ph.D. diss., University of California, Los Angeles, 1969.

Deverell, William, and Tom Sitton, eds. *California Progressivism Revisited*. Berkeley: University of California Press, 1994.

Duffus, R. L. *The Tower of Jewels: Memories of San Francisco*. New York: W.W. Norton, 1960.

Ethington, Philip J. *The Public City: The Political Construction of Urban Life in San Francisco, 1850–1900*. Berkeley: University of California Press, 2001.

Gentry, Curt. *The Madams of San Francisco*. New York: Ballantine Books, 1964.

Gira Grant, Melissa. *Playing the Whore: The Work of Sex Work*. Brooklyn: Verso, 2014.

Goldman, Emma. *Living My Life*. 2 vols. New York: Dover Publications, 1970.

———. *Red Emma Speaks: An Emma Goldman Reader*. Compiled and edited by Alix Kates Shulman. New York: Schocken Books, 1982.

Hapke, Laura. *Girls Who Went Wrong: Prostitutes in American Fiction, 1885–1917*. Bowling Green, OH: Bowling Green State University Popular Press, 1989.

Holtz, William. *The Ghost in the Little House: A Life of Rose Wilder Lane*. Columbia: University of Missouri Press, 1993.

Johnson, Katie N. *Sex for Sale: Six Progressive-Era Brothel Dramas*. Iowa City: University of Iowa Press, 2015.

Lotchin, Roger W. *San Francisco, 1846–1856: From Hamlet to City*. New York: Oxford University Press, 1974.

Lowrie, Donald. *My Life in Prison*. New York: Mitchell Kennerley, 1912.

———. *My Life Out of Prison*. London: Forgotten Books, 2015.

Markwyn, Abigail M. *Empress San Francisco: The Pacific Rim, the Great West, and California at the Panama-Pacific International Exposition*. Lincoln: University of Nebraska Press, 2014.

Mowry, George E. *The California Progressives*. Chicago: Quadrangle Books, 1963.

Nagle, Jill, ed. *Whores and Other Feminists*. New York, London: Routledge, 2010.

Older, Fremont. *My Own Story*. Oakland: Post-Enquirer Publishing Co., 1925.

Pinzer, Maimie. *The Maimie Papers: Letters from an Ex-Prostitute*. Edited by Ruth Rosen and Sue Davidson. New York: Feminist Press, 1977.

Sabraw, Liston F. "Mayor James Rolph, Jr. and the End of the Barbary Coast." Master's thesis, San Francisco State College, 1960.

Sewell, Jessica Ellen. *Women and the Everyday City: Public Space in San Francisco, 1890–1915*. Minneapolis: University of Minnesota Press, 2011.

Shumsky, Neil, and Larry M. Springer. "San Francisco's Zone of Prostitution, 1880–1934," *Journal of Historical Geography* 7, no. 1 (December 1980).

Sides, Josh. *Erotic City: Sexual Revolutions and the Making of Modern San Francisco*. New York: Oxford University Press, 2009.

Soderlund, Gretchen. *Sex, Trafficking, Scandal, and the Transformation of Journalism, 1885–1917*. Chicago: University of Chicago Press, 2013.

Stanford, Sally. *The Lady of the House: The Autobiography of Sally Stanford*. New York: Putnam, 1966.

Ralston, John C. *Fremont Older and the 1916 San Francisco Bombing: A Tireless Crusade for Justice*. Charleston, NC: History Press, 2013.

Rosen, Ruth. *The Lost Sisterhood: Prostitution in America, 1900–1918*. Baltimore: Johns Hopkins University Press, 1982.

Walkowitz, Judith R. *Prostitution and Victorian Society: Women, Class, and the State*. Cambridge, U.K.: Cambridge University Press, 1980.

Wells, Evelyn. *Fremont Older*. New York: D. Appleton-Century Company, 1936.

Yamazaki, Tomoko. *The Story of Yamada Waka*. Translated by Wakako Hironaka and Ann Kostant. Tokyo: Kodansha International, 1985.

Yung, Judy. *Unbound Feet: A Social History of Chinese Women in San Francisco*. Berkeley: University of California Press, 1995.

About the Authors

Ivy Anderson is a San Francisco–based writer by way of Ojai, California. Focused on issues of Bay Area ecology and radical history, her reportage on water management issues has been published in *Water Efficiency Magazine,* and her poetry has appeared in *Poecology.* She holds a B.A. in environmental studies with a minor in geography, runs a community garden, and is on the board of a bookstore collective in San Francisco.

Devon Angus is an artist, activist, and historian based in San Francisco. In collaboration with Hazy Loper and Closer to Carbon, he cowrote and performed a conceptual folk operetta based on San Francisco history, *The Ghosts of Barbary,* throughout the Bay Area, Switzerland, and Italy in 2014. He organized and published a series of oral histories of immigrants in the Catskills region, and he was the recipient of an arts grant through the New York State Council on the Arts for his show *Songs and Stories of Old New York.* He is currently pursuing a master's degree in history.

For additional content and announcements about book events, please visit the editors' website at www.voicesfromtheunderworld.com.

About the California Historical Society Book Award

In 2013, after a twenty-year collaboration and with a shared commitment to finding new and inclusive ways to explore California's history, the California Historical Society and Heyday established the California Historical Society Book Award as a way of inviting new voices and viewpoints into the conversation. Each year we bring together a jury of noted historians, scholars, and publishing experts to award a book-length manuscript that makes an important contribution both to scholarship and to the greater community by deepening public understanding of some aspect of California history. For more information, visit www.heydaybooks.com/chsbookaward or http://www.californiahistoricalsociety.org/publications/book_award.html.

CALIFORNIA
HISTORICAL
SOCIETY since 1871

About the California Historical Society

Founded in 1871, the California Historical Society (CHS) is a nonprofit organization with a mission to inspire and empower people to make California's richly diverse past a meaningful part of their contemporary lives.

Public Engagement

Through high-quality public history exhibitions, public programs, research, preservation, advocacy, and digital story-telling, CHS keeps history alive through extensive public engagement. In opening the very heart of the organization—our vast and diverse collection—to ever wider audiences, we invite meaning, encourage exchange, and enrich understanding.

CHS Collections

CHS holds one of the state's top historical collections, revealing California's social, cultural, economic, and political history and development—including some of the most cherished and valuable documents and images of California's past. From our headquarters in San Francisco to the University of Southern California and the Autry National Center in Los Angeles, we hold millions of items in trust for the people of California.

Library and Research

Open to the public and free of charge, our North Baker Research Library is a place where researchers literally hold history in their hands. Whether you're a scholar or are simply interested in learning about the history of your neighborhood, city, or community, you have hands-on access to the rich history of our state.

Publications

From our first book publication in 1874, to our ninety-year history as publisher of the *California History* journal, to the establishment of the annual California Historical Society Book Award in 2013, CHS publications examine the ongoing dialogue between the past and the present. Our print and digital publications reach beyond purely historical narrative to connect Californians to their state, region, nation, and the world in innovative and thought-provoking ways.

Support

Over the years, the generosity and commitment of foundations, corporations, cultural and educational institutions, and private donors and members have supported CHS's work throughout the state.

Learn More

www.californiahistoricalsociety.com

HEYDAY
into California

About Heyday

Heyday is an independent, nonprofit publisher and unique cultural institution. We promote widespread awareness and celebration of California's many cultures, landscapes, and boundary-breaking ideas. Through our well-crafted books, public events, and innovative outreach programs we are building a vibrant community of readers, writers, and thinkers.

Thank You

It takes the collective effort of many to create a thriving literary culture. We are thankful to all the thoughtful people we have the privilege to engage with. Cheers to our writers, artists, editors, storytellers, designers, printers, bookstores, critics, cultural organizations, readers, and book lovers everywhere!

We are especially grateful for the generous funding we've received for our publications and programs during the past year from foundations and hundreds of individual donors. Major supporters include:

Anonymous (3); Advocates for Indigenous California Language Survival; Arkay Foundation; Richard and Rickie Ann Baum; Randy Bayard; Jean and Fred Berensmeier; Joan Berman and Philip Gerstner; Nancy Bertelsen; Barbara Boucke; Jamie and Philip Bowles; Beatrice Bowles; California Historical Society; California Humanities; California Rice Commission; California Wildlife Foundation / California Oaks; The Campbell Foundation; Candelaria Fund; John and Nancy Cassidy; Graham Chisholm; The Christensen Fund; Jon Christensen; Lawrence Crooks; Nik Dehejia; Topher Delaney; Chris Desser and Kirk Marckwald; Frances Dinkelspiel and Gary Wayne; The Roy & Patricia Disney Family Foundation; Tim Disney; The Durfee Foundation; Endangered Habitats League; Marilee Enge and George Frost; Richard and Gretchen Evans; John Gage and Linda Schacht; Wallace Alexander Gerbode Foundation; Patrick Golden; Walter & Elise Haas Fund; Penelope Hlavac; Charles and Sandra Hobson; Nettie Hoge; Donna Ewald Huggins; Inlandia Institute; JiJi Foundation; Claudia Jurmain;

Kalliopeia Foundation; Marty Krasney; Abigail Kreiss; Guy Lampard and Suzanne Badenhoop; David Loeb; Judith Lowry-Croul and Brad Croul; Sam and Alfreda Maloof Foundation for Arts & Crafts; Manzanar History Association; Nion McEvoy and Leslie Berriman, in honor of Malcolm Margolin; Heather Mcfarlin; The Giles W. and Elise G. Mead Foundation; Richard Nagler; National Wildlife Federation; The Nature Conservancy; Steven Nightingale and Lucy Blake; Northern California Water Association; Julie and Will Parish; Ronald Parker; The Ralph M. Parsons Foundation; Jeannene Przyblyski; James and Caren Quay; Susan Raynes; Alan Rosenus; The San Francisco Foundation; San Francisco Heritage; San Manuel Band of Mission Indians; Greg Sarris; Ron Shoop; Stanley Smith Horticultural Trust; William Somerville; Liz Sutherland; Roselyne Swig; Thendara Foundation; Jerry Tone and Martha Wyckoff; Sonia Torres; Michael Traynor; Michael and Shirley Traynor; Lisa Van Cleef and Mark Gunson; Stevens Van Strum; Marion Weber; Sylvia Wen and Mathew London; Valerie Whitworth and Michael Barbour; Cole Wilbur; Peter Wiley and Valerie Barth; and Yocha Dehe Wintun Nation.

Board of Directors

Getting Involved

To learn more about our publications, events and other ways you can participate, please visit www.heydaybooks.com.